JUL 1999

B

WILLIA

WITHDRAWN

ROBIN WILLIAMS

ROBIN WILLIAMS

Andy Dougan

THUNDER'S MOUTH PRESS
NEW YORK

First THUNDER'S MOUTH PRESS edition 1998
Published by THUNDER'S MOUTH PRESS
841 Broadway, 4th Floor, New York, NY 10003

First pubished in 1998 by Orion Media
An imprint of Orion Books Ltd
Orion House, 5 Upper St Martin's Lane, London WC2H 9EA

Library of Congress Cataloging-in-Publication Data
Dougan, Andy.
  Robin Williams : a biography / by Andy Dougan.
      p.   cm.
  Filmography: p.
  Includes bibliographical references and index.
    ISBN 1–56025–196.4
    1. Williams, Robin, 1952, July 21– 2. Comedians—United States—
  –Biography. 3. Actors—United States— Biography. I. Title.
  PN2287.W473D68   1998
  791.43′028′092—dc21
    [B]   98–34078
                                                                     CIP

ISBN 1–56025–196–4

Typeset in Minion by Selwood Systems, Midsomer Norton
Printed and bound in Great Britain by Butler & Tanner Ltd,
Frome and London

Distributed by PUBLISHERS GROUP WEST
1700 Fourth Street
Berkeley, CA 94710
(800) 788–3123

CONTENTS

To Christine, Iain and Stuart

AUTHOR'S NOTE AND ACKNOWLEDGEMENTS

This is an unauthorised biography and does not pretend to be anything other than an unauthorised biography. This book has actually been in the pipeline for a number of years. As a film journalist one of the great joys of my professional life is to watch Robin Williams work a room. It is a pleasure and a privilege and it was as a result of this that I first started to think about this book. When I started to make contact with a number of his colleagues and co-workers I very quickly received a fax from his lawyers advising me that he would not 'authorize [sic] a biography of him to be written or encourage his close associates to cooperate in the writing of such a book'.

Since the purpose of the book was to try to explore some of the influences behind the creative process of 'the funniest man alive', this was discouraging but not altogether unexpected. However over the past few years I have interviewed a number of Robin Williams' co-stars and directors as well as, of course, interviewing him on his frequent publicity junkets for his films. This book draws from these interviews as well as subsequent conversations with friends and colleagues, some named, some not.

I would particularly like to thank those who took the time to talk to me, especially Adrian Cronauer, Barry Friedman and Dan Holzman. I am also grateful to those who were so helpful on my trips to New York and San Francisco, especially the staff at the Billy Rose Theater Collection in New York and Susan Krauss in California. My grateful thanks too to Kristine Krueger from the National Film Information Service at the Center for Motion Picture Study in Los Angeles, for once again guiding me through the maze.

A number of colleagues were also kind enough to help. I would like to thank Siobhan Synnot of BBC Radio Scotland for making available her interviews with Robin Williams for *Flubber* and *Good Will Hunting*, as well as Chris Columbus for *Mrs Doubtfire*, and Alison Maloney for access to her interview with Gus Van Sant as well as for asking questions on my behalf. My thanks too to Anwar Brett for having a better filing system than me and invaluably managing to retrieve the transcripts of press conferences for *Hook* and *Mrs Doubtfire* which I had misplaced.

For their help and encouragement along the way I would like to thank my agent Jane Judd, as well as Trevor Dolby and Pandora White at Orion.

And finally, once again, my thanks to my wife and children for putting up with the beast in the attic for another three months.

Andy Dougan

Be Sure to Wear a Flower in your Hair

America in 1969 was in the middle of tremendous civil unrest. At its heart was an unpopular war in Vietnam. American involvement in Vietnam reached a peak in 1969 with 541,000 US troops committed to serving in South East Asia. In addition to the notion of their boys being slaughtered in the jungle, Americans at home had also become sickened and horrified by revelations about the conduct of their troops in Vietnam. Only a year previously American soldiers had slaughtered Vietnamese villagers at My Lai. By the end of 1969 the mood on the home front had changed dramatically, with millions of Americans taking part in protest marches against the most unpopular war in the country's brief history.

The average age of the American combat soldier in Vietnam was only 19. By comparison the average age of a GI in the Second World War was 26. The youthful nature of the combatants was matched by the equally youthful nature of the protesters. This was very definitely a student revolution as millions of young people demonstrated and protested about their classmates and contemporaries being sent overseas to fight. The heart of this revolution could be found on the West Coast, specifically in the colleges and universities in and around San Francisco. The American protest movement has its origins in the so-called Summer of Love which was centred in San Francisco two years previously. That summer of 1967 was seen by the establishment as a symbol of the moral decline of American youth. Instead it would go on to define a whole generation as well as the ones which followed.

Since it was taken from Mexico in 1846, the whole of what became the state of California has had a frequently tenuous association with the rest of the country. Self-styled sophisticates in New York will refer disparagingly to California as America's 'left coast'. They do things differently out there to be sure, and this is largely because of the strong European influences on their culture and politics. Los Angeles, for example, had become the home of Stravinsky, Isherwood and Huxley. San Francisco similarly had been subject to strong European influences from the hundreds of thousands who came from all over the world, drawn by the discovery of gold in the Sierras in 1846, and later settled there because they had struck it rich or were too poor to go home. As a consequence of this melting-pot of cultures San Francisco has always taken a perverse pride in being *in* America without necessarily being *of* America.

In the Fifties, the city had become the home of the Beat Generation and its charismatic poets and writers such as Alan Ginsberg, Neal Cassidy and Jack Kerouac. They had turned the city's North Beach into the western annexe of New York's Greenwich Village. Their world revolved around the City Lights bookstore in Columbus Avenue and the bars and cafés which dotted the nearby streets. The word 'beatnik' was originally coined as a derogatory term by Herb Caen, one of San Francisco's best-known newspaper columnists. Within a few years the Beat Generation had grown up and moved on and left behind another movement which would shape America's future.

The hippies were an offshoot of the Beats. The word was originally a not altogether complimentary beat term to describe those well-intentioned young people who followed in their footsteps without always understanding what they were really about. Both groups believed in the rejection of materialism, but their rejection took different forms. While the Beats wrote novels and poems raging against the capitalist nine-to-five life and extolling the virtues of personal freedom, the hippies were more heavily influenced by drugs and music. They were more inclined to light up a joint than to write a poem. The hippie movement began in the coffee bars of the university campuses of the Bay Area but quickly found a home in the Haight-Ashbury district just to the west of downtown San Francisco. Here they established communal squats in formerly impressive but now run-down mansion houses and took the advice of their guru Timothy Leary by turning on, tuning in and dropping out.

The hippie movement was based on three things: music, love and drugs. And the greatest of these was drugs. The writer Hunter S. Thompson estimates that in 1965 almost everyone on the streets of Haight-Ashbury 'between twenty and thirty was a "head", a user of either marijuana, LSD, or both. To refuse the proffered joint is to risk being labelled a "nark" – a narcotics agent – a threat and a menace to almost everybody.'

The hippies had discovered LSD, a powerfully hallucinogenic, 'mind-expanding' drug. Not only that, many of them were bright enough to manufacture it safely and cheaply. A tab of good-quality acid would cost around $5 and leave you high as a kite for hours at a time. The money for the drugs could be quickly raised by begging on the streets. This so-called 'panhandling' was the principal source of income for many hippies, and the money was easily obtained from the tourists who were beginning to flock into the area. For their part it was a cheap price to pay for what was the best freak show in town.

Music was also an important part of hippie culture. Bands like Jefferson Airplane and The Grateful Dead were required listening for those who were not hearing the music of the spheres after dropping a tab or two. The defining moment of the hippie movement came in the summer of 1967 when their non-materialistic instincts led them to put on a free concert in San Francisco's Golden Gate Park. What was intended to be a tiny local event drew a crowd of 20,000 and took the media by storm. Suddenly world-wide attention was focused on this small Californian neighbourhood, and by the end of the year there were an estimated 100,000 hippies living in and around Haight-Ashbury.

The hippie lifestyle was a protest, however mild, against the American Way of Life. Elsewhere in San Francisco, at the universities of Oakland and Berkeley on the other side of the Bay Bridge, a more hard-line protest was taking shape from another group of disaffected young people. The Free Speech Movement was founded at Berkeley in 1964 as a means of evading a ban on student political activity. Within a few years this had hardened into a protest against America's involvement in Vietnam. In 1968 there had been pitched battles in San Francisco's Telegraph Hill area when rioting broke out after students attempting to show solidarity with their protesting contemporaries in Paris were met by a strong show of force from the police. The fighting and rioting went on for several days before order was eventually restored. Another protest at the so-called People's Park, a piece of university land which had been taken over by the students, ended when the police moved in to end the four-day occupation, firing tear gas into the crowd and wading in with night-sticks. One person died and more than 100 were injured.

The campus of the University of California at Berkeley became a symbol for America's rapidly increasing protest movement. It was the heart and soul of a new generation which was finding its own voice and fighting for a say in its own destiny. At first dismissed by the establishment as a bunch of rabble-rousing malcontents, the students from California rapidly began to define the mood of the country. Encouraged by the students' example, there were other protests in San Francisco in 1969. Under cover of darkness a group of American Indians took over the now abandoned former Federal penitentiary at Alcatraz in the middle of San Francisco. Their plan, among other things, was to convert the building into their own university. Their aims were idealistic and their methods were non-violent. Recognising that they were buoyed up by public opinion, the authorities decided to wait them out. It was a long wait, but eventually internal dissension on the part of the protesters and a rising tide of public indifference meant that Alcatraz was eventually reclaimed in 1971.

Even though the Indians finally surrendered these were heady times in 1969. The hippies were getting stoned, the students were getting tear-gassed, and the Indians were on The Rock.

Into the midst of all this came a shy, slightly overweight teenager from an exclusive private school in Detroit.

'That was the transitional year for me,' Robin Williams would later recall. 'San Francisco in 1969 changed everything.'

1

I Love You in Blue

The dawning of the American Century, that period when America began to dominate the world economically, politically and culturally, came with the end of the Second World War. After the restrictions of the war years America suddenly found itself in the years immediately after 1945 with one of the greatest consumer booms of modern times. Men who had fought and killed on the battlefields of Europe and the Pacific Theatre for four years returned home with new dreams and desires. Those dreams and desires boiled down to two things: their own car and their own home.

A new car was a convenient status symbol in the immediate postwar years. A plentiful domestic supply of petrol from the oilfields of Texas and Oklahoma meant that fuel was cheap and the automobile industry was set for its golden age. The mass production techniques originally pioneered by Henry Ford were honed and refined but they would not be used to churn out boxy, basic black Model Ts. This was the age of automotive opulence, where bigger was definitely better.

If one company came to symbolise American industrial might of that period it was General Motors, which dominated the automobile industry and with it America's manufacturing sector. This was the period when one of the company's senior executives, Charlie Wilson, was misquoted as saying that what was good for General Motors was good for America. What he actually said, when he left GM to become Secretary of Defence for President Eisenhower, was 'We at General Motors have always felt that what was good for the country was good for General Motors as well'.

Regardless of what he actually said, everyone knew what he meant and his point was well made. General Motors had a near monopoly on the car industry. Their main rivals Ford had deteriorated markedly from the company which Henry had founded. Indeed Ford's performance had fallen so badly that GM bosses genuinely feared that, such was their dominance, they might one day be liable to an anti-trust suit. In 1953, GM had 45 per cent of the American market, and by 1956 this had risen unchecked to a staggering 51 per cent.

The symbol of GM's power was the car which became America's dream machine, the Cadillac. This was the ultimate aspirational target for the American working man. Everyone dreamed that, in the land of opportunity, they would one day be driving their own Caddy, just like their boss. A Cadillac in the early Fifties would cost around $5000. Wages in the manufacturing sector ranged from $2400 to $3000 a year, with those in the motor industry not surprisingly at the top end of the scale. However, with an annual trade-in a Cadillac could be owned for a net cost of $700 per year. This meant that with hard work and a little initiative the dream car could become a reality.

It was hard for America's other automobile manufacturers to compete with the glamour, the price and the reliability of the Cadillac. Ford, even though it was second by a long way, was GM's chief rival and it attempted to lure motorists away from the Cadillac with its own luxury car, the Lincoln Continental. It was a hard row to hoe, but all they could do was try.

Robert Fitzgerald Williams was a senior executive at Ford in charge of the Midwest sales division of the Lincoln-Continental operation. He was a ramrod and a trouble-shooter. It was his job to go where the problems were and make sure that Ford could hold their own in the battle with General Motors at the top end of the market. Although he was a captain of industry, Robert Williams was cut from a different cloth from most of his fellow executives in the car industry. Williams had been born in Evansville, Indiana to a family which was a mixture of English, Welsh and Irish stock. The Williams family was seriously wealthy, having made its fortune in the lumber and mining industries. But like so many family fortunes, the businesses had fallen on hard times during the Depression. Eventually things had reached such a poor pass that Williams had to work in the family strip mines himself for a time. He was, by all accounts, possessed of talent and a fierce will, and through the combination of these and sheer hard work he was able to reach the upper echelons of industry once again. The experience had scarred him, however, and he would remain deeply cynical and mistrustful for the rest of his life.

Williams was a tall, imperious, patrician man who is said to have resembled the broadcaster Alastair Cooke. His wife Laurie was a former model and society beauty. Her family was French from New Orleans and she was blessed with the fine bone structure and gamine charm of Audrey Hepburn or Leslie Caron. They were the perfect couple who had found each other relatively late in life – each had been married before – and in the summer of 1952 they produced a son.

Robin McLaurim Williams first saw the light of day on 21 July 1952 in Chicago, Illinois. Robert Williams was a senior executive and was paid accordingly, so the family were not exactly short of a dollar. When his job required that he move to Detroit, the capital of the American auto industry, he took his wife and child to a 30-room mansion in 20 acres of grounds in the exclusive Bloomfield Hills district. This was the real deal for Robert Williams. It was the American dream writ large, with the big house, the good job, the servants and the high income. The problem was that he was frequently not around to share it with his family. Williams' work took him all over the Midwest and he spent days and weeks at a time away from the family home. Even when he was working in Detroit the hours would be long, requiring him to leave early in the morning and not return until late at night.

While he was away, young Robin had to grow up without him. And with his mother also busy modelling and organising charity benefits he spent a great deal of time without either parent. He had the whole third floor of this huge mansion to himself. Literally to himself. Bloomfield Hills was not exactly teeming with school-age children, and as Williams remembers there were no other children in the neighbourhood at all. There was just him, his dog Duke, and Carl his pet turtle. On a good day the son of the family's maid might come over and play. Duke was a constant companion but his value as a playmate was somewhat limited.

> We would play hide and seek [Williams recalled] and I would always find him. Duke thought that if he couldn't see me then I couldn't see him. Duke was dumb. I could always see – or at least hear – his big tail going whop! whop! whop! on the parquet floors. Pretty early on I banished myself to the attic where I had a huge army of toy soldiers. I had about 10,000 of them and I would have them all separated by periods in boxes. I would have time-machine battles with Confederate soldiers fighting GIs with automatic weapons and knights fighting Nazis.

As well as his toy soldiers – an army whose size appears to vary from 2000 to 10,000 depending on who he was speaking to – Robin Williams also

had a full and rich fantasy life. When he tired of mock battles he would
retreat into his imagination and fill his days with imaginary friends. But
imaginary friends are no substitute for the real thing. Even when he was
ten and discovered that he had in fact two half-brothers from his parents'
previous marriages, the excitement was tempered by the fact that they
were both much older than him. Lauren, his mother's son, was four years
older, and Todd, the son of his father's first marriage, was 13 years older.
Williams never saw them much when he was growing up, and his recollection of Todd in particular is of someone who would come into his
room and 'borrow' from his piggy bank for beer money.

  Although he was lonely, Robin Williams insists that he still felt loved.
However, many years later, and with the benefit of therapy, he would
look back and recall that his childhood was not necessarily as he had
remembered it.

> I'm just beginning to realise that it wasn't always that happy [he told *Esquire*
> magazine in 1989]. My childhood was kind of lonely. Quiet. My father was
> away, my mother was working, doing benefits. I was basically raised by this
> maid and my mother would come in later, you know, and I knew her and
> she was wonderful and charming and witty. But I think maybe comedy was
> part of my way of connecting with my mother – 'I'll make mommy laugh
> and that will be okay' – and that's where it started.

Williams did, he realises now, grow up with an acute fear of abandonment.
Such feelings are not uncommon in young children, but in his case, with
his father coming and going so much, the fear must have been that little
bit more real. Performing was a means of getting attention as well as
providing a little bit of added value. He wasn't just their son, he could be
entertaining too. If Williams' love of performing came from being eager
to please his mother, he also acknowledges the debt he owes to both
parents in contributing to his talent.

  Laurie Williams was the perfect audience for her son's fledgling efforts
as a performer. She is bubbly and effervescent, with a bizarre sense of
humour which belies her Southern Belle upbringing. She once turned up
at a society ball in an exclusive Illinois country club dressed to kill but
with her two front teeth obscured by tape as a joke to make it appear that
they were missing. Naturally all the women there were wondering, to her
delight, why someone who could dress so well would not be able to afford
to get her teeth fixed. Laurie Williams would regale young Robin with
tales from a favourite book which was supposedly written by a nineteenth-
century English society hostess which she insisted was called *Balls I Have*

Held. And among the inexhaustible supply of jokes and stories with which she would amuse her son, there was also her penchant for faintly *risqué* doggerel. One favourite rhyme was

> Spider crawling on the wall
> Ain't you got no sense at all
> Don't you know that wall's been plastered
> Get off that wall you little . . . spider.

Another of his mother's rhymes which amused the young Williams was

> I love you in blue
> Love you in red
> But most of all
> I love you in . . . blue.

Robert Williams on the other hand was stern without actually being strict. He was a great believer in children knowing their place and wasn't wild about the notion of youngsters acting up. Williams, however, cannot recall his father raising his voice to him, except on one occasion, when he made a rude gesture of defiance to his mother. That was the only time he remembers being smacked – but only once. According to Laurie Williams, Robert Williams was 'strict but fair' and his son absolutely adored him. She and Robin would affectionately refer to her husband as 'Lord Stokesbury, Viscount of India' for his elegance and patrician manner.

Williams himself recalls the advice his father gave him, a relic of the bitter cynicism which his own family's misfortunes had left in him. 'He was this wonderful elegant man who thought the world was going to hell in a hand basket. It was basically "You can't trust them. Watch out for them. They'll nail ya. Everybody's out to nail ya".'

There is no doubt that Robin Williams loved his father deeply and the feeling was reciprocated. It would be false to assume that Williams grew up feeling rejected by a cold and aloof paterfamilias. What there was between them was distance; sometimes geographical, sometimes emotional. There was also the problem of Robert Williams approaching middle age – he was 46 – when his son was born. It is often difficult for older parents to match their children's energy levels, and children of older parents frequently grow up feeling a little more distant from their families than they would like.

But between them Robert and Laurie Williams have passed on to their son the gifts which he has used to make him the man he is today. His mother gave him an extravagant sense of comedy, and the still, wry humour of his father gave him a sense of theatre. The combination of the two is what makes Williams a unique package.

'I got her energy and funkified sense of humour,' Williams concedes, 'and I got a grounding thing from Dad. I never met my grandmother on Mom's side, but Mom says she was a great character who just loved to watch men wrestle. There's probably a lot of happy madness which has been passed down in the family, with characters from *Arsenic and Old Lace* all over the place.'

School Daze

For someone who had effectively grown up in isolation, no matter how privileged that isolation may have been, school must have been a brave new world for Robin Williams. It was a whole exciting realm of adventure, stimulation and – most important – other children. Williams must have thought he had died and gone to Heaven on his first day of school.

Although he remembers his early days at Gorton Elementary School in Chicago as being unspectacular, his classmates have a slightly different recollection of the period. One former classmate remembers him as having a perpetual smile as early as the fourth grade when he was taught by Miss Granice, a teacher with a reputation for discipline. That was also, one assumes, the beginning of his talents for vocal mimicry. Friends recall that Williams would sit engrossed in his school work but at the same time emitting a variety of strange sounds – a forerunner of Mork from Ork – as he went about his business. Miss Granice would move his desk further and further away from the other children to minimise the distraction to them, but there was nothing to be done until eventually the desk ended up out in the corridor, where Williams would spend the rest of the lesson. Later on, by the time he reached the sixth grade at Gorton, Williams had found a favourite teacher. Miss Turner, who had a penchant for playing opera when the children were supposed to be studying maths, obviously appealed to the eccentric side of his nature.

If the story of Williams' noise-making is true, and there seems no reason why it shouldn't be, it is also perfectly understandable. Having spent hours occupying himself at home on his own, he was probably unaware of the habit. Whatever disruptive effect he might have had on the class can be put down to excitement and exuberance rather than mischief. Here was a whole new group to pay attention to him to over-compensate for the loneliness he frequently felt at home. It's also worth remembering that growing up without other children would also have left Williams' social and play skills considerably underdeveloped. That often meant that school could be a painful experience for the young Robin Williams, who was terminally shy. Class photographs of the period show Williams as a sturdy, pale, round-faced child with a rather severe crew cut. He sits with his back straight, his arms folded across his lap and his hands thrust between his thighs. And there is, as his classmates reported, just the hint of a sly smile; a suggestion that he knows something that no one else does. But for Williams, who was a quiet little boy, school could also be a trial.

'Kids can be quite cruel to one another, we all know that,' Williams concedes. 'And at one time I did get bullied at school, because I was little and I was fat, and I got called names.'

Occasionally the bullying manifested itself in more physical ways. Perhaps because they were aware that he had grown up without other kids, his parents had made a conscious effort to educate their son through the public school system rather than the more cocooned environment of a private school. For a short, fat kid with crippling shyness there were times when every day was sheer purgatory. There was, he realised, only one way to deal with it.

> I started telling jokes in the seventh grade as a way to stop getting the shit kicked out of me [he remembers]. Mom and Dad had put me in a public school and most of the kids there were bigger than me and wanted to prove they were bigger than me by throwing me into the walls. There were a lot of burly farm kids and sons of auto plant workers there. I'd come to school looking for new entrances and thinking, 'If only I could come in through the roof.' They'd nail me as soon as I got through the door.

It can't have been easy for Williams, the rich, well-spoken new boy, to be such an obvious fish out of water. Frequently, as Williams also recalls, the humour only worked up to a point. The school toughs thought he was funny but they decided they were going to pick on him anyway. Williams' physical torment was ended by a stroke of luck. For once the peripatetic nature of his father's job worked in his favour. The move to Bloomfield Hills in Detroit meant that Robin Williams ended up at the Detroit

Country Day School, a private school where he could at least mingle with boys of his own background and finish the seventh grade. To his horror he quickly found out that he had merely switched one form of abuse for another. The privileged pupils of his new school would never have soiled their hands with the physical battering Williams had suffered previously. But, in the casually callous manner of children all over the world, they found a new and possibly even more hurtful form of torture.

'I was picked on not only physically but intellectually too,' says Williams. 'People used to kick George Sand in my face,' he says trying to make light of it. 'It's a whole other thing when you get both.'

The irony is that Williams was by no means an intellectual lightweight. He was a studious and intelligent boy who was more than a match in terms of academic ability for any of his schoolmates. Where they had the advantage, however, was in terms of confidence. Williams was still hampered by his shyness, which meant he was less likely to say anything in his own defence, and more likely to say the wrong thing at the wrong time.

> All these hyperintellectuals would lay into me with lines like 'That was a very asinine thing to say, Williams' [he remembers]. I remember one kid was into heavy calculus in the seventh grade and everyone would go, 'Wow, cross sections of a cone. Gee, Chris, I wish I could do that.' That was one side. The other side was physical abuse. The real problem was that everyone was going through puberty or just about to, which produces a lot of tensions.

Perhaps as a defence against the bullying of his WASP classmates, Williams found himself gravitating towards the Jewish boys at the school. They were obvious targets for discrimination because of their background and that perhaps provided some common ground between them. Most of his school friends were Jewish and they proved to be much more accepting of Williams than the other classmates had been. Williams says, with some pride, that as an 'honorary Jew' he went to 14 bar mitzvahs in a single year. His new friends also provided him with a working knowledge of Yiddish which survives now in the words and phrases that sprinkle his conversations and his stage act.

It would be fair to say that Robin Williams endured rather than enjoyed his early years at school. But now with high school looming a number of important decisions would have to be made. One of the first was that he was going to have to do something with his life. Robin Williams had finally had enough of being bullied physically and intellectually. He had decided to take charge of his life and do something about it. At roughly the same time that he was due to go to high school he had started to get into shape. He took up running, which has remained a lifelong passion, he was doing calisthenics and had lost weight, and in addition he had begun playing sport.

One of the sports he had taken up was wrestling and he found that it brought him immediate and uncharacteristic popularity; the shy young-ster who had been a target for everyone was now maturing into a suc-cessful and well-adjusted young man. Williams made the wrestling team and was undefeated in his freshman year. He was good enough to reach the state finals but there he met someone older, more experienced, and probably a bit heavier. Williams lost that bout and also picked up a shoulder injury which led to him having to give up the sport in his sophomore year. But wrestling had been good for him. He was naturally small and compact – by now he weighed just 103 pounds – which gave him an advantage, but he was also tenacious. More importantly, wrestling meant something to him. After years of being pushed around and picked on, he now had the chance to get his own back. It wasn't just about being big and tough, wrestling was also about guile and agility. This was a sport where quickness of the mind was as important as brute strength. Williams admits he got rid of a lot of pent-up aggression and frustration on the wrestling mat.

Although his shoulder injury meant he had to give up a promising career in wrestling, Robin Williams was by now well and truly hooked on sport. His running helped to keep his weight down and his mind focused. It was only a matter of time before he found another arena in which he could excel as he had at wrestling. Before that though there was the obligatory and disastrous try-out for the school football team. Williams was put in at safety with the job of stopping the other team from scoring. Given that he weighed just over 100 pounds and the average running back can weigh twice that, the experiment was not a success. By the end of the first game Williams was left with stud marks up one side and down the other. His football career lasted only a week. Such was the reputation of Detroit Country, however, that it attracted a lot of foreign-exchange students. This meant that as well as playing football they also played soccer. Again it is a sport where the small and nippy can excel against the large and slow, providing they are willing to take their lumps. Williams quickly made his mark in the burgeoning sport and became a team favourite.

His time at high school had changed Robin Williams completely. Gone was the shy, tubby boy who had been tormented in grade school. He was now a sturdy and compact youth who was not only scholastically bright but athletically successful and popular with it.

'By the end of my junior year I had my act together,' says Williams. 'I was a good student – a member of the Magna Cum Laude society, in fact – and I was going to be president of the senior class. I was looking forward to a very straight existence and was planning to attend either a small college in the Midwest or, if I was lucky, an Ivy League school.'

A bright and shining future beckoned Robin Williams. He could have gone on to study law, business, economics, whatever he chose. The world was pretty much his oyster. But while he was looking forward to his career, his father was becoming more and more disillusioned with his. The car industry in the late Sixties was not the industry that Robert Williams had joined. He was becoming increasingly frustrated with the declining standards and lack of concern for quality and value for money which he had once held so dear. As in almost every other industry, the grey men in suits were starting to take over and he wanted no part of it.

In 1968, at the age of 62, Robert Williams decided he had had enough and announced that he was retiring. Not only that, he was retiring to California. The family was on the move once again, and Robin Williams was about to find out that his way in the world would not be along the path he thought he had chosen.

3

In Old Tiburon

Tiburon is a quiet, residential town just 18 miles north of San Francisco on the other side of the Bay. It's a 40-minute rush-hour commute by car or bus to downtown San Francisco. The ferry sailing takes half the time and on a fine day it's an enjoyable trip. Tiburon is a pleasant retreat for the upwardly mobile, and during working hours the town empties as most of its population heads to either San Francisco or nearby Oakland.

The Spanish discovered Tiburon when they first explored San Francisco Bay in 1776. They named the peninsula Punta de Tiburon or Shark Point, *tiburon* being the Carib Indian word for shark. Some 220 years later Tiburon is a quiet residential community but it is one with an interesting past. Tiburon Town was created in 1884. It sprung up when the Northwestern Pacific railroad reached the north side of San Francisco Bay and completed a rail-ferry link with the city of San Francisco. Wealthy San Franciscans had been steadily migrating to the North Bay to buy property in nearby Belvedere, which had been subdivided as a 'residential park' and leisure retreat for those who could afford it. The rail-ferry link provided a fast, safe and convenient service across the Bay, and Tiburon grew steadily over the years. Sailing was another popular pastime and during Prohibition the town achieved a deal of notoriety because its safe harbour provided the ideal landing site for bootleggers smuggling booze.

Bootlegging was a lucrative but short-lived revenue source but it did attract the tourists, who continued to visit even after the Volstead Act was repealed in 1933. The heart of Tiburon remained the railroad yard and through the years the town grew around it. It was a thriving community. As well as the railroad there was good dairy farmland and herds of cattle grazed on the lush green hills surrounding the cove. It seemed that the railroad would be there for ever, but eventually it fell victim to the nation-wide drift to private transport and the last train left the depot in 1967.

Tiburon has responded well to the challenge of change. A visitor to the town now would be hard pressed to recognise its railroad origins. The railyard is long gone. A clutch of chic shops and restaurants and a discreet row of condos now nestle where the trains once ran. The former pasture land has similarly been turned into high-priced housing. The old water-front is now a shoreline park and the only trace of its heritage is in the historic Ark Row. In the old days the more Bohemian houseboat-dwellers of Tiburon would moor their boats here in the winter. A couple of the originals are still here, surrounded by shops and stores built in the same design. It's a quiet town, an upmarket Bedford Falls, and if it's not quite at the stage where everyone knows everyone else, it has a strong and well-developed sense of community. It's the sort of town where shops can close for maternity leave and the birth of the new baby is announced in the shop window to the delight of passing customers. It's the sort of town where a business can announce it's closing early because the entire staff are going on a skiing weekend. It's the sort of town, in fact, which guarantees a quiet and contented life.

It was to Tiburon that Robert Williams came when he retired from the rat race which the motor industry had become. Tiburon was in something of a period of transition then. The railyard had just closed and the redevel-opment was about to begin. Tiburon and Belvedere have now reached maximum density, but in the late Sixties there was still plenty of space for a home befitting the Williams's status. In Tiburon Robin Williams very definitely was a rich kid. He has acknowledged as much in his act with gags to the effect that he wasn't really that rich – after all he had to wait until he was 16 for his first Mercedes.

Although he had been doing well at school, there was no resentment on Williams' part over being taken out of boarding school in the Midwest and shipped half-way across the country to California. For one thing, he wanted to go home to be with his family, and for another he would relish the chance to spend more time with his father. Williams completed his high-school education at Redwood High School in Larkspur, just a ten-minute drive from his new home. The drive was made not in a Mercedes, but in a Land Rover which his parents had bought for him. Williams admits that compared with the Midwest his new home in Marin County was something of a culture shock, but nothing was quite as shocking as

his new school. At Detroit Country Day School he had worn the uniform –
a fetching blue-and-gold blazer – and carried a briefcase. At Redwood the
dress code was a little different.

> Well at first I still carried my briefcase [he remembers] and guys would
> either ask, 'Who's the geek?' or stare at me and say, 'Wow, a briefcase – how
> unmellow. You're really creating negative energy.' In the Midwest if your
> classmates thought you were creating negative energy, you'd hear 'Yo!',
> followed by a right cross to the jaw. It took me a few weeks before I showed
> up at Redwood without a tie on, and within a couple of months, I finally
> took the big step and went to school in jeans . . . Right after I started wearing
> jeans, somebody gave me my first Hawaiian shirt and I was gone; I got into
> a wild phase and I learned to totally let go.

The atmosphere inside the classrooms of Redwood High was every bit as
different from Detroit Country as the dress code. The school had courses
in film-making and psychology courses based on group encounters where
the entire class would stop what they were doing for a group hug.
Redwood also had a Black Studies department, although Williams insists
there was only one black student at the school and he wanted nothing
to do with it. The overall effect was an eye-opening and invigorating
experience for the teenage Williams.

> I went from this all boys private school to a gestalt high school where some
> of the teachers were taking acid [he remembers]. It was great to go into a
> history class and find teachers saying 'I'm Lincoln'. It changed me, [going]
> from this private school which was very rigid to this full-out crazy school
> which was amazing. I thought, 'This is certainly different. I guess we won't
> be speaking Latin here.' This was in 1969 when there was rioting in certain
> places, when people were tripping their heads off. That was the transitional
> year for me. That was the year that changed everything.

Things were different in California in 1969 from almost anywhere else in
the United States. The drug culture was almost *de rigueur* and it was at
Redwood that Williams began to experiment with drugs for the first
time. Before he came to California he claims he didn't even know what
marijuana looked like; now he was smoking it. But at that stage he never
got into it in a big way. Williams' hero at the time was the marathon
runner and Olympic champion Frank Shorter – Williams even grew a
moustache to look more like him – and he thought smoking grass might
harm his endurance. He had just made the school cross-country team

and didn't want to do anything which might damage his stamina. His only experience with serious drugs came just before he graduated when someone gave him some peyote without telling him. Watching his friend's face turn to rubber and melt before his eyes was apparently a salutary experience.

Redwood also did one more thing for Robin Williams. It made him realise that he was funny. Up till then he had been entertaining his mother with his routines at home. Obviously the strict regime at Detroit Country was not conducive to Williams' character 'schtick', but in the liberal surroundings of Redwood he blossomed.

'In the last year of high school it just sort of kicked out,' Williams explains. 'It wasn't like I had gone all through school being the class clown. It was like being a closet comedian – better latent than never – and then it finally happened in my first year at college and it was such fun.'

After his mother, his schoolmates at Redwood were Robin Williams' first serious audience and he left them rolling in the aisles. When he graduated he was voted 'Most Humorous Boy in School' and hand in hand with that he was also voted 'Least Likely to Succeed'.

In terms of his success after high school both Robin Williams and his parents had a fair idea what they wanted from life. When they sat down to choose a college his parents were keen that it should be one which would equip their son for a useful working life. His background thus far meant he would be studying liberal arts, but the idea of education in abstraction did not appeal to either Williams or his parents. They wanted their son to be able to take his obvious academic talent and wed that to some useful application in the working world. The syllabus and outlook of Claremont McKenna College seemed to fit the bill exactly. It was relatively new, having been founded in 1946, and was perfectly in tune with America's muscular take-charge view of the postwar world. The founder of the college, Donald McKenna, had envisaged an institution which would provide the basic grounding and preliminary training for business and the law. His 'Statement of Purpose' from 1946 explains his aims succinctly.

Business administration and public administration are to be taught in combination so that their numerous interlocking aspects can be clearly studied from a bi-partisan viewpoint. The emphasis on training for leadership in public and private administration does not, however, imply a narrow vocational training. The new School will require its students to complete courses in the same broad fields of human knowledge as do the social science majors in the customary liberal arts college … It is a fundamental part of the purpose of this institution that all who engage in the life and work of the college shall experience some of the great ethical and spiritual influences which are essential in building the character and effectiveness of individuals. For those who are to guide the corporate and public affairs in modern society, the importance of ethical foundations can hardly be overestimated.

At Claremont, Robin Williams would be groomed to take his place among America's élite. His parents were already looking to their son taking up a career in the diplomatic service where he could fully utilise his mother's grace and charm and his father's pragmatism. Claremont McKenna seemed to be the ideal place to equip him for that life. Williams had a sharp mind and was keen on politics and philosophy, and since Claremont specialised in political science it seemed like an ideal fit. In addition, the college also set great store by athletic achievement. Although it is a small school with around a thousand students, more than one in three of those students take part in team sports, so his new-found athletic skills would also be challenged.

The choice of this relatively staid college after a year at Redwood may seem surprising. According to Robin Williams his career choice was the last vestige of his Midwestern upbringing before becoming a fully-fledged Californian free spirit. He went to Claremont, which is some 35 miles north of Los Angeles, with the intention of studying politics and joining the foreign service. Williams took eight classes in his freshman year, mostly political theory and economics, but his choices also included one elective in theatre studies. After only an hour in class he was hooked. It was, as he remembers, 'a gas'.

'The school theatre seated about 80 people and we formed an improv group called The Synergy Trust and we filled the place every Friday night. I'd never had so much fun in my life, which was probably why I didn't show up for any of my other classes.'

Williams' work did suffer drastically and his absences from his other classes became so noticeable that at the end of the year some of the teachers who were supposed to be lecturing to him hadn't even met him. Williams maintains that his answer to the end-of-year essay in his macroeconomics course consisted of the five words 'I really don't know, sir'. It was obvious that Williams and Claremont would not remain in each other's company for long. Claremont was in the business of producing America's élite, not improvisational artists, and, having failed every course, Williams left at the end of the year. His sojourn at Claremont had been enough to convince Robin Williams that the life of a diplomat was not for him – he wanted to be an actor. When he broke the news to his parents his mother's reaction was entirely as you might expect. Laurie Williams, who believes that 'man was put on earth to know great joy', wished him good luck and told him his grandmother would have been very proud of him.

Under the circumstances his father's response was remarkably restrained. Robert Williams understood what it was like to have a dream; his had been beaten out of him by an industry obsessed with the bottom line. He was not therefore about to stand in the way of his son's dream. His only caveat, quite reasonably, was that there was no point in him paying Claremont's pricey tuition fees if Williams wasn't going into the foreign service.

'My father was wonderful,' remembers Williams. 'He said, "I'm not going to pay for you to go to that college, but if you want to come home and keep going with it [acting], that's okay. I also want you to study welding, just in case."'

Robert Williams was nothing if not a practical man. He knew that nothing could be achieved other than alienating his son by standing in his way. On the other hand he also knew that in a fickle business like acting his son would do well to have a second string to his bow – a career like welding would be perfect to fall back on. Both aims could be satisfied at Marin Junior College, a community college on Williams' side of the Golden Gate Bridge and within easy travelling distance of the family home. Robin Williams was delighted with his parents' reaction, and he was eager to fall into line with his father's wishes, but welding proved a little more than he was capable of.

'I went for one day to welding class and this man put on a mask and said, "Basically, you can be blinded if there's an accident." So I thought I would pass on that and keep on with the theatre.'

At Marin College, Williams threw himself whole-heartedly into learning more of the craft of acting. Improvisational theatre had appealed initially, he says, because there were no lines to learn. Now he was becoming more disciplined. Marin College had an excellent theatre department which would make demands on Williams' ambition. The school auditorium also had a replica of the Globe Theatre stage, and it was here that Robin Williams got his first taste of Shakespeare. He loved every minute of it.

'I was off and running,' he says about the adrenalin rush of his early days in improv. 'It was a chance to build on all the knowledge that you had acquired in school. When it works it's wonderful, but when it doesn't it's really a little scary.'

Williams' experience at Claremont had been a cathartic one. The whole world had opened up to him with the discovery that he could act and he could make people laugh. The shy little boy had been banished to the background, the grown-up Robin Williams had found a way to compensate and a way to ensure that he would never be picked on again.

4

It's a Helluva Town

The theatre course at Claremont McKenna College had opened up Robin Williams' eyes to a lot of things, and not just creative ones. In his short time in California Williams had discovered girls in a big way. Back in Michigan at the all-boys Detroit Country Day School, girls were like strange creatures from another planet. They were encountered once or twice a year when they were bused in for school dances. Having been placed in front of them they were then whisked away again, usually just as things were getting interesting, leaving behind a testosterone-drenched hall full of hormonally excited pubescent males.

But in California things were different. Williams jokes that the difference between a California girl and a Michigan girl is a handgun, but he certainly found that California girls were everything that the Beach Boys had led him to believe they might be. And they found him every bit as attractive as he found them. Williams was in good shape physically, the running and the wrestling and exercising having all contributed to a compact but athletic physique. More importantly, he could make them laugh, always a plus in any courtship ritual. The scales started to fall from Williams' eyes in the summer of 1969 when he took a holiday job before going to Claremont. Williams was working in the Trident restaurant in Sausalito, a place which would effectively be his finishing school in terms of California culture. Sausalito is now a glorified tourist trap and popular ferry destination about half-way round the coast between San Francisco and Tiburon. When Williams first knew it, the small coastal town was firmly in the vanguard of the counter-culture. It still retained much of the atmosphere of the Bohemian haven which had given the world such disparate talents as Jack London and William Randolph Hearst. Williams remembers the Trident – which is now long gone – as having the most beautiful waitresses in the world.

> It also had the strangest waitresses in the world [he recalls]. They wore spray-on two-piece macramé outfits that looked like a pair of socks. It was like 'Sonja, your nipple's hanging out'. And she'd say, 'I know, I'm trying to get tips'. Girls literally had to audition for their jobs. They'd come in and get their pictures taken and most of them were these lovely earth princesses. They'd go up to a table and say, 'Hello, I'm your waitress. How's your energy today?'

The effect of all of this on a boy from the Midwest who was dealing with the last remnants of his sexual repression must have been considerable. Not even a year at Redwood High had prepared him for this. And by the time he got to Claremont at the end of the summer his sexual hang-ups were well and truly behind him. The trip to Claremont wasn't just the beginning of college, it was a rite of passage.

> I really made the transition to manhood when I went away to college, moving away from home to where there was no one dictating what choices I had to make and I went berserk for one year. I just went 'Fuck this! There are girls to sleep with! And improvisational theatre classes where you don't have to learn any lines and people laugh.' I did all the shit that I ever wanted to do. Flunked out of all the political science classes but found what I'm doing now. It was this weird catharsis. Total freedom . . . Everything opened up. The whole world just changed in that one year.

By the time Robin Williams went to Marin Junior College he had more or less come to terms with his new identity. He was not as wild and he was much more focused on doing what he now knew he wanted to do with his life. He was, he believed, going to be an actor. Although he could make people laugh, he was convinced that his talents lay in the more legitimate theatre. And he wanted to learn and stretch himself. When they did *Romeo and Juliet* Williams chose to play Mercutio, Romeo's sidekick, rather than Romeo himself. The reason was simple: although Romeo is the one with his name in the title, Mercutio is the one with all the best lines. Robin Williams thrived on Shakespeare although his acting idols were people like Marlon Brando and Jason Robards. Privately he fancied himself following in the footsteps of someone like Robards, perhaps the quintessential American actor of his generation.

By day Williams was studying Shakespeare at Marin Junior College, but by night he was honing his improvisational skills. One of the country's leading improvisational groups, The Committee, was based in San Francisco. The first time he saw them Williams was completely knocked out. He had some experience of improvisational theatre from The Synergy Trust at Claremont, but by his own admission he was still a little naïve about the way things actually worked: 'I always thought, "Oh God, that's so brilliant." I didn't realise that some of it was scripted and they may have been doing that scene for the past three years.'

The Committee with its ground-breaking work was definitely the group to be with in the early Seventies, and Williams combined his time at Marin with studying with The Committee as well. It was an intense two-and-a-half-year period in which he did a lot of performing in almost every type of production it was possible to mount. He also came to realise that if he was serious about his ambitions as an actor then he would have to leave San Francisco. For all its European influences, San Francisco is something of a backwater theatrically. It could not compete with New York, Chicago, or even its deadly rival Los Angeles – the self-styled Athens of the West. If he stayed in San Francisco Williams faced the dubious prospect of becoming world famous in the Bay area. He could earn a living but he would not be stretched as an actor. There would be no way of maintaining the forward momentum which is vital to the growth of a performer.

The heart of the American theatrical establishment is New York, with the bright lights of Broadway as well as the chance to try out off-Broadway or, if you're really ambitious, off-off-Broadway. Either way Robin Williams knew that sooner or later he was going to have to leave San Francisco, and with his course at Marin Junior College coming to an end it was a decision that would need to be made sooner rather than later. The Juilliard School in New York is a world-wide centre of excellence as far as training in the arts is concerned. The school itself is a concrete oasis just beside the Lincoln Center in Columbus Circle at the north end of Broadway. As they make their way along its corridors and across its plazas, students can hear the roar of traffic coming from the Great White Way; they can see the glare of the neon and almost smell the greasepaint. Juilliard had primarily been concerned with teaching music, but in 1968 it had set up a drama department for those for whom the lure of Broadway was irresistible. Juilliard prides itself on its high standards and it will go to almost any lengths and travel any distance to find a promising student.

As a matter of course it regularly holds auditions in major cities through-out the United States.

Williams had heard that Juilliard had started a drama school. He had also heard that they were auditioning in San Francisco. If he could get an audition and if he was successful then he would qualify for a full schol-arship which would take him to New York without being a drain on his family. Any audition is a daunting process, and even though Williams had got over his shyness it was still a fear-drenched experience, especially with so much riding on the outcome of those few minutes. The regional auditions usually attract hundreds of would-be students and on the day Williams was told to attend there were about fifty others trying out. Williams had prepared two contrasting pieces for his audition. The first piece was a speech by Malvolio from Shakespeare's *Twelfth Night*, the second a scene from John Knowles' novel *A Separate Peace*. Both were legit pieces – the Knowles book is an allegory about love and death in the Second World War which is a standard high-school text – and there was no improvisational comedy. In any event the audition was successful and Robin Williams was offered a three-year scholarship to the Juilliard School.

Going to Juilliard in September 1973 was the biggest step of Robin Williams' life. He was 21 years old, and despite his having reached the age of maturity, his family could not have been anything but concerned. He had lived a life of privilege, he had been born to money, and although he had been away from home before there was a world of difference between surviving at boarding school or college and surviving on his own in New York. There would be no support system, no schoolmates – even bullying classmates are better than none at all – and no friends. He would be completely alone. For all that, however, Williams was perversely keen to go. He knew it would be difficult and possibly emotionally painful, but he also knew that he was in danger of 'becoming terminally mellow' if he remained in San Francisco. New York held a sense of danger, a threat which Williams genuinely found appealing. He suspected the city would force him to toughen up mentally as well as physically, although he couldn't have expected it would have happened quite so quickly.

On my first day in New York [he remembers] I went to school dressed like a typical California kid. I wore tie-up yoga pants and a Hawaiian shirt, and I kept stepping in dog shit with my thongs. My first week there I was in a bus going uptown to see an apartment when an old man two seats in front of me suddenly collapsed and died. He slumped over against a woman sitting next to him and she said 'Get off me!' and moved away. Somebody told the driver what had happened, so he stopped the bus and ordered everybody off, but I wanted to stay and help. The driver told me, 'He's dead, motherfucker, now get off! You can't do shit for him, so take your raggedy California ass and get outta my bus!' I knew that living in New York was certainly going to be different.

That's a story which sounds as though it may have been embellished somewhat over the years, but the point is still well made. Life in New York was different and, like Dorothy, Robin Williams knew he wasn't in Kansas any more. One thing helped; he found a friend very quickly. Because he was 21 when he went to Juilliard, Robin Williams was much older than most of the other students. He was being taken in as an advanced student which meant he would then have to work much harder to catch up with those who had already been at Juilliard for at least a year. Williams was one of two advanced students, the other being a young man called Christopher Reeve who had similarly been studying elsewhere.

Christopher Reeve was the ideal Juilliard student. He was dashing, handsome and prodigiously talented. Like Williams he was a privileged child; his mother was a journalist and his father a college professor. Unlike Williams he came from a broken home; his parents divorced when he was four although his mother was later married again, to a stockbroker. He had also started in the public school system but was so gifted that he switched to a private school so he might be more challenged academically. Something of a prodigy, Reeve studied music and voice and worked as an assistant orchestra conductor. When he was only nine years old he made his stage début in a professional production of a Gilbert and Sullivan operetta at the McCarter Theater in Princeton. By the time he was 16 he had an agent and immediately after graduating from high school he played Hollywood star Celeste Holm's leading man in a touring production of a play called *The Irregular Verb to Love*. He continued to combine professional acting with his studies at Cornell University thanks to an understanding agent who arranged auditions to suit his academic schedule.

Reeve had been at Cornell – where he majored in English and graduated with honours – while Williams had been at Marin. However, when they were thrown together in adverse circumstances they became fast friends. Reeve, who is a native New Yorker, is a few months younger than Williams but it seems reasonable to assume that Williams would have been somewhat in awe of a man who could be so effortlessly talented and still so likeable. Reeve for his part recalls being both amused and intrigued by 'this California kid who walked around in tie-dyed shirts and a track suit

and knew about Eastern religions and Tai Chi'. Reeve was fitting in pretty
well at Juilliard, but Williams was finding the work more difficult than he
could have imagined and it was only his friendship with Reeve which
made life bearable. They were near-neighbours, as it turned out, and after
a day of being mauled by his teachers, Williams would walk the half-mile
or so to Reeve's apartment building. The two young men would open a
bottle of the cheapest wine they could stomach and talk about cabbages
and kings long into the night.

 If the first few months in New York were hard, there was worse to come
for Robin Williams. Christmas rolled around and everyone, including
Reeve, had gone home for the holidays. Williams couldn't afford to go
back to Tiburon and was too proud to ask his parents for the cash they
would doubtless have gladly given. Instead he chose to stay on his own in
New York.

It was the first cold winter I'd experienced in many years and New York
seemed unbearably bleak and lonely. One day, I started sobbing and I
couldn't stop. When I ran out of tears my body just kept on going; it was
like having emotional dry heaves. I went through two days like that and
finally hit rock bottom and realised I had a choice; I could either tube out
or level off and relax. At that point, I became like a submarine on the bottom
that blows out some ballast and gets back up again ... Once in a while it's
good to have a nervous breakdown. A little emotional house cleaning never
hurt anybody. Once all my anxieties were behind me, the rest of the year
was easy.

5

Damaged but Interesting

Robin Williams' breakdown in December of 1973 was simply an accident waiting to happen. He had gone to New York just three months earlier convinced that he was doing the right thing, determined that he was no longer going to be a big fish in a small pond. What he found was that he didn't know a fraction of what he thought he knew and if Juilliard was the pond in which he was now swimming, then he was barely at the level of plankton. Basically his teachers at Juilliard told him in pretty short order that almost everything he thought he had learned up to this point was completely and totally wrong.

'It's a little like the Army,' says Williams by way of comparison. 'They break you down and then they build you back up. In my first few days at school I learned that I didn't project out, that I talked too fast, and that I swallowed my words.'

Williams' confidence was shot to pieces. It also wasn't helped by the fact that, coming in as advanced students at an age where they should have been in their third year, he and Christopher Reeve were frequently in classes by themselves. Williams would almost certainly have suffered in comparison to Reeve at this stage, but now his shortcomings were being exposed almost on a one-to-one basis. The teaching methods at Juilliard contributed to this. At Marin Junior College and at The Committee, the method was to take scenes, break them down, and then discuss them. At Juilliard, however, the teaching focused on the individual skills and techniques that were required for an actor. Williams at this stage was

an intuitive performer rather than a disciplined one, and he was quickly
very aware of how much he needed to learn.

> One of the first things I tried in class was a religious monologue Dudley
> Moore had done in *Beyond the Fringe*. I thought I had done fine but my
> teacher, a man named Michael Kahn, hated it so much that he said to me,
> 'You have two choices. Come back and do it again or give up any thoughts
> you have about an acting career.' He really was furious with me and it was
> because I had only imitated what I had heard and hadn't tried to find new
> things that would make the piece mine.

Williams was shocked by Kahn's criticism but he also acknowledges that
it had the desired effect. It was supposed to shake him up and make him
think about what he wanted to do, rather than regurgitate other people's
ideas.

> A lot of teachers were intense [Williams continues], including a New Yorker
> named Gene Loesser who would stop you in the middle of a reading and
> shout, 'What the fuck do you think you're doing?' What we were doing was
> working our asses off; between all the acting, speech, movement and even
> fencing classes, we'd be at Juilliard from eight in the morning until nine or
> ten o'clock at night.

Although Michael Kahn may have loathed Williams' monologue, there
were others, including Christopher Reeve, who did not share that opinion.
'John Houseman had an idea of what the Juilliard actor should be, well
spoken but a bit homogenised, so it's not surprising the teachers were
thrown by Robin,' according to Reeve. 'That monologue from *Beyond the
Fringe* made us laugh so hard we were in physical pain. They said it was
a "comedy bit, not acting".'

John Houseman was the head of the Juilliard drama department.
Houseman was one of America's most distinguished and respected actors
and writers. With Orson Welles he had founded the Mercury Theater and
helped write and produce some of their most famous work, including the
notorious *War of the Worlds* broadcast in 1938. Houseman had also
contributed significantly to *Citizen Kane* both as a writer and producer,
but he and Welles parted company when Welles insisted on taking all the
credit. Undeterred by the acrimonious split, Houseman went on to a
successful career as a producer working with directors such as Vincente
Minnelli, Max Ophuls and John Frankenheimer. In 1973, the year that
Williams went to Juilliard, Houseman had made his film début at the age

of 70 when he starred in *The Paper Chase*. The role of a sadistic law professor was originally intended for Edward G. Robinson, but terminal illness prevented Robinson from taking the part. When it was offered to James Mason he said he wasn't interested, so director James Bridges then went to Juilliard to find Houseman. The part made Houseman an international name and he won an Oscar for Best Supporting Actor, joining an élite band who have won Oscars for their film débuts. He would also reprise the role in a short-lived but highly-praised television series based on the film. By any standard Houseman was the jewel in Juilliard's drama crown.

It was undoubtedly at Houseman's suggestion that Williams was taken out of the third-year advanced class and made to start all over again at the first-year level. Christopher Reeve believes it was simply because they didn't know what to make of Williams. Reeve was always convinced of Williams' ability. The first time he saw his friend act it was in *The Night of the Iguana* in which Williams played Nonno, the old man. According to Reeve it was 'an amazingly full characterisation'. It seems certain that although he was a long way from the finished article, Houseman saw something in this young man whom he described as 'damaged but interesting'. By taking him back and grounding him in the basics he perhaps hoped that the talent he recognised would reach its potential. In many ways it was a real-life version of his screen persona as the tyrannical Professor Kingsfield.

Whatever the reason, Williams responded to Houseman, whom he took as a kind of role model. He admired Houseman's passion and saw the sense in Houseman's argument that if he was classically trained then he could go anywhere. During his early days at Juilliard Williams was having particular problems with an English Literature course which he looked liked failing. It was Houseman who took the time to sit him down for a very elegant pep talk in which he advised him that perhaps it was time to pull himself together. Williams quickly became one of John Houseman's biggest fans. He knew that he was having a hard time at the hands of his mentor, but at the same time he could see what Houseman – described by Williams as 'a card-carrying radical' – was trying to do.

'I don't think he wanted us just to crank out classical actors,' says Williams – at odds with Christopher Reeve for once – 'but people who would go out and change things.'

Houseman by this stage, with the Oscar and the television series, had become a man of some influence as well as something of a household name. Williams could not have been the only one who saw the irony in the situation.

'John Houseman gave a speech one day,' Williams recalls, 'in which he said, "The theatre needs you. Don't be tempted by television or the movies. The theatre needs new plasma, new blood." And then a week later, we saw him [on television] in a Volvo commercial.'

Although it was never completely easy, life at Juilliard became progressively easier after that first cathartic Christmas. Williams' comedy may not have gone down well with the teachers, but his fellow students loved it. Between classes and after school the locker-room became an impromptu improv comedy club as Williams and his friends tried constantly to outdo each other – the atmosphere was intensely competitive. Money worries had also eased quite considerably. Williams took his new-found skill in movement classes and began to perform at lunchtime as a mime on the steps of the Metropolitan Museum. Williams' skill and gift for physical comedy made him a very successful draw for the tourists and office workers. On a good week he could make up to $100, which helped to pay for his food, clothes and rent.

During his second year at Juilliard Robin Williams fell in love. He had been in love before, having had a spectacular crush on a young girl he had met at Marin Junior College, but this, he felt, was the real thing. The girl in question – Williams has never revealed her name – had come to New York from California and Williams was completely captivated by her. She was, he remembers, a free spirit, and when the two of them went back to Marin County at the end of his second year the relationship really deepened. His girlfriend was staying in California and Williams was so much in love that he did not want to go back to Juilliard.

As he saw it there wasn't a lot to go back for. Christopher Reeve had graduated from Juilliard the previous year and had gone first to England and then to France, where he worked at the Old Vic and the Comédie Française. When he came back to the United States he landed a leading role as Ben Harper on the long-running daytime soap opera *Love of Life*. Without his best friend Juilliard held little charm for Williams, and he was also concerned about the amount of actual training that he would now be getting. In their third year Juilliard students spent a lot of time out on the road performing shows in community theatre projects. They could go from playing the toughest neighbourhood in the Bronx one night to playing the rarefied social climes of Park Avenue on the next. Life was hard for Williams. Maintaining a long-distance romance was an incredible strain. He was racking up phone bills of around $400 a month just to keep in touch and by the time he paid these there was barely enough money left to pay the rent.

As Williams saw it there was only one thing left to do. He would leave

Juilliard and go back to California to be with the woman in his life. He was just over two years into his three-year course, but it was not as difficult a decision as he had thought it might be. Once again, as he had in San Francisco, Williams felt he had reached a point where he had gone as far as he could. It was time to move on. He wasn't sure where to in career terms, but he knew he had reached the end of the line at Juilliard. Geographically at least he was moving on to San Francisco. When he got back, however, things didn't work out anything like he had planned. He and his girlfriend set up home together, but after little more than a month of living with each other they parted company. The relationship ended and Williams went into a massive depression, which only got worse when he couldn't find any work.

Juilliard had been good for Robin Williams. He is not slow to acknowledge the debt he owes to the institution for providing him with the grounding which enabled him to make such a success of his career. But it undoubtedly also exacted its pound of flesh from the young man. He was a square peg whom they had resolutely but unsuccessfully tried to force into a round hole without much regard for the consequences.

'They were trying to mould Robin into a standardised Juilliard product,' says Christopher Reeve, citing Kevin Kline as the perfect example of what he believes they were looking for. 'But Robin was too special, too original, to be that. They kept breaking him down. It's amazing how he tried, how much he took.'

6

Fly Like an Eagle

O nce again Robin Williams was in the middle of a deep depression. His early days back in San Francisco after dropping out of Juilliard were among the unhappiest of his life. His relationship with his girlfriend, which had seemed so full of promise back in New York, had now come to a sudden and abrupt end. It's interesting to speculate on the reasons, even though Williams himself seldom speaks publicly about it. In an interview in *Playboy* magazine some years later, the subject turned to the Bush administration's stance on abortion. Williams agonised about the plight of the poor who would be forced into a terrible dilemma of either having an unwanted child or consulting a potentially deadly backstreet abortionist. Williams offered that making the decision to have an abortion was not an easy one, which begged the obvious question from interviewer Lawrence Grobel about whether he had ever found himself in that position.

'Long, long, long time ago,' Williams replied candidly, 'and it was because we were too young and it wasn't right.'

The time period between the 1992 *Playboy* interview and the break-up of his relationship in 1976 would certainly constitute a 'long, long, long time ago'. That being the case, did Williams and the love of his life split up because she had become pregnant?

Whatever the reason, Robin Williams' relationship had come to a dead end, but so too, it seemed, had his career. Williams had set aside the promise of a successful career three years earlier to go to New York. Surely, he reasoned, with almost three years of training at one of the world's finest schools behind him it would not be difficult to find work in his home town. As it turned out, however, when he tried to join some of the city's professional theatre companies, no one wanted to know. Williams couldn't get arrested in San Francisco in 1976. If he thought he had come to the end of the line in Juilliard, he must have begun to realise that in San Francisco he had well and truly hit the buffers.

Williams' only recourse was to go back to the only other thing he knew he could do. He put his legitimate acting career on hold and decided he would try his hand at making people laugh. San Francisco in 1976 was one of the breeding grounds for America's nascent generation of stand-up comedians. The city teemed with comedy clubs, and if Williams could be as successful with an audience as he had with his school fellows at Redwood and Marin and his classmates at Juilliard then he might have a chance.

> Comedy had always been an outlet for me [he explains], but I'd always treated it a bit like a guerrilla activity. It became primary for two reasons. It was a form of therapy which helped me get over the relationship and it also allowed me to support myself for the first time. I'd do $25 a night gigs and I'd actually make enough to pay my $100 a month rent. I was self-sustaining and I could say, 'No Pop, I don't need that cheque. But thanks.'

Williams' comment about his parents is interesting. Obviously they would not have been unconcerned about how their son was feeling, but they were caring enough to stay at arm's length to let him work out his problems for himself. The fact that his father was more than willing to subsidise him in order for his son to follow his dream also gives the lie to the notion of Robert Williams being aloof and uncaring.

Robin Williams quickly joined a comedy workshop which was run by a man called, appropriately, Frank Kidder. While the students worked in classes during the week, Kidder encouraged them to put what they had learned into practice by performing at the weekend. Williams quickly put a stand-up routine together and made his comedy début at a now defunct club called The Intersection on Union Street. The club was a former coffee-house in the basement of an old church. Since the comedians would generally come on after some avant-garde feminist poetry readings it wasn't necessarily the easiest room he would ever play. Another veteran of The Intersection, Lorenzo Matawaran, remembers it being a tough room. But he also remembers how Williams made it his own: 'Robin got up and blew everyone away, but he was meek the way he still is. He'd do a monster set and then come sit down and ask us in that little voice, "Did

I go over?" We used to have an Indian name for him – "Squirrel-Boy-Who-Turns-Into-Golden-Eagle-Onstage". When that grew too long we just shortened it to "Eagle".'

Williams quickly established himself and began to make the rounds of the clubs, touring the 'open mike' nights – generally in the quieter earlier part of the week – when just about anyone could get up and do their stuff. As he became more successful the bookings started to get better. The Boarding House was a San Francisco comedy club which prided itself on bringing in the best comedy talent from Los Angeles, New York and right across the country. Robin Williams became the first local comedian to play The Boarding House in what amounted to a major coup. His success there meant that he had opened the doors for other local comics to follow.

'Robin has a tremendously inquiring mind,' says David Allen, the owner of The Boarding House, who became a close friend of his new find. 'He was a street performer back in New York, so he knows how to look into people's lives, but he's got a number of other interests. He roller-skates, has a very serious concern about environmental issues, has a deep and abiding interest in the theatre, and he gets a kick out of sports cars. Everything he does for fun seems to end up in his act somehow because he is such a fantastic observer.'

Robin Williams was nonetheless still a fairly troubled young man at this stage. He admits himself that, had he not been doing stand-up, he shudders to think what the consequences might have been. The comedy was a release which enabled him to deal with the frustrations of the world. What he referred to as his 'duck and cover' technique allowed him to hide his real self away while dealing with his problems through a variety of different characters. The traditions of stand-up comedy are rooted in verbal violence. Old-time vaudevillians and the comedians who plied their trade in the early days of radio and television would talk of their work in the most aggressive terms. Audiences were 'killed' or 'slayed' or 'murdered'. It was almost an act of gladiatorial defiance as the lone comedian stepped into the spotlight in front of the baying mob.

But in the case of Robin Williams his stand-up comedy was a defence. Even when he went into his complete, frenetic, borderline psychotic routine – what he describes as 'full tilt bozo' mode – it was an act of self-defence. Williams was hiding from his problems, just as he had at school. His solution was to make people laugh while showing nothing of his real self for fear it might be used against him. His routines were a collection of fears, neuroses and repression – usually sexual repression.

'You're trying to keep the world out by being aggressively funny,' says

Williams, 'or by mocking it. Because somewhere along the line, when you let it in, it will hurt.'

Although the quickfire synaptic rhythms of his word-associative patter routines quickly became his trademark, the basis of Williams' comedy at this stage came in portraying different characters. The comedians he most admired were Peter Sellers and Jonathan Winters.

'Jonathan because of the pure madness,' he says of a man who used to do a routine in which he played King Quasi of Quasiland, a country which was five feet wide and eleven miles long. Its main exports were string and spaghetti. 'Jonathan transforms himself. He's like Buddha meets Gumby. He becomes it. With Sellers it's mostly the characters, that he could become so many different things. People who knew him said he just locked off and became the character.'

Those who knew Sellers would also point out that he was a man who would hide behind a number of comic personae, so that when the characters were stripped away there was almost nothing left of Sellers himself. Williams put together a rapidly expanding repertory company of weird and wonderful characters to hide behind. Over the years these would come to include Nicky Lenin, the Soviet Union's only entertainer, the Rev. Ernest Lee Sincere, a holy-rolling evangelist, Little Billy, a child who performed the Death of a Sperm ballet, a blind bluesman, and himself as an older man looking back on his life. These characters gave him a platform from which to free-associate and work the room while at the same time giving him something to hide behind. The characters also gave him a chance to develop a rapport with his audience; Williams' relationship with those who've paid money to see him is a good deal more gentle than that of some of his colleagues.

> I don't like to attack them [he explains]. There's a real fine line there, but if someone attacks me, like a heckler, then it's open season. I guess at the end you have to be prepared to take it yourself. If you're a character then you can get away with it, but if you're yourself then it's you who's doing the attacking and that's different. I used to do an evangelist who would heal people. I could do 'You with the bad wig, come forward. You could fly to Persia on that rug. Let's get a tight weave for Jesus.' You can do that when you're a character, you can play with those kinds of things.

Having left The Intersection behind and having cracked The Boarding House, Williams continued to ply his trade at a number of well-known clubs. One of the toughest was the Salamander in Berkeley, where he claims a bartender once shot a customer for having the temerity to ask

for change. He was also becoming a regular at the Holy City Zoo, a club
near Golden Gate Park where he had begun in the open mike nights on
Mondays and Tuesdays. It was a small club which would hold no more
than 60 people on a good night, but Williams liked the atmosphere. He
built up something of a following and began to work in the club as a
barman to supplement his comedy income. Also working in the same
club was a cocktail waitress called Valerie Velardi. Like Williams she had
her eye on bigger things while she was working at the Holy City Zoo. Her
waitressing work was helping to put her through school. She was a dancer
with ambitions to become a choreographer, and through a mixture of
talent and determination she finally earned her Masters degree in Modern
Dance.

The first night that Robin Williams and Valerie Velardi met he was
coming on for 24 and she was 26. He pretended to be a Frenchman and
she let him maintain the pretence even though she knew better. They
quickly started a relationship and were soon inseparable.

'Was it love at first sight?' Williams wondered later. 'More like lust. She
was this Italian woman, a Napoletana girl. She didn't dress sexy, she just
looked . . . hot. Caliente. We hung out, we started living together.'

After the collapse of his last relationship Valerie Velardi was exactly
what Robin Williams needed. Valerie was, by all accounts, a hard-headed
and pragmatic young woman. The way her life had panned out up till
now had given her little option to be anything else. She was the daughter
of a building contractor, whose parents split up when she was 12 years
old, leaving her to become a surrogate mother to three younger siblings.
Valerie was used to providing a maternal influence; emotionally Robin
Williams was still a mess and she provided a centre and a focus for his
life. But it wasn't always easy.

'Since he didn't grow up with other children, he [Robin] is an only
child as far as I'm concerned,' she said. 'The result is that he has a very
rich private life, and it's hard to filter in. It's hard to get in deep with
someone who's used to taking care of himself only. It's such a cliché but
they make their own world.'

Within a month of meeting in the Holy City Zoo, Robin Williams and
Valerie Velardi had moved in together. He thrived on the new-found
stability in his life, and the work started to pour in. The money was
getting better, the clubs were getting bigger, and the audiences were
growing more and more enthusiastic. Once again Williams was faced
with the prospect of being a big fish in a middling-sized pond. Both he
and Velardi knew there was only one thing to do. They would have to
make the leap of faith and try their luck in Los Angeles. It's debatable

who actually had the idea of going to Los Angeles. In different interviews both Velardi and Williams have taken the credit. It seems more likely, however, that with so many other comedians from San Francisco heading for Los Angeles, Williams would naturally have wanted to prove himself in the bigger arena. The notion of heading south probably just grew organically out of the events of their daily lives. But no matter who made the decision, there was no doubt that it was Valerie Velardi who was making the sacrifice. She was mid-way through her studies and she would have to put her ambition on hold to further her boyfriend's career. In interviews of the period she never seems to have had less than 100 per cent faith in Williams' ability to succeed.

'I guess I always knew Robin was spectacularly talented,' she says, 'but I didn't trust the show business industry to pick up on it so quickly.'

Williams was well aware of what he was asking Valerie to give up. He knew that she would be passing up the chance of a career for herself because there wasn't a lot of call for choreographers in Los Angeles, a city not noted for its dance companies.

> Val supported me . . . kept me sane and most important she kept me happy.
> I always wanted to hit it big, but I thought it would be easier in San Francisco,
> where there was less competition. It was Val who made the sacrifice. She
> dropped her own career to help me with mine. She encouraged me, almost
> ordered me, to go to Hollywood. I trust Val completely. She's the best friend
> I have. Because she is on the outside looking in she sees things a lot clearer
> than I can ever possibly see them. Every so often she'll tell me to come and
> wash the dishes, and I like that because she knows it will keep my feet on
> the ground.

Of such mundane domesticity are show-business careers made. Six months after they met, Robin Williams and Valerie Velardi were on their way to Los Angeles and the Mecca for all stand-up comics, The Comedy Store on Sunset Boulevard. With its three showcase rooms The Comedy Store is effectively a multiplex for comedians. Agents, managers and other comics trawl the club like a comedy meat market looking for a hot comic or a routine they can lift. Robin Williams described his first viewing of it as 'a terrorising combination of the Roman arena and The Gong Show'. In the space of a week some 200 comedians will get up in front of the microphone and look for his or her fifteen minutes of fame; that magic moment which will propel them to sitting on the late-night couch swapping anecdotes with Dave or Jay or Conan. Robin Williams' audition was scheduled for only a few days after they had arrived in Los Angeles.

Typically he would have to show his mettle on open mike night on a Monday and prove his worth against anyone who wanted to pick up the microphone and tell a gag. The worst moments of Robin Williams' life have always been just before he goes on-stage. These are the moments when the fear has to be recognised, acknowledged and locked away before he goes out to face a crowd of complete strangers.

'My stomach was in my shoes, I was so scared,' he remembers of that first night in Los Angeles. 'But after less than a minute I felt comfortable. I knew I could make these people laugh.'

To borrow a phrase from the vernacular of Henny Youngman or Milton Berle, Williams slayed them. He had them laughing themselves sick and he was hired on the spot for a residency at a basic $200 a week. The Comedy Store was just one stop on the LA circuit. Williams worked the circuit vigorously, sometimes being billed as Robin McLaurim Williams. Among his early triumphs was an audition at the equally famous The Improv. This was typical Williams – a five-minute penis joke. The routine involved a man masturbating and watching his penis grow so large that he couldn't get out of the room. Once again they laughed until they were begging for mercy. Within weeks of leaving San Francisco to seek the big time Robin Williams was basking in the glow of being the hottest new talent in town. Williams hooked up with the late Harvey Lembeck who was running one of Los Angeles' best-known improvisational comedy ensembles. The Harvey Lembeck Comedy Workshop was the place to be if you wanted to be noticed. Lembeck was rigorous in his methods. He would simply stand there and yell out a subject and the comedians would then have to come up with a funny routine. One of his topics was a request that the class members improvise a phone call to explain that they were going to be late for an appointment. While the other comedians came up with the predictable responses, Williams improvised a routine about calling God. Lembeck knew that he had a rare talent on his hands.

Among his fellow comedians at the Lembeck company was John Ritter, who was still some years away from his TV fame on *Three's Company*.

> I saw the way this dude was dressed [remembers Ritter of their first meeting]. In baggy pants, suspenders, a beaten-up tux over high-topped sneakers, a straw hat with the brim falling off, and John Lennon glasses with no glass in the frames. I thought, 'Well, this guy is definitely going for the sight gag.' I was almost a big suspicious. So I watched carefully and he turned out to be the funniest guy I've ever seen.

Ritter and Williams became fast friends, behaving like poster boys for arrested development. They would run around like overgrown kids with water pistols or firing suction dart guns at each other. But at the same time they were capable of crafting the most brilliant improvisations. Ritter naturally settled into the classic role of the comic feed, providing Williams with the wind beneath his wings and allowing him to transform from Squirrel Boy to Golden Eagle. Ritter never once resented the arrangement. He says he saw right from the start how talented Williams was and how much potential he had. He hadn't a moment's hesitation in taking the part of the straight man. 'The first bit I ever saw him do,' remembers Ritter, 'was as a kiddie-show host. And it was the most demented thing you can imagine. He brought these puppets on-stage and did those weird voices and wound up doing an S&M routine with the puppets which is indescribable.'

Wherever he went Robin Williams was making a big impression. Nowhere more than at The Comedy Store, where his resident spots were among the biggest draws of the week. One of the people who had caught word of the buzz about the new kid in town was television producer George Schlatter. He came in one night and found that everything he had heard was true, and then some. 'I saw Robin doing a fragmented free-association act that was very, very funny,' says Schlatter. 'He was doing what I'd call dirty material. He had a full beard and hair down to his shoulders, he was barefoot and he wore overalls and a cowboy hat. But it was his originality that knocked me out.'

With the memory of that performance fresh in his mind, Schlatter approached Williams sometime later at The Comedy Store to pitch an idea to him. He was putting together a revival of *Rowan and Martin's Laugh-In* with an entirely new cast and he wanted Williams to be in it. Williams agreed almost immediately and found himself as the first cast member in what was supposed to be a pioneering new comedy show.

Williams was signed for six shows at the princely sum of $1500 a week. He was about to go from being a big fish in a small pool to being a household name. Or at least, that was the theory.

7

Sock it to Me

In 1968 radio announcer Gary Owens took American audiences for the first time to 'beautiful downtown Burbank' and brought possibly America's most revolutionary television show into their homes. Not since the great days of *Your Show of Shows* with Sid Caesar, which virtually defined television comedy in its earliest days, had a show had the impact of *Rowan and Martin's Laugh-In.*

Hosted by Dan Rowan and Dick Martin, a couple of actor-comedians in the classic pairing as suave straight man and dumb stooge, the show broke the mould as far as American television was concerned. Its formula of fast-moving, often pointless sketches with inanely repeated punchlines took America by storm. The humour, with its references to sex and drugs, was *risqué* by the standards of the period, and the whole psychedelic layout of the studio set was directly influenced by the West Coast drug culture. It made household names of Arte Johnson, Ruth Buzzi and Judy Carne, who became known as the 'Sock it to me' girl since her sole function seemed to be saying the line and then getting smacked in the head with a gag boxing glove. Other jokes were delivered by a body-painted go-go dancer, but those few moments of fame launched Goldie Hawn to stardom.

America loved it. It was a show which was directly in tune with the mood of the period. Sex and drugs were on the agenda and the establishment was there to be lampooned in the form of big-name guests who would turn up to get the treatment every week. One memorable show featured John Wayne no less in a giant pink bunny suit. *Rowan and*

Martin's Laugh-In was an instant success. Phrases like 'Sock it to me', 'You bet your bippy' and Dick Martin's lascivious 'Blow in her ear and she'll follow you anywhere' became part of the national vocabulary. The show was launched in the 1968–69 television season and stayed at number one in the Nielsen ratings for two years. But it was a programme which was very definitely of its time. After two years at the top the ratings bombed in the third season. What had once been fresh and pioneering now seemed stale and repetitive, and the show was cancelled. Even so, it left behind a rich legacy both in terms of the talent it produced and the influence it had. Rowan and Martin paved the way for shows like *Saturday Night Live* and comedians like Chevvy Chase, Eddie Murphy, John Belushi, Carrie Fisher, Dana Carvey and indeed Robin Williams himself.

Since he was away at boarding school in the great days when *Laugh-In* was in its pomp, it is debatable whether Robin Williams would have been able to see the show in first run. But he was certainly aware of its image and its reputation, which is why he was so enthusiastic when George Schlatter approached him that night at The Comedy Store. Williams was so keen that he even took Schlatter's advice and spruced himself up by shaving, getting his hair cut, and wearing something approximating to a conventional suit for his meeting with the television executives. Schlatter is a veteran television writer and producer with a number of shows such as *The Cher Show, Funny People,* and a Sinatra 80th birthday tribute to his credit before and since. He had a fair idea that with the growth of comic talent in the mid-Seventies there might be a possibility to recapture some of the magic of *Rowan and Martin's Laugh-In* with a whole new cast. After spotting him in The Comedy Store, Schlatter suspected that Williams would be the corner-stone of his new show, called simply *Laugh-In.*

Williams was as excited as he had ever been. When he knew he'd landed the part and realised that it paid $1500 a week, he thought he had made the big time. Mentally he was dreaming of the big house and the pool and everything else that comes with the trappings of a smash hit TV show. It didn't take long before his illusions were shattered.

'Unfortunately doing a remake of a show which had been one of the milestones of TV was a little like doing *Jaws VI*. How are you going to top the original? Are you going to have the shark come up on land and gum people to death? *Laugh-In* sure sobered my ass up. The show lasted 14 weeks and most of the time I played a redneck or a Russian.'

Schlatter had hired Williams and then put him in a show which stopped him doing what he did best. He simply wanted a clever mimic and a character comedian and there was nowhere in the show to use the more mercurial side of Williams' comic nature. *Laugh-In* became a personal if lucrative purgatory for Williams, but he never once gave anything less than his total effort. He was not happy but he wasn't about to stop working. Joan Rivers, who met Williams for the first time in the *Laugh-In* revival, says he seemed to be living off his nerves.

'You know how it is. You're struggling, you want to be noticed, and the only way to be noticed is to be the funny boy,' she recalls. 'We took a picture together and he never stopped mugging. You wanted to tie him down and say "Stop".'

George Schlatter quickly found that Dan Rowan and Dick Martin had caught lightning in a bottle with their show. It simply could not be repeated. The mood of the country had changed, and the mood of the television audience had changed along with it. Comedy in 1977 was bland and safe; it was *Welcome Back Kotter* and *Three's Company.* Within weeks it was obvious that the show was not going to work and Schlatter announced that he would be cancelling the run. It was something of a pre-emptive strike on his part: to cancel before they were cancelled, and also to try to attract the attention of the other two networks. There was no response, so *Laugh-In* ended, but its demise would have repercussions for Robin Williams further down the track.

Laugh-In had done nothing for Williams in career terms except to give him experience of working in television. It also provided him with what he now believes may be one of the single most embarrassing moments of his life. Like the original show the *Laugh-In* revival featured big-name guest stars coming on to act effectively as stooges for these young comics. Williams got to work with Hollywood legends like James Stewart, Frank Sinatra and Bette Davis, which was the up-side of the job. It also, unfortunately for him, provided a down-side which almost ended his fledgling career in ignominy.

'Frank Sinatra was on *Laugh-In* one week,' Williams recalled later. 'I went up to him and said, "Mr Sinatra, I'm so happy to meet you I could drop a log." I was afraid they would want to fire me and that I would have to explain that I never meant to upset Uncle Frank. Thank God he laughed,' said a relieved Williams.

Williams left *Laugh-In* after 14 weeks a little older, a whole lot wiser, and quite a bit better off financially. Whatever doubts he may have felt about appearing in a flop show were quickly quelled when he was hired almost straight away for another show. This time he would be working with one of his comedy idols, Richard Pryor.

For many Pryor is possibly the greatest stand-up comedian America has ever produced. He is certainly among the most influential, and his work has been an inspiration to a generation of black American comedians such as Eddie Murphy, the Wayans brothers, Martin Lawrence and Chris Rock. Given Pryor's background, it's astonishing he survived, far less became a comedian. He was born in Peoria, Illinois and raised by his grandmother in the brothel where his mother worked. He was abused physically and sexually as a child and abandoned completely by his mother when he was ten years old. The acorn plainly did not fall far from the tree in Pryor's case, and he dropped out of high school, became a teenage father himself, and spent many of his waking hours stoned on drink or drugs. Surprisingly, when he began stand-up comedy at the age of 17 his routines were safe and non-confrontational, in the mould of his role model Bill Cosby. Pryor was carving out a solid career for himself on stage and in cabaret until one night in 1969 when he had a breakdown on stage in Las Vegas.

When Pryor returned to performing he was a changed man. In 1969 he moved to the West Coast, became a black activist and was heavily involved in the counter-culture. His new stage act reflected his newly politicised status. His unashamedly excoriatingly confrontational routines about white versus black, especially in the twin areas of sex and drugs, were both shocking and rib-achingly funny. Before he ruined his health and his career with substance abuse – the lowest point came when he set himself on fire while free-basing – Pryor was as good as it got; he was the comedian to whom all others aspired. He took no risks and he took no prisoners. His 1979 concert movie *Richard Pryor – Live in Concert* is generally held to be the best stand-up routine ever committed to celluloid and one of the rare examples of Pryor's uncompromising genius caught on camera. Comedians idolised Pryor, and Robin Williams was no exception. There are comedians who make him laugh, such as George Carlin or the late Sam Kinison or Jay Leno. But Pryor was one of the few comedians that he actively envied, especially in his daring and courage in doing what Williams after all could not – talking about his own life on stage in the most frank and candid terms.

'When he kicks there is no one in the world better,' says Williams of Pryor. 'No one has ever done what he does. He is the king of that . . . And his stand-up, he sets the rules. Then he destroyed the boundaries.'

NBC, the network which had bombed with the *Laugh-In* revival, had signed Pryor to a weekly series, and Williams was also signed as a regular member of the supporting cast. Pryor had worked in television before. In his Cosby clone days he had starred in the *Kraft Summer Music Hall* for NBC in 1966. Even after his conversion Pryor had been successful as part of the Emmy-winning writing team for *The Lily Tomlin Show* and *Lily.*

Looking back, it is astonishing that anyone could have thought even for a moment that the scatology of Richard Pryor could fit on prime-time television in those pre-cable days. He had been on his best behaviour for a successful comedy showcase *The Richard Pryor Special?* Nevertheless both the network and Pryor felt that it could be made to work. NBC was obviously gambling on his new-found status as a wholesome film star in *Silver Streak*, the first of a successful series of films with Gene Wilder. It took only the first shot of the first episode of *The Richard Pryor Show* to prove both the comedian and the network catastrophically wrong. Pryor had planned to start the series by poking fun at the fact that he, possibly America's most threatening and seditious comedian, was now on prime-time television. The idea was to start with a tight shot on Pryor's face with him saying, 'I'm on TV – me, Richard Pryor – and I didn't have to give up a thing.' The camera would then simultaneously pull back and track down to reveal that Pryor was in fact naked. Not only was he naked but from the waist down, he had no genitalia, making him look like a Motown version of Barbie's boyfriend Ken. The point being, of course, that he hadn't given up a thing for prime-time television except that which every man holds dear.

The shot was instantly seized on when the show was previewed for the media, and it appeared in almost every newspaper in the country and on every television news show. But when the first episode of *The Richard Pryor Show* screened it wasn't there; the network had ordered that it be removed. This was the beginning of a long-running battle with the network which would bring Pryor close to breaking-point.

Richard got nailed by the censors in the opening shot of the first show and that was the beginning of his frustration with TV [says Robin Williams]. It was sad, because he went into it with such hope . . . After six or seven weeks he was so disillusioned that he would just do his old night club act as his monologue. They'd run film on him for 45 minutes and by the time the Broadcast Standards people got through with editing it, they could use maybe three minutes.

In spite of all that, we had some great times on the show. In one sketch I played a liberal white Southern lawyer defending a black man charged with raping a girl who was a steaming hunk of white trash. I had a couple of ideas for lines but I wasn't sure if I should use them, but Richard said 'Just go for it', so I did. At one point in the trial I got up and told the jury, 'Negro – what a wonderful word. Say it with me: Negro, from the Latin word "negora" meaning "to tote".'

Williams would have given the Standards and Practices people as many headaches as Pryor with that particular sketch. It wouldn't be the last time he would be engaged in a battle of wits with the network censors over the next few years. Naturally, as Pryor became more and more disenchanted, the ratings slipped and the show was cancelled. Williams had now been on two shows which were cancelled in the space of a year, but it didn't matter. Richard Pryor had succeeded where *Laugh-In* had failed in allowing a little of Williams' natural humour to be transplanted from the stage to the tube. It was the first time Robin Williams had really had the opportunity to let himself go in comedic terms on television. It wouldn't happen again for a while, but at least he now knew that it could be done.

All the while that he was appearing on television, Williams had not neglected his stand-up work. Stand-up was where he felt most alive, and he continued to appear in Harvey Lembeck's troupe to keep the creative juices flowing and develop new material. Like The Comedy Store, Harvey Lembeck's Comedy Workshop was another required stop on the circuit for managers and agents. It was a tough gig for the comedians. They would effectively compete against each other in 'improv wars', trying to top their opponents before time-up was signalled by a buzzer or the lights going out. One night in the spring of 1978 Larry Brezner happened to stop by. Brezner was part of Joffe, Rollins, Morra & Brezner, one of the major management organisations which already looked after the interests of the likes of Woody Allen and Martin Mull. Brezner, who hadn't got where he was by not being able to spot talent, settled into his seat and quickly became absorbed in the proceedings.

> Harvey ... would throw out situations and the students would react [he recalls]. I watched this one kid get up and, no matter what situation was thrown at him, he never got lost. In an improv, right before the black-out, you've either won or lost; you either hit the big line or it lays there. I watched two hours of this kid never losing, reacting off the top of his head, working off nerve impulses – not intellect at all. Incredible.

The kid of course was Robin Williams, and Brezner was so impressed with what he had seen that night that he signed him as a client and became his first manager. 'He wasn't that different on-stage then; the attitudes were the same,' Brezner remembers. 'He's like Holden Caulfield, a guy walking around with all the nerve endings completely exposed.'

8

My Favourite Orkan

Despite two failed television shows Robin Williams was still a spectacularly talented comedian; possibly the most talented in America. But talent frequently is not enough on its own; sometimes talent needs a helping hand. Two men are responsible for making Robin Williams the success that he is today; one of them directly, the other indirectly. Williams may well be one of San Francisco's most famous citizens, but he owes a great deal to another near neighbour. George Lucas, who also lives across the Golden Gate Bridge in Marin County, is the man who is indirectly responsible for Robin Williams' meteoric rise. It is debatable whether we would ever have seen Mork, the alien from planet Ork, had it not been for two phenomenally successful films by George Lucas.

The influence of Garry Marshall on Robin Williams' career was felt much more directly. Marshall is the son of a classic showbiz mom who desperately wanted her son to be a dancer. Marshall had rhythm but not much aptitude for dance, and as a young man his ambition was to be drummer in a jazz band. He'd become a drummer when his mother finally despaired of him ever being a dancer and bought him a drum-kit so he could keep the beat for his sisters. Between gigs he supplemented his income by writing jokes and skits for the comics he met on the cabaret circuit. Marshall could turn a phrase and eventually he became a gag writer for the comedian Joey Bishop. On his own account Bishop was a good comedian without ever threatening to be a great comedian. But as one of Frank Sinatra's notorious Rat Pack, the men who defined

masculinity for a generation of postwar Americans, Bishop was, by association, one of America's hottest funnymen. As his star rose, so too did
Marshall's, and he eventually became a full-time writer supplying the
gags on *The Dick Van Dyke Show*, the programme which became the
prototype for American television comedy. From writing Marshall moved
into production and became the producer of *The Odd Couple*, the television series based on the Neil Simon play which had also been a hugely
successful film. By the early Seventies he was a recognised hyphenate, a
writer-producer, a man of some weight who had done his duty in the
trenches of television's ratings war. And it was with this kind of pedigree
behind him that he made a reasonably confident pitch to the ABC
network in 1971 for a new comedy.

Marshall's show was called *New Family in Town*, but no one at ABC
seemed sufficiently interested to commission a series. The show eventually
aired on the anthology comedy series *Love, American Style* on 25 February
1972 under the title *Love and the Happy Day*. In this case the happy day
in question was the arrival of the first TV set into the lives of a Fifties'
family played by Marion Ross, Harold Gould, Ron Howard and Susan
Neher. Although it had not been commissioned as a series, *Love and the
Happy Day* was not a total loss and would, bizarrely, play a key role in the
development of American cinema. It had been seen by George Lucas and
inspired a rites of passage movie he was developing about a group of
teenagers in a small American town. Lucas was one of the new breed of
American film-makers whose passionate love for cinema had led them to
film school as a way of breaking into the business. Lucas, from Modesto
in northern California, had been the *de facto* leader of an emerging group
of diverse talents at the University of Southern California which also
included John Carpenter, Robert Zemeckis and John Milius. From there
he had gone on to be an assistant to Francis Ford Coppola, who in turn
had now agreed to produce a movie which Lucas would direct from a
script he had co-written with former college friends Willard Huyck and
Gloria Katz. Lucas' film, *American Graffiti*, was set on a single night in an
American small town in the summer of 1962 as the graduating class take
their first tentative steps towards the adult world. Ron Howard, a popular
TV star in his own right, had been cast in the film after appearing in
the *Love, American Style* episode. *American Graffiti* also starred Richard
Dreyfuss, Charlie Martin Smith, Candy Clark, Cindy Williams and, in a
small role, Harrison Ford. With the exception of Howard, who had
become something of an institution through his appearances on *The
Andy Griffith Show*, all of them were unknown. That did not stop *American
Graffiti* from being a runaway hit in the summer of 1973. It had cost just

over $1 million and made more than $55 million at the US box-office. Suddenly it seemed that nostalgia was a hot property after all. Garry Marshall got the call from ABC; and happy days would soon be here again.

Marshall retooled his original proposal. For one thing the title was deemed to be a loser and the show would now be called *Happy Days* after the *Love, American Style* episode. It would now focus on the lives of one family – the Cunninghams – in small-town America in the Fifties. There were some changes from the pilot, but Marshall still put together a talented and likeable cast. Ron Howard is now at the top of Hollywood's directorial 'A' list as the man behind films such as *Splash, Cocoon, Apollo 13* and *Ransom*. In the Seventies this was all still in front of him but he was then one of American television's best-loved stars and he took the key role of Richie Cunningham. Marion Ross again played his mother, Tom Bosley was drafted in as his father, and his sister was played by Erin Moran. In the early shows Richie also had an older brother, played by Gavan O'Herlihy, but he was quickly written out. The series added two best friends – Potsie and Ralph Malph – who were played by Anson Williams and Donnie Most. But the one who would make most impression was Henry Winkler as Arthur Fonzarelli – The Fonz – who lived above the Cunninghams' garage. With a nod to Marlon Brando's biker-chic in *The Wild One*, Fonzie instantly became the coolest role model in America. A leather-clad stud muffin who was a cross between Elvis and James Dean with a heart of gold to boot, he became the idol of millions, male and female alike.

Happy Days débuted on 15 January 1974 and after a season and a half of solid ratings it eventually cracked the top ten and then remained one of America's most watched shows. It would stay in the top three in the Nielsen ratings for three years and spawn its own spin-off show *Laverne and Shirley*.

This spin-off, which starred Garry Marshall's sister Penny and Cindy Williams, came about when The Fonz and Richie Cunningham double-dated with Laverne Di Fazio and Shirley Feeney in an episode in series three of *Happy Days*. The girls ended up with their own series which was also a top-three show. If anything it was more popular than *Happy Days*, charting in the top three for four consecutive seasons. In the 1977–78 season *Laverne and Shirley* took over from *Happy Days* as America's top show, and it was about this time that Marshall started looking for fresh material. Like all sensible producers he did some market research and asked a sample of TV's biggest demographic group what should be on *Happy Days*. The sample actually consisted of Marshall's own son.

My seven-year-old son, Scott, was reluctant to watch *Happy Days* or *Laverne and Shirley* or any show that I did [recalls Garry Marshall]. So I asked him, 'What do you like?' He said, 'I only like space.' I told him, 'I don't do space.' 'Well you could do it,' he said. So I asked him, 'How would you do space in *Happy Days*?' And he said, 'It could be a dream.'

Scott Marshall's choice was probably influenced by the massive legi-timisation of science fiction in American popular culture which had been inspired by the huge success of another George Lucas film. The box-office clout of *American Graffiti* had allowed Lucas to make his long-cherished sci-fi saga *Star Wars*, until recently the most successful film ever released domestically in the United States. This had led to an explosion of science fiction-related films and television shows as space opera suddenly became the in thing.

Garry Marshall saw the potential for the idea. The show was now in its fourth year and they were running out of intriguing situations for Fonzie. An alien might be just what the show needed. America had been crazy about flying saucers in the Fifties after all, he reasoned, and he and his *Happy Days* writers came up with an episode called 'My Favourite Orkan', its title a reference to the popular Sixties' TV show *My Favourite Martian* which had starred Bill Bixby and Ray Walston. The basic plot was that an alien visitor from outer space would drop in on The Fonz while he was house-sitting for the Cunninghams. The visitor had come to take back a typical earthling for closer study. He had Richie Cunningham in mind but found The Fonz instead. The visitor would ask Fonzie's advice on terrestrial dating rituals, which would set up a slapstick sequence with the alien being fixed up with an Earth girl. The Earth girl in question was Laverne Di Fazio from *Laverne and Shirley*, alias Penny Marshall. All that remained was finding the right alien.

Garry Marshall's first choice for the role of the alien, who would be called Mork, was an established actor called John Byner. Byner was well known in the industry as an impressionist and a good ensemble player. He had done a number of sitcoms in the Sixties and Seventies, but none of them had gone on to be successful. His best-known role was probably as Detective Donahue in the cult comedy series *Soap*. Byner was perfect for what Marshall saw as basically a bit of fun. He was a seasoned pro, a recognisable face for the TV audience, and would do a good job on what was no more than a one-shot deal. Byner, for reasons best known to himself, turned the job down. Time was tight and the popular myth is that the casting dilemma was resolved by the tried and trusted formula of the cattle call, an open audition. From this audition, the story goes, a young man whom no one knew walked in off the street and announced himself as Robin Williams. He then, so the publicity material would have it, proceeded to slay them in the aisles and landed the part which would make him a household name.

In fact, Williams was nowhere near as unknown as the later *Mork and Mindy* publicity material would have had people believe. He did have a fair amount of television experience from *Laugh-In* and *The Richard Pryor Show*, and his new manager Larry Brezner had done a fair amount of shopping him around town. He would bring film and television executives to wherever Williams was playing in the hope that they would get a taste of his happy madness.

'Robin was doing stuff from Shakespeare, carrying on, dancing on tables,' says Brezner. 'I brought some United Artists executives to see him at The Comedy Store. They said "He's crazy" and walked out.'

Brezner in the meantime had found Williams more television work with guest spots in *Fernwood 2 Night*, *The Great American Laugh-Off* and *The Alan Hamel Show*. This was really just a question of trading on volume and getting experience in front of the cameras. With the exception of *Fernwood 2 Night*, none of the shows was especially distinguished. *Fernwood* is a neglected gem in America's television canon. Martin Mull, another Brezner client, starred in a parody of a small-town talk show. It was one of the first of the 'show within a show' genre which Garry Shandling has now made his own. As well as Mull and co-star Fred Willard, Williams also got to work with people such as Harry Shearer, Jim Varney and Kenneth Mars, who would all go on and establish themselves as major comedy names.

The real version of Robin Williams being cast as Mork is nowhere near as romantic as the press release would have it, although luck still played a part. Marshall is a man who in his work as a producer and director – he has gone on from television to direct movies such as *Pretty Woman*, *Soap Dish* and *Frankie and Johnny* – likes to surround himself with people he can trust. In many key positions these people turn out to be members of his family. He has cast his sister Penny many times and he uses another sister, Ronny Hallin, as his most trusted casting adviser. It was Ronny who suggested Robin Williams, whom she had found at Harvey Lembeck's Comedy Workshop in Los Angeles. Lembeck had pointed him out specifically when she had asked to see his top comedian. Because of her recommendation Williams found himself auditioning for Garry Marshall along with 20 other young comedians who were just as keen to land the part. Marshall was a little sceptical of his sister's choice, though he conceded that Williams did at least look as if he might be from another planet after the actor turned up wearing a pair of glasses made from two soupspoons with a white feather hanging from each of them. By good luck Williams had recently seen Steven Spielberg's *Close Encounters of the Third Kind* and had incorporated a character called 'The Alien Comedian' into the repertory company which was his stage act. Williams admits he was intimidated by the audition process, which is hardly surprising when you consider the shyness which had dogged him all his life. In addition he didn't think much of his chances and seems to have compensated for his lack of confidence by simply not taking things too seriously.

'When I auditioned for Mork I made every bizarre noise and gesture I could think of,' he recalls, 'and the director Jerry Paris hired me and pretty much let me play it the way I wanted to. The show got some positive feedback and for whatever reason ABC decided to use the Mork character in a spin-off series.'

Guest stars had come and gone on *Happy Days*, but Robin Williams made a big impression, especially with Henry Winkler. 'My job stopped being about remembering lines or moves, but to keep from laughing,' says Winkler of his guest star. 'And yet Robin was so shy, it was hard for him to speak. He did ask me, "After a day of this, how do you perform at The Comedy Store?" I told him, "After this, you really don't have the energy to perform at night".'

Garry Marshall jokingly insists Williams got the part because 'he was the only Martian who applied'. But only weeks after that episode had aired, he knew what he was going to do with his favourite Martian. 'We said, "No it's not a dream, it's real",' recalled Marshall in response to his son's original suggestion. 'It's another series.'

Marshall and ABC were simply giving the public what it wanted. Mork's lesson in love from The Fonz and his pursuit of Laverne around the Cunninghams' sitting-room had been a huge and entirely unexpected success. The network had received more letters about that one show than any other in the series and since almost all the letters wanted to see more of Mork, the next step seemed obvious. In the Seventies, American television followed the trends set by the movies, but where cinema had sequels, television had spin-offs. Ed Asner was one of the early successes when his Lou Grant character was successfully spun out of *The Mary Tyler Moore Show*; *Three's Company* would give rise to *The Ropers*; and *Happy Days* had already been responsible for *Laverne and Shirley*. No show had ever produced two spin-offs, until now.

While Marshall was negotiating with the network for his new spin-off show, he was also trying to put the show together. His first priority was to hire good writers, but the first two he approached – writer-producers

Dale McCraven and Bruce Johnson – were not keen. McCraven told him in no uncertain terms that he 'didn't do Martians'. Marshall had a trump card in the shape of the *Happy Days* episode which neither man had seen. Once they saw 'My Favourite Orkan' both McCraven and Johnson were so impressed with Robin Williams and his comic potential that they agreed to take on the writing responsibilities. McCraven and Johnson's first order of business was to work out a format for the show. Obviously three series set in the Fifties might strain credulity somewhat, so it was decided to place the show in a contemporary setting. Williams, who was brilliant at improvisational comedy, would also need someone to play against. What he needed was a straight man who didn't appear to be a straight man.

Pam Dawber was born in Detroit in October 1951. She grew up in the suburb of Farmington, which was only a half-hour drive from Bloomfield Hills, where Williams grew up. She had moved to California and begun a modelling career while she was at Oakland Community College. After becoming tired of what was essentially a small-town modelling scene, she headed for New York, where she joined an agency and became a busy and successful model. Dawber also had notions of a theatrical career and had started taking singing lessons. In 1977 she made her début in a production of *Sweet Adeline* in Connecticut and the following year she was cast by Robert Altman in *A Wedding*. In her movie début Dawber plays the jilted girlfriend of Desi Arnaz Jr, who has to ride a horse into the reception and announce that she may be pregnant. In between *Sweet Adeline* and *A Wedding*, Dawber had also auditioned for the title role in *Tabitha*, a proposed series based on the daughter of Elizabeth Montgomery's character in *Bewitched*. Dawber didn't get the part, which, given the short life of the series, was no bad thing. Instead she was given a one-year contract with ABC which led to another pilot. In *Sister Terri* Dawber would play a feisty nun whose mission was to bring God to the streets, but – perhaps not surprisingly – the show was not commissioned. Like all young actresses Dawber was anxious but reassured by the soothing promises of her agent who assured her that there was something much more satisfying in the offing. A few days later without ever, to her knowledge, having met or auditioned for Garry Marshall – or even having heard of Robin Williams – Pam Dawber read in the industry trade papers that she and Williams were being signed to do a show called *Mork and Mindy*.

McCraven and Johnson had come up with a comedy staple for the new show. It was a basic 'fish out of water' format, with Williams as Mork arriving from Ork on a scouting mission. He would then meet up with a sweet-natured Earth girl Mindy McConnell and eventually – in a prime-time friendly, sexually non-threatening way – move in with her the better to observe our quaint customs. Once the format had been decided on, Garry Marshall realised that he needed a female foil for Williams' free-wheeling humour. He was looking around for the right girl when he came across the *Sister Terri* pilot. With the help of a skilful editor, Marshall had Williams' scenes from the *Happy Days* episode cut together with Dawber's scenes from *Sister Terri*. The finished product looked as if the two characters were appearing in the same scene, and Marshall instinctively knew that the chemistry would work.

Garry Marshall now had his cast, his writers and his format. He was ready to launch his show but, even coming on the back of the huge response to 'My Favourite Orkan', they were still taking a big chance. Everyone knew that the show was risky, not least Williams and Dawber.

Williams is on record as voicing doubts about how the character of Mork could be developed satisfactorily for a series, while Dawber was reportedly worried that the show would turn out to be some 'real dumb thing'. Even ABC seemed a little uncertain about the show's ability to deliver an audience. They were initially going to schedule the programme in a notorious ratings graveyard. It was originally planned to run against *Monday Night Football*, a time slot which was effectively the kiss of death for any new show. With the bulk of the male television-watching, remote-controlling population watching the NFL's game of the week, there was next to no chance to build an audience. The show went into production in July 1978, still with that graveyard slot in mind. It was only when an ABC executive saw the finished versions of the first couple of episodes that the network realised they might have another hit on their hands. On the strength of these first few shows *Mork and Mindy* was switched to Thursday night at eight. This is historically the plum slot in American prime-time television, and Robin Williams was about to add another jewel to television's crown.

9

Nanoo, Nanoo

The summer of 1978 was an extremely important period for Robin Williams both personally and professionally. Being cast in *Mork and Mindy* – his first leading role – meant that his career was poised on the launch pad, but before it would finally take off there was something more important that he had to do. He and Valerie Velardi got married. Williams had spoken of Velardi in nothing but glowing terms, he was aware of all that she had sacrificed for him, and now he wanted to make a public declaration of how much she meant to him. He called her his 'stabilisation point', and perhaps their wedding near the family home in the hills above Tiburon in June 1978 was exactly what he needed. Velardi was much more pragmatic and hard-headed than Williams and, at a time when he was about to be exposed to all sorts of temptations, having at least one anchoring force in his life was no bad thing.

That same summer in San Francisco Williams performed the comedy gig of his life. He was part of a bill which also included Steve Martin and Joan Baez, but it was Williams who got the standing ovation from a crowd of more than 7000 people. This was a pre-*Mork and Mindy* appearance when Williams was very definitely a supporting act. The combination of television success and the audience reaction would mean that very soon he could play to crowds like this on his own.

Robin Williams had never actively sought television success. It had never been his ambition to star in his own TV show, far less a sitcom about a funny alien. But now that the opportunity was here he was not about to pass it up. However, even before he got the chance, the opportunity was almost snatched from him by a piece of legal red tape. When Williams had signed on to do the *Laugh-In* revival, his initial contract was for six shows, but he had also signed an option agreement. This agreement gave George Schlatter the right to renew his services annually for up to five years if the show was picked up as a series. NBC of course did commission a series, which meant that the option clause in Williams' contract could be activated. The consequences of this contract would not be felt for some time and in the process it would involve Williams in a serious political wrangle between producer Schlatter and the network. It was obvious within a few weeks that the new *Laugh-In* was not going to work, audience tastes had changed and the ensemble collected for this one, Williams notwithstanding, was nowhere near as talented as the original cast. George Schlatter announced that he was going to cancel the show. It seems, though, that this was simply a fishing expedition. He had got word that NBC was not going to renew the show, so he decided to go public in the hope that one of the other two networks would pick it up. The strategy came to nothing, and the show ended with Williams free of any obligation, or so he thought, and about $20,000 better off for the experience.

Once Williams had been confirmed as ABC's choice for *Mork and Mindy*, George Schlatter appeared on the scene again to announce that Williams was still tied to him under the terms of the *Laugh-In* contract. That being the case, then he would not be available for the series. It seems pretty certain that Schlatter was attempting to exert a little leverage on ABC, who could not, he reasoned, do the show without Williams since the whole concept was built around him. Whether he wanted some sort of financial settlement, or whether he wanted some kind of screen credit for what he would have perceived as a hit show, or whether he wanted a piece of Robin Williams is not clear. It is significant, however, that when Williams was cast in *The Richard Pryor Show* there wasn't a word from Schlatter. It seems reasonable to assume that the deciding factor was the huge buzz from the *Happy Days* appearance and the fact that Williams was now the star of the show. Robin Williams was undoubtedly stunned and surprised by the development. He insisted that he had, perhaps naïvely, believed Schlatter when he announced that *Laugh-In* was being cancelled and also believed that his contract was terminated. At the end of the day the issue was settled at a hearing held under the auspices of the American Arbitration Association. At the hearing Schlatter was very candid about his intentions with *Laugh-In*. He told the hearing that his announcement that he was scrapping the show was indeed merely a negotiating tactic to alert the other two networks in the hope that they might pick it up. Williams again argued that he believed he had no obligation to Schlatter whatsoever. The arbitrators agreed that Williams had acted in good faith and they dismissed Schlatter's claim. Williams was now free to star in *Mork and Mindy* without any legal encumbrances.

The first episode of *Mork and Mindy* was broadcast by ABC at 8.00 p.m. on Thursday, 14 September 1978. The show drew heavily on the *Happy Days* guest appearance which had played so well earlier that year. Initially Mork is given something of a back story in which it is revealed that life on Ork is rather dull. Orkans, according to Mork, are the white bread of the universe. Mork is something of a free spirit and his unconventional behaviour has brought him to the attention of the authorities more than once. The show opens with Mork awaiting another interview with Orson, supreme leader of Ork. Mork's sin this time is to have painted a moustache on The Solar Lander – whatever that is – and to have referred to Orson variously as 'Fatso', 'Rocketship Thighs' and 'Star-Twit'. As a punishment exercise Mork is sent to Earth – 'an insignificant planet on the far side of the galaxy' – where he will study our primitive ways and, conveniently, report back to Orson telepathically each week.

Mork arrives on Earth on the outskirts of what turns out to be Boulder, Colorado. It is late, and through a combination of darkness and cluelessness he manages to put on the one suit he has with him – his luggage was lost somewhere in the vastness of the universe – back to front. As he begins to walk into town he meets Mindy, who has been ditched by her date after being less than enthusiastic about his amorous advances. Seeing Mork and mistaking him for a priest because he has his collar back to front, Mindy is relieved to find some company out there on the road, and the two walk back into town together. Mindy invites him back to her apartment for a sociable drink, but when they get there she realises to her horror that he is not a priest, he simply has his suit on back to front. Once the rest of his luggage arrives at her front door, in an egg powered by some sort of anti-gravity device, Mork comes clean and reveals that he is in fact an alien. After the obligatory comic histrionics Mindy takes the news quite well, considering, and offers Mork a place to stay, temporarily, and realises that it will do her budding career as a writer the world of good if she studies him while he is studying us.

One of the first things Mindy has to do is make Mork more like a human by getting rid of his Orkan voice, which sounds a bit like Mickey Mouse on helium. This gives Williams the chance to engage in a wild improvisational riff in which he assumes the voices of variously Jackie Gleason, Shirley Temple and both Lucille Ball and Desi Arnaz. Later in the show he would settle on a modified Shakespearean accent which was modified still further to approximate to Williams' own soft-spoken tones. In the process of doing all of this Mork reveals that he has been to Earth before when he was sent by his biology class to collect a specimen. This is the cue for a flashback episode in which the bulk of 'My Favourite Orkan' with Henry Winkler and Penny Marshall is repeated. Once Mork's reminiscence is out of the way the story moves on to introduce the remainder of *Mork and Mindy*'s ensemble cast. Conrad Janis plays Mindy's father Fred, who runs a music store; Elizabeth Kerr plays her grandmother Cora; and young Jeffrey Jacquet plays Eugene, a kid from the neighbourhood who becomes one of Mork's first friends.

The formalities of introducing the dramatis personae completed, the plot, such as it is, for the rest of the show concerns Mork's ability to stay on Earth. Fred McConnell, grabbing the wrong end of the stick, is concerned about Mork and Mindy cohabiting. Not knowing that Mork is from Ork, he begins to suspect he might be at best mentally ill or at worst some kind of dope-head. His policeman friend Officer Tilwick – a guest appearance by Geoffrey Lewis – also has suspicions and eventually arrests Mork. Tilwick's excuse is that he thinks Mork is insane. A competency hearing has been arranged for the following day at which Mork's fate will be decided.

Mork conveniently spends the night before the hearing watching *Perry Mason* re-runs and the courtroom drama *Inherit the Wind*. He elects to conduct his own defence, which consists of another sparkling improvisation based on a Frederic March speech from *Inherit the Wind*. He is getting nowhere, however, and seems destined to be thrown into gaol. Eventually Mindy and Fred McConnell burst in to act as character witnesses for Mork, who is eventually found to be eccentric but sane. The episode concludes with Mork's first report to Orson – the heard but never seen Ralph James – in which he marvels at the human emotions which led Mindy to rush to his defence. Orson is similarly intrigued and modifies Mork's mission to study human emotions without getting involved with them.

One of the more prescient lines in this first episode of *Mork and Mindy* comes from Michael Prince, who plays the judge at the competency hearing. Mork, he concludes, 'adds a new dimension to the word eccentric'. Whether the line was written by Dale McCraven or Bruce Johnson, they were right on the money. Williams as Mork did take an audience to new realms of comic fantasy, much as his own hero Jonathan Winters had done for Williams as a boy. It was a question of looking at the world and seeing it exactly as it was, taking everything at its face value. One memorable moment from that first show remains a highlight of the programme's entire run. It comes when Mork encounters eggs for the first time. Having seen him and his luggage arrive in eggs, the audience already knows that on Ork eggs, like everything else, are different.

'Little hatchling brothers, you must revolt against your oppressors,' Williams tells a bowl of eggs which he finds on a kitchen worktop. 'You have nothing to lose but your shells. Fly, be free,' he encourages one egg, throwing it into the air where it demonstrates its natural aerodynamic properties and smashes on to the bench. Mork then offers it a quick burial at sea – in the sink – before sorrowfully telling the remaining eggs, 'Your brother bit the big one.' It's a piece of vintage Williams improvisation and was typical of the sort of humour which Williams brought to *Mork and Mindy*. It was humour born out of the freedom which he had been given by Garry Marshall.

> I wasn't restrained at all [Williams recalls], because they basically took what I did and put it into TV. They would take whole sections of my act and write episodes around them. They would come in and watch me perform and then write an episode of Mork doing this. There used to be a thing I did in my act about what it's like when a comedian bombs and I would talk about that, and they put that into an episode of *Mork and Mindy* where he split up into different personalities. The fact is I was very lucky to break through at a time when they [the network] didn't know what was happening. The fact that we had a live audience was the only thing that saved us – they saw it working. They didn't know what it was and they were scared but they said, 'People are laughing. Let's see what happens.' They gave me total freedom, carte blanche, and the first year was incredible because they didn't know what hit them.

People were indeed laughing. Within two weeks *Mork and Mindy*, the show destined for the graveyard opposite *Monday Night Football*, had broken into the top ten most watched programmes in the United States. By the end of its first season it would finish at number three in the charts with a weekly average audience of around 55 million viewers. In some weeks it reached as high as 70 million.

But Williams insists the men and women in suits at ABC were never quite certain what to make of the show. And were even less certain what to make of him.

> They really didn't know what I was [he remembers]. When we started the series the network guys would come in and sit together and, at first, they didn't laugh, but then they couldn't help laughing. Starting with the first

taping in front of an audience it seemed like everyone was having a good time, and the more freedom I was given, the more I enjoyed it. It was the kind of playfulness I had experienced in night clubs, but never thought I would be able to get on television. I had guested on certain TV shows where they were very specific: 'Mr Williams, your line is "Lola, Jimmy's home".' There was no deviating from the script, but in *Mork and Mindy* I was allowed to work the way I do on-stage. In the middle of a monologue, I could suddenly go off into different accents and characters and nobody would blink.

Whether they understood him or not, the network certainly knew the series was a hit, and by the end of the first season Williams' salary had doubled from an initial $15,000 per show to $30,000 per show. As Williams has hinted, however, there was still some doubt about who was responsible for what on the show.

Certainly the physical characterisation of Mork was entirely the product of Williams' imagination and theatrical talent. The striped shirts and rainbow braces favoured by Mork were a direct reflection of Williams' own off-screen preferences for thrift-store attire. Williams also brought his own influences to bear on the way Mork moved. His strangely flat-footed childlike gait and the equally childlike manner in which he would cock his head quizzically at our Earth customs are a throwback to his days as a white-faced mime on the steps of the Metropolitan Museum in New York. Certainly it was a winning combination. The rainbow braces became fashion items, and Mork's everyday Orkisms – the greeting 'Nanoo, nanoo' and the all-purpose expletive 'Shazbot' – became Seventies' catchphrases.

As for the content of the programme, Williams continued to insist that much of the humour on the show was inspired either directly or indirectly by his improvisation. He maintains, probably with some accuracy, that the show would not have been as successful had it been completely scripted. Whether it would have been off the air in seven weeks, as he maintained, is debatable. In a 1982 interview with *Playboy* magazine Williams alleged that Garry Marshall and the other producers on the show had been aware of a chemistry between himself and Pam Dawber which they didn't want to interfere with. Williams would be encouraged to do his own thing while she was also encouraged to be completely natural in her reactions to it. According to Williams, it eventually reached the stage where the writers would simply offer notes in some scenes and he would then extemporise on the themes they had suggested. In another interview Williams claimed to improvise about a third of his dialogue and that he did so to prevent the TV writers from being forced into constant repetition.

Williams agreed that this was an unusual way to run a TV show.

> As far as I know it is [he conceded]. But you have to remember that Mork was basically an open book, a sieve who had picked up his knowledge of the planet from years of watching Earth television. He was a little like a comic-book character called Zippy the Pinhead, someone who absorbs everything that comes in but who puts it back out a little out of context, like a word processor with dyslexia. It helped that Mork was an alien, because in some ways there were no real boundaries as to what he could say or do.

This sounds like a perfect arrangement, but it's an argument which, whether Williams intended to or not, undervalues the contribution to the show made by McCraven and Johnson. Although Williams was the star, there was more to the show than just him. *Mork and Mindy* still had an ensemble of other characters who all had to be written for, and written for skilfully, so that they could provide springboards for Williams' humour while still remaining interesting to the audience.

> A half-hour TV show couldn't possibly be done that way [said Dale Mc-Craven of Williams' explanation]. Robin contributes a great deal but we don't leave holes in the scripts. Robin can take lines which have been written and make them sound like ad-libs, which is great. He comes off as being spontaneous but he is a very studied man. He may try some ad-libs during rehearsals, but when we film the show on Thursday he knows exactly what he's doing.

The real truth is probably somewhere between the two. Williams has always been one to be fairly unrestrained during rehearsals and between takes, and there is no doubt that a lot of his own zaniness would have acted as inspiration for the scripts that Johnson and McCraven wrote. Those who know Robin Williams' stand-up work also suggest that one of his great strengths is the ability to take familiar lines and make them sound like ad-libs. But because of the logistics of camera set-ups and other actors' cues, the show cannot be improvised to the same extent as a stand-up set. What Williams was doing was improvisation, but only within some pretty well-defined parameters. And it was Williams' genuine improvisations which came closest to landing the show in trouble with the network.

We were sneaking in with a lot of stuff [Williams remembers]. They had to get new censors every other week because they kept going 'What's he saying? What does he mean?' We would sneak in lines like 'Mindy, I just bought this book, the Catherine the Great story called *My Friend Flicka*.' They would get them a week later and realise, 'Damn, he got another one through.' It was a nice time because the network executives were just lost. Another part of the censorship is not the nudity or the words but the products you can't mention because you might upset a sponsor. Like you couldn't make jokes about McDonalds not serving red meat. I used to say things like 'Mindy, do you think McDonalds are using kangaroo meat, because I bought a hamburger and it had a pouch with another hamburger inside it.' And they went 'What?' and they cut out stuff like that. You couldn't do anything about religious groups either because they were such a powerful lobby. They would lobby against the products and then the sponsor would cut off the money, so that was it.

But it was nice because parents could still watch it with their children. There were enough adult references and the children loved the innocence of it. I would have kids come up and throw an egg in the air and shout 'Fly' and you could hear their parents go, 'Our kitchen's all screwed up because of you.'

Mork from Ork was an instant success. Williams brought an innocence to what would be the first of a series of what might be termed 'man-child roles' that he would play both on television and in film over the next two decades. That mixture of naïveté and a literal interpretation of everything that was said to him struck a chord with audiences and critics alike. When the show first appeared there were some who compared it unfavourably with *My Favourite Martian*, but within a few episodes they were raving about the programme and hailing Robin Williams as a remarkable new talent.

One of the first to champion the show and Robin Williams in particular was *People* magazine, the ultimate arbiter of American popular taste. 'Even earthlings prepared to sneer,' it said, 'were won over by the elastic-faced, ineffably alien Robin Williams.' In a later article *People* would claim that Williams' 'brilliantly sophisticated mixture of wisecracks, double-talk and improvisations make *Mork and Mindy* sizzle'. *TV Guide* also heaped praise upon the show. 'What keeps it from bogging down is Williams' hundred inventions – his eerie vocal noises, babyish walk and crazy handshake, his virtuoso mangling of Earth language and his straight-faced ability to carry on a conversation with a talking space suit ... The moments are a lot funnier than the plots but so far they are enough.'

Even the *New York Times*, America's newspaper of record, could not fail to notice the new kid on the television block. 'The season's biggest new face,' said the *Times*, 'undoubtedly belongs to Robin Williams of ABC's *Mork and Mindy*, another singularly unmemorable series except for the bizarre antics of its decidedly off-beat aggressively hilarious star. Mr Williams ... not only exhibits a fine madness, but he also nurtures and protects it fiercely.'

While lavish in its praise for Robin Williams, the *Times* had noticed the show's fatal flaw. Robin Williams was bigger than *Mork and Mindy*. Without him there was no show. No single memorable moment was contributed by any other member of the cast. Every highlight of the series involved Williams and, more frequently than not, only Robin Williams. And the *New York Times* was not alone in noticing this. The suits in the ABC network offices, the ones Williams insisted didn't have a clue, were slowly wising up.

10

'Mork, Robin . . . Robin, Mork'

By any standard the first season of *Mork and Mindy* was a runaway success. Audiences loved it, critics were crazy about Robin Williams, and the show ended its first run in December 1979 as the number three show of the year. The success of *Mork and Mindy* helped give the ABC network an almost total ratings dominance. The top six shows on television were products of the so-called 'alphabet web', and with *Laverne and Shirley* in first position and *Happy Days* in fourth, three of the top four shows were Garry Marshall productions. Overall ABC had 12 of the top 20 shows, and the bulk of them were the half-hour sitcoms which were the network's speciality at that time.

Fast forward a year and the picture is entirely different. ABC finishes the 1979–80 season with only two shows in the top ten and a mere six in the top 20. The network had taken a big gamble and it had failed disastrously. Network television programming depends on holding an audience throughout the commercial breaks, especially those breaks between shows. The successful scheduler will carve out a whole slab of television time by carefully programming individual shows into what amounts to a whole evening of viewing. One of the most impressive examples in recent years is NBC's creation of 'Must See TV' on Thursday nights by packaging shows such as *Seinfeld*, *Friends* and *e.r.* together. This is standard practice now, but at the end of the Seventies it was less common. Most networks were happy to sweep certain nights, but ABC decided that with so many top-rated shows it could use these as a platform to sweep the ratings on consecutive nights, maybe even the whole week. So at the end of the

1978–79 season the schedulers started changing things around. Shows which had been popular in one time slot were suddenly switched to a different slot, sometimes even a different night, and often against stronger opposition in the hope that they could take their audience with them. *Mork and Mindy* was one of those shows which ABC hoped would be a hard-hitting weapon in the ratings arsenal. It was taken from its winning slot on Thursday night, where it had had barely three months to establish itself, and ended up on Sunday nights opposite *Archie Bunker's Place*, a hugely popular spin-off from the ground-breaking *All in the Family*. The redneck, politically incorrect Archie, played by the much-loved Carroll O'Connor, beat *Mork and Mindy* like a drum. For the rest of its run *Mork and Mindy* would never again feature in the ratings top 20. And, as it plunged in the ratings, the quality of the show suffered drastically.

> It was a simple case of greed and it didn't work out [says Robin Williams]. Then when the network realised things were going poorly for our show, it got panicky and started putting in all these sexually-oriented stories: 'Mork becomes a cheerleader for the Denver Broncos'. I think people who had always watched the series just looked at that stuff and said 'Jesus, what's this?' . . . It didn't piss me off so much as make me wonder why. Everyone was then doing T&A [tits and ass] shows, so I guess the network guys said 'Let's put Mork in drag – that's always funny.' But that was going far away from what we had originally had, a gentle soul who was suddenly becoming kind of kinky. The producers were torn between the network's saying 'We need stories we can promote' and their own feelings about supporting the characters. Well, because the network wanted a show it could promote, there I was with 32 cheerleaders.

The supporting cast was also changed to try and boost the flagging ratings in the second series. Conrad Janis was dropped as Fred McConnell, though the character was later restored in series three. Elizabeth Kerr had also been dropped as Mindy's trendy grandmother, as had Jeffrey Jacquet as Eugene, the kid who had proved an effective comic foil for Mork. Jay Thomas, Gina Hecht and Jim Staahl were added to give Mork and Mindy some friends of their own age, and Tom Poston joined the cast as grumpy downstairs neighbour Mr Bickley, who allowed Mork to examine less wholesome sides of the human condition. But the strangest addition was that of Robert Donner as Exidor, a man who believed that the Venusians were coming to reclaim him and a character who was even more bizarre than Mork. Donner is a fine comic actor with an excellent sense of timing, but the whole point of the show was how Mork interacted with normal people; to have someone behaving even more strangely than him seems odd to say the least. The network presumably felt that if one weird guy was funny, two would be even funnier. The real effect, however, was to make Mork look a little more normal by comparison, which was hardly the point of the show.

> I think the stories just got too complex and we got away from the simplicity of the character [explains Williams]. *Mork and Mindy* originally worked because it was about this cheerful man from outer space doing very simple things – 'Mork buys bread' or 'Mork deals with racism'. Mork and Mindy were both very strait-laced, and the charm of the show, I think, was in having Pam Dawber deal with me in normal, everyday situations to which I would react in bizarre ways. The show began with very human roots and Pam was responsible for a lot of that; she's a fine actress and a friend, and there was a wonderful exchange of humanity between us.

The second series of the show was also beset by rumours of professional jealousy between Williams and Dawber. She strenuously denied this, and his comments to *Playboy* magazine in 1982 also seem to give the lie to those suggestions.

> I think people really connected with the characters we played [Williams continued], and in our first year, the series was exactly what it was designed to be, a situation comedy. When you think of, say, *The Honeymooners*, you know who Ralph Kramden was and you know who Norton was; they were at their best in everyday situations and the simpler the better. If the stories ever became too complex – as they did on *Mork and Mindy* – there still would have been some funny things going on, but the show wouldn't have been nearly as effective. I didn't want to see *Mork and Mindy* bastardised in that way, but it was.

Shows in the second series did become increasingly off-beat. As well as having Mork almost join the Denver Broncos cheerleaders, another two-part episode had him fighting for his survival against the Necrotons, a race who had declared war on Ork. The fact that the Necrotons were led by Raquel Welch and included *Playboy* playmate Debra Jo Fondren among their number puts it fairly and squarely in the T&A category. In other shows Mork was shrunk and ended up in an alternative universe, brought home an abandoned chimpanzee, and even considered plastic surgery.

There's a certain irony here, because when they were developing the show McCraven and Johnson had consciously toned down Mork's abilities. Mork in the series has very few alien 'powers' compared with his appearances on *Happy Days*. They felt it was important dramatically that Mork be strange, but not too strange. Now the series was thrashing around, with its writers desperately searching for ideas and gimmicks of any kind that the networks could sell in a one-line teaser. According to Williams, by the time the show reached its third series it was all about getting a story which could be reduced to one line and then promoted to the audience. Williams himself was beginning to tire of the show by this stage. He still loved the character but was becoming increasingly frustrated at being used as a glorified network hustler to drum up audiences. He was also driving himself at an increasingly hectic pace. He would finish his day's shooting on *Mork and Mindy* at the Paramount lot and then spend his evenings doing gigs at local comedy clubs before making the one-hour journey back to his home in Topanga Canyon. It was not uncommon for him to work until two or three in the morning and then head for home – to be back on set a few hours later. In the autumn of 1978, not long after *Mork and Mindy* had become a ratings success, Williams collapsed from sheer exhaustion. His new wife Valerie Velardi, who had put her career on hold to support his, had to nurse him back to health. And, as Williams himself admitted, his sudden rise to fame so soon after getting married had caused some early tensions in their relationship. 'It was a little trying at first because Valerie felt like she was riding on my coat-tails,' he says. 'It has to cause tensions, but we came through that with flying colours.'

Velardi for her part seemed to realise that there was only so much you could do to control Robin Williams. He needed the free rein to exhaust himself if necessary; performing was for him like a drug which he could not do without. 'I love to see him work,' she says. 'I think it's a gift and so does he. If I knew what it was I'd package it. You have to take everything as it comes. You've got to live minute to minute.'

Although he was among the hottest names on television Williams was still, in many ways, an innocent abroad in showbusiness. The naïveté of Mork was not that much of a stretch from his own trusting nature. The incident with the *Laugh-In* contract had made that abundantly clear. 'He's still naïve about the business,' said screenwriter friend Bennett Tramer. 'He'll still talk to anyone who comes up to him.'

Valerie Velardi was equally aware of her husband's constant accessibility to fans, to agents, to bookers, to almost anyone who had a cause they needed to raise funds for. Williams was still a fit man who continued to run several miles a day, but she introduced him to health foods and mineral and vitamin supplements. She also put him in touch with a chiropractor to deal with chronic tension-induced back pain. But, more importantly, she was teaching her husband to say no.

There was one area where Williams was still not saying no. He had begun to take drugs. He admitted in the 1982 *Playboy* interview to smoking marijuana and taking cocaine but, in an eerily prophetic statement which echoes the views of addicts everywhere, he insisted he was in control. To be fair to him, at the time he probably thought he was. He told the magazine he had never got into hard drugs – and 'I never will', he insisted. 'Most times, anything I try, I have the opposite reaction to what I'm supposed to have,' he told interviewer Lawrence Linderman.

He was equally categorical about the effect cocaine had on him. 'I get passive and just hold back,' he said. 'Most people get talkative, I don't say anything to anybody. It's always weird, because I don't have regular reactions to any of these things. I don't like doing any of the heavies, because normally my energy is just up when I'm performing.'

There is nothing inherently contradictory in Williams' statement. In Hollywood in the late Seventies cocaine use was endemic in the film industry. It was almost a social grace and those who used it did not really consider themselves to be drug users. This is why on the one hand Williams can freely admit to doing coke, but on the other hand excuse himself because he isn't doing anything heavier like heroin, morphine or speedballs. It was a fine moral tightrope to walk and it would not be long before he would fall off.

Professionally, however, Williams was rapidly gaining the reputation as a man who just couldn't say no. Show him a crowd and he just had to perform. One close friend reckoned that if you had a kid and you had a way of getting to Williams, you could probably book him for a birthday party. For all that, Williams has always been an intelligent man with a fair amount of self-knowledge, and his own awareness of his problem led to what is probably the most remarkable *Mork and Mindy* show of the entire run.

'Mork Meets Robin Williams' was transmitted mid-way through series three. Although there may have been some doubt in the early days about who contributed what to the show, there seems little doubt that Williams was the guiding hand in this particular show. The set-up is simple. Mindy, who is now working for a local television station, has to get an interview with Robin Williams, who is doing a benefit concert in Boulder. Mork asks who Robin Williams is, and Mindy explains, pointing out that he and Williams look a lot alike. This is the cue for Mork/Williams to have a lot of fun at his own expense.

'You could pack a family in that nose, Mind,' says Mork of the cover of Williams' top-selling comedy album *Reality ... What a Concept*. 'And look at that mouth! They had to airbrush this guy's entire face. I'm bright and cheery – this guy's got big problems.'

Mindy isn't the only one who notices the resemblance, and when Mork goes out into Boulder that afternoon he is spotted, mistaken for Williams, and mobbed. Mork barely manages to escape and, with his clothes in tatters through the efforts of souvenir hunters, it is a deeply traumatised alien who finally makes it back to their apartment. Mindy is having no luck arranging an interview, so she decides to go and doorstep Williams at the gig, and Mork tags along. The old mistaken identity bit works once again, this time in their favour. Mork, with Mindy in tow, is quickly ushered into Robin Williams' dressing-room by an eager security guard. A few moments later Williams himself walks in. The split-screen effect that was used to place Williams as Mork and Williams as himself in the same frame at the same time is crude and unsophisticated. Indeed its lack of subtlety is surpassed only by Mindy's interview technique which, through probing questions such as 'What's it like to be a celebrity?', finally elicits the fact that Williams is indeed the comedian who can't say no. Mindy thinks this may be a great line for her article and asks Williams why he thinks that might be.

I don't know why I can't say no [says Williams as himself]. I guess I want people to like me. I hate myself for that. I used to be able to say no. Before all this craziness started my friends used to call me up and say 'Robin, come on, we're all going outside. There are some really gnarly waves. We can all hang out.' And I'd have to go, 'No, my momma says I have to stay inside and read Nietzsche tonight.' Later on I guess I felt really afraid to say no to them because then they'd all say, 'Oh, Robin Williams. Mr Smarty Pants. Big shot. You forgot your old friends. You can't lend me ten thousand dollars for a new car. You won't do the Save the Shrimp benefit.'

Seldom has a performer's sheer need to be liked and even loved by his audience been more nakedly exposed. And there was more to come, as Williams went on to describe how he had come to start out as a performer in the first place.

Actually I became a performer by accident [he tells Mindy]. You see, my dad used to have this job where he had to move around a lot. And sometimes he'd leave a forwarding address. Just kidding [he said, presumably remembering this is supposed to be a comedy show] – actually he'd pack me in the crates with the dishes.

I was always being the new kid in the neighbourhood. And since I was suffering from a case of the terminal shy I couldn't make friends that easily, and I always spent a lot of time in my room and I created my own little world full of all these little characters that had strange and unusual qualities. After a while, I realised that people found these characters funny and outrageous, and then it got to the point where I realised the characters could say and do things that I was afraid to do. And after a while, here I am.

It's interesting to consider the effect this scene would have had on the studio audience. By the time it was transmitted, in common with every other American comedy, a laugh track had been added to beef up the slow moments. To be honest 'Mork Meets Robin Williams' is self-indulgent, unsophisticated and not terribly funny to those who are unaware of his background. But, to those who are, it is an astonishing insight into what makes Robin Williams the performer that he is. The fear which had defined his stage act for years is articulated in one short speech. It was a catharsis via public confession to an audience of millions. It may also have been designed as something of a swan-song, because Williams had pretty well made up his mind that he wanted to leave the show. But the network had one powerful bargaining chip still to play. Williams would get the chance to appear regularly beside his comedy hero, Jonathan Winters.

The show had fallen to 49th in the ratings by the end of the second season, and not even a move back to its original Thursday time slot had been enough to halt the slide. Now Mork and Mindy were to be married in a move which smacked of sheer ratings desperation. Not only that, biological incompatibility aside, they were to have a baby only two shows later. The baby, Mearth, would be played by Winters, and Mork had to explain to Mindy that on Ork, unlike Earth, people are born old and grow younger over the years. So the audience was treated to the sight of the husky form of Jonathan Winters running around in romper suits and dungarees. Williams had nothing to do with getting Winters on the show, even though the older comedian had appeared as a different character in an earlier show and he and Williams had been terrific together. Given their particular comic chemistry it is surprising that Winters hadn't been introduced to the show sooner than this. But the network executives plainly felt that the presence of Winters would be enough now to get at least one more season out of Williams.

'Having him on the show was one of the main reasons I stayed with it,'

Williams agreed. 'For me, it was like the chance to play alongside Babe Ruth. I'd always wanted to just meet Winters. When I was a kid my parents would say, "All right, you can stay up a little longer to watch this wonderful man fly around the room and do all this crazy stuff".'

Winters appeared as Mearth in the final 18 episodes of *Mork and Mindy*. The chemistry between him and Williams is at times nothing short of magical. There is the occasional sense of the torch being passed between two of the great absurdist comedians of their respective generations. But even though Williams and Winters were inspired, the network was not, and it announced in the middle of the fourth series that *Mork and Mindy* was not being renewed. Winters, whose shows have attracted cult success rather than huge audiences, apparently blamed himself for the cancellation. But even though series three finished 60th in the ratings, Williams insists that the figures actually went up when Mearth was introduced to the show.

> But then [he adds] we got back to doing bizarre stories that had no semblance of reality, and the show's ratings went way down. For a little while I thought, 'God, maybe I'm not goosing up like I used to; maybe the old mad energy is gone.' But I decided it wasn't true, because people still liked my performances. I think the show just had a confused base. The combination of that and going up against *Magnum P.I.* was finally too strong.

Williams did at one point suggest that he thought ABC had deliberately manipulated things to get the show off the air, but that, he insists, was the initial rage against the coldness of the decision. No one had the decency to tell him in person. Everyone knew that the show was under threat, but Williams finally found out that it was cancelled from a newspaper.

> It was cancelled on 3 May [he remembers] ... I think they tried to call me the day before; I just didn't return the call because I kind of knew what it was about. I knew it was coming. The ratings started off incredible with Pam and me going through the courting period. I guess the biggest was the honeymoon period – 'Mork is gonna get laid' – and then they stopped promoting it, and it went down the ratings list; the twenties, the thirties, the forties. It finally sort of bounced off the bottom. In the end it was like the last days in Berlin. We even shot one episode in 3-D.

When news of *Mork and Mindy's* demise finally reached Williams he was filming a children's special, *The Frog Prince*, for his close friend the comedian Eric Idle. 'The end of that show wasn't unexpected,' says Idle, 'but you don't think you'll find out by having someone hand you a newspaper when you're on a set. Robin gathered the technicians around him and did a routine about TV executives. Everyone was on the floor and it was behind him. I thought that was the most useful example of comedy that I'd ever seen.'

Once his anger passed, Williams was at least grateful that *Mork and Mindy* was allowed to depart with some dignity, its 91-show run brought to an end with a three-part story in which Mork's existence is revealed to the world. The last show was broadcast on 12 August 1982. It had lasted four seasons; one more than *My Favourite Martian.*

'It was wonderful while it lasted, but I wouldn't want to bring the character back,' Williams said a few months later. 'The show was a crap shoot that worked out and the freedom I had on it was incredible.'

11

I Yam What I Yam

Robin Williams had always had his doubts about *Mork and Mindy*. He had never really believed that the character could be developed sufficiently well to last a single series, far less 91 shows. By the time ABC finally decided enough was enough, Williams was eventually branching out into other areas. With his success on the TV show it was inevitable that movies would be the next logical step. Already he and his now manager Larry Brezner were looking around trying to find the right vehicle to showcase his singular talents. By one of those happy Hollywood accidents it looked as though fate had steered them to the right project.

Popeye the Sailor Man was one of America's best-loved comic characters. He first made an appearance in 1929 in *Thimble Theatre*, a daily newspaper strip created by E. C. Segar. The previous star of the strip was the rake-thin Olive Oyl, but on 17 January 1929 Popeye made his début. Olive's brother Ham was looking for a sailor to take them on a trip when he spotted the unfeasibly muscled hero.

'Hey there,' he asked, 'are you a sailor?'

'Ja think I was a cowboy?' asked Popeye, before promptly telling Olive to get to the ship's galley. The first words she spoke to him – 'Shut up, you bilge rat' – were no indication of the decades-long romance which was to follow. After that first adventure Segar dropped Popeye from the strip, but reader demand was such that he was brought back at the expense of Ham. Popeye soon became the centre of a rich and varied repertory company of characters which included Olive Oyl, the villainous bully Bluto, the hamburger-mooching Wimpy, the evil Sea Hag and many others. *Thimble Theatre* was a weird and wonderful world where just about anything could and did happen, and only Segar's rules applied. The comic strip was a huge success and the spinach-guzzling seafarer became the star of a popular series of cartoons from Max Fleischer in the Thirties and Forties. The first of these appeared in 1933 and was called *I Yam What I Yam*, the phrase which would become his signature. In later years there would also be TV shows and hundreds of merchandising spin-offs from one of America's most enduringly appealing characters.

The huge box-office success of *Superman* in 1978 had made comic books and comic characters suddenly hot in Hollywood. Fantasy heroes were being optioned right, left and centre in the rush to jump on to a new bandwagon. One of the properties being actively pursued was *Popeye*, which producer Robert Evans wanted to turn into a live action movie. Evans was a mercurial New Yorker who had gone from being a child actor to a successful clothing manufacturer to a hot producer. With his lean, tanned good looks Evans looked more like a movie star than most movie stars, and his marriages to actresses Camilla Sparv and Ali McGraw, among others, merely cemented his Hollywood image. But beneath the tan and the dapper exterior, Evans possessed razor-sharp instincts. He had become head of production at Paramount Pictures in 1966 and over the next decade would turn out a stream of films which included *Rosemary's Baby, Love Story* and the first two *Godfather* films. In 1974 he started producing films for himself with a remarkable string of hits which began with *Chinatown*, and included *Marathon Man* and *Black Sunday*. *Popeye*, as far as he was concerned, was merely to be the next jewel in the crown.

The jewel, however, was proving a little too rich for Paramount Pictures' blood. *Popeye* was going to cost $20 million, a huge amount in 1979, and Paramount was unwilling to commit that much. Then Disney offered to share the load by taking on half the budget, so Paramount's exposure would only be $10 million. This was deemed more acceptable and the film got the go-ahead.

The production hit a snag early on when Evans' first choice for the role, Dustin Hoffman, decided that he didn't want to do it. Hoffman is an actor with impeccable instincts and he seems to have been right on the money here. It's hard to see him as the muscle-bound sailor man mixing it with Bluto. As they were looking around for a replacement, *Mork and Mindy* was going into its second series and Robin Williams was hotter than steam. You can see the attraction for Evans in having America's newest favourite comedian ready to make his screen début playing one of the country's most popular cartoon heroes. Everyone concerned felt that

Williams' physical comedy and his natural gifts as a mimic would be perfect for the role, and he was duly signed. Some of the other casting was not quite so smooth. Director Robert Altman wanted Shelley Duvall to play Olive Oyl. The slender Duvall could have passed as Olive's twin, but Paramount was holding out for *Saturday Night Live* star Gilda Radner. In the end, however, Altman got his way.

Although he was keen to make a film, Williams wasn't necessarily looking for a showy role that would net him hundreds of thousands of dollars; he simply thought it would be a good part. *Popeye* was not technically his screen début. He had recorded some skits for a lame sex revue called *Can I Do It . . . Till I Need Glasses*. The film was released in 1977 without Williams' contribution, but after the success of *Mork and Mindy* it was hastily re-edited to include Williams and re-released. *Popeye* was an entirely different proposition, and Charles Joffe from Joffe, Rollins, Morra and Brezner, who was an experienced negotiator, handled the deal with Paramount. Williams was so unconcerned with his actual pay-cheque that Joffe claimed it was three months before his client even asked him about the terms of his contract. So, having signed on, Williams spent his down time on the second series of *Mork and Mindy* punishing himself in the gym to learn the acrobatics which would be required for a very physical film. And when he wasn't in the gym he was taking dancing and singing lessons for this musical version of Segar's creation. Harry Nilsson was providing the music, and Williams as Popeye had one big number, *I Yam What I Yam*, based on the sailor man's oft-stated philosophy 'I yam what I yam and that's all that I yam'.

Popeye was to be directed by Robert Altman from a screenplay by writer-cartoonist Jules Feiffer. In retrospect you would have to question Altman's suitability for this particular job. Altman had gained rave notices and huge box-office returns for his first major movie, *M*A*S*H*, in 1970. Since then his work had been eclectic, ranging from the sublime *McCabe and Mrs Miller* to the frankly bizarre *Quintet*. Although he had established himself as a genuine American original, there was nothing to suggest that he was ideal to handle a musical comedy based on one of America's best-loved newspaper strips. Paramount executives were also less than thrilled by the choice of Altman, who was reported to have drink problems. Nonetheless Evans prevailed because of his fondness for hiring name directors after a flop, and there was no question that the bizarre *Quintet* had been a total disaster at the box-office.

Altman and Feiffer conceived *Popeye* as a morality tale about a young man searching for a lost father. Williams pitches up in the small seaside town of Sweethaven, impossibly muscled and with a permanent squint in one eye, looking for his pappy. He falls in love with the flighty Olive Oyl even though she is betrothed to Bluto, the man who rules Sweethaven with a fist of iron and a voice like thunder. Eventually Popeye and Bluto duke it out, Popeye wins and both gains the hand of his beloved Olive and is reunited with his pappy. Having been cast in the title role, Williams found himself surrounded by a quality selection of the Altman repertory theatre. Shelley Duvall played Olive, Paul Smith was Bluto, Paul Dooley played Wimpy, and respected Broadway star Ray Walston was Popeye's father, Poopdeck Pappy. Since Walston had starred in *My Favourite Martian* this was the first recorded meeting of a Martian and an Orkan.

Williams admits that he not only thought it was a good role, he also felt *Popeye* was the movie which could do for him what *Superman* had done for his good friend Christopher Reeve. His decision to wear the cape and tights and fly at the end of a Chapman crane in front of a blue screen had made him an international star. Williams took his research seriously, and he and Reeve had long talks about the difficulty of bringing a cartoon character to life and making him believable.

> When I was training for *Popeye* [says Williams], I thought this is it. This is my *Superman* and it's gonna go through the fuckin' roof. I also had the dream of getting up and thanking the Academy, but I got beyond the 'this-is-it' stage as soon as we started shooting. After the first day on *Popeye* I thought, 'Well, maybe this isn't it', and I finally wound up going, 'Oh God, when is this going to be over?'

Filming *Popeye* was a miserable experience for everyone concerned. Shooting took place in Malta, which has one of the world's largest marine tanks and is ideal for films with a nautical theme. A replica of Sweethaven was built on the coast, and the cast were more or less marooned for six months in a place which Williams describes as 'San Quentin on Valium'. Because Paramount were concerned with security, the cast and crew lived in a compound with wire fences and guards on the gates. This only added to the feeling of being held against their will and it was quickly dubbed 'Stalag Altman'. It was hardly surprising that drug-taking, especially cocaine use, was rife on the set.

> We were there for six months, working six days a week, and soon after we got to Malta it started raining and hardly ever stopped [recalls Williams]. That stretched out our shooting schedule, and we would just sit there for days, going bats and feeling trapped … there are no great entertainment centres on Malta, and on weekends we used to drink. They had this very

strange wine available on the island; cabernet muck ... When the English
had a naval base on Malta, they built a few pubs which are still there. We'd
visit them on Saturday nights and get a little loaded and then sleep all day
Sunday and go back to the grind on Monday.

It was a nightmare experience for anyone making their film début,
especially someone who was obliged to carry the film by playing the title
role. The pressure on Robin Williams must have been enormous, and it
wasn't helped by the physical demands which the role made on him.
Transforming him into Popeye took 90 minutes in the make-up chair
every day, after which the trademark grotesquely inflated muscular forearms would be applied.

'They tied me off almost like a junkie,' he says. 'In some of the fight
scenes I'd lose all the circulation in my arms and they'd lock up. I'd ask
for a little blood and they'd untie me and say "Relax, Robin. Relax". Once
the circulation got going they'd tie up my arms again so I could fight for
another half-hour. It was very strange and very strenuous.'

Williams and the rest of the cast were not the only ones feeling the
strain. As the shooting schedule wore on with no immediate end in sight,
the executives at Paramount – who had never been keen on the project
to begin with – started to become more and more anxious. Without
warning they simply decided enough was enough, and Altman was told
basically to finish up in Malta, come back with what footage they had and
see if it could cut together into some kind of film. Williams in particular
was devastated. He had felt the pressure throughout the film but hoped
that, finally, as he had on *Mork and Mindy* and *The Richard Pryor Show*
before that, he would get the chance to break free of the strait-jacket in a
rousing finale. He had visions of a special-effects-laden final sequence in
which he would perform impossible feats of spinach-fuelled derring-do
and save the day. It wasn't to be. The final scenes, which involved Popeye
rescuing Olive from a giant octopus, bordered on the farcical.

On the last day of shooting we were struggling desperately to come up with
an ending [remembers Williams], and we all knew it would take great
special effects to pull it off ... I know that I was supposed to punch an
octopus out of the water and have it go whirling into space, but that didn't
happen either ... when we were ready to shoot the ending the special effects
guys had already left Malta. We were backed against a wall and we all knew
it. Shelley Duvall, who was terrific as Olive Oyl, was supposed to be attacked
by an octopus, but the one they built for the movie couldn't do anything.
The Disney studios had half investment in *Popeye* and if anyone had let

them know that the octopus couldn't even manipulate its arms, I think they would have sent over a couple of guys and we would have had an octopus that could blink, wink, blow bubbles and smoke underwater. Shelley had to do a scene with the octopus grabbing her, so she literally wrapped its tentacles around her like a wet rubber boa and had to sell the fucker as hand-to-hand combat. That's when I was supposed to show up and launch the octopus into outer space. We blew it up instead, but you couldn't tell what really happened.

Despite the Ed Wood-style finale there were more problems in store in post-production. Altman's obsession with the use of natural sound which he had pioneered in his earlier films meant that Williams had to re-dub his dialogue twice to get the right effect. He had spent a long time working on Popeye's voice, which he described as sounding like 'a frog farting under water'. But even with the benefit of two dubbing sessions much of his dialogue still sounds garbled and indistinct.

When the movie was released it was slaughtered by most of the American critics. Williams believes they went into the movie looking for the cartoon they had grown up on and were then instantly antagonistic to Altman's 'very gentle fable with music and a lot of heart', as Williams described the finished film. Given the circumstances under which the film was shot and the production was shut down, it's remarkable that there was anything to release at all. Williams for his part received generally non-committal reviews which praised his intuitive mimicry while pointing out that he had never really got into the character. It was a classic case of the prosthetics wearing the actor and not the other way round. Although some of the reviews wounded him deeply, Williams must have suspected that they were going to be like that. Especially after he had watched the film play in near total silence at its Hollywood première, an experience which he compared to a waking nightmare. But he also claims that he felt all along during shooting that something was missing.

For instance [he explains], we needed a couple of slam-bang musical numbers that really tore the tits off the place. Same with the action. When the cartoon Popeye started dancing, walls would come down, windows would break, people would go flying out of the door, and Popeye would swinging Olive Oyl around with her body parallel to the floor. Instead of all that we shot in a real small space where you couldn't kick out the jams. A lot of the movie was filmed on a sunken steamer that was sitting on the end of the bay in Malta, and that kept things confined. So we wound up seeing the softer side of Popeye.

Williams dealt with the pain of the critical rejection of his efforts in *Popeye* by doing what he does best. He went on-stage and worked it out as a form of therapy. There were the inevitable heckles about the movie, and Williams would take them in his stride, zinging back with a one-liner. One of his favourites was to tell whoever asked 'What about *Popeye*?' that it was playing on a double bill in Hollywood with *Heaven's Gate*, the 1980 Michael Cimino folly which almost bankrupted United Artists. Williams felt aggrieved and hard done by about *Popeye*. His own feeling was that he had given a strong performance with some depth, but he had simply not been allowed to express himself. However, looking back on the film now you have to concede that the whole venture of a naturalistic *Popeye* was ill-conceived, with a clumsy script which was going to defeat even the most experienced of actors.

One thing that *Popeye* did teach Williams, however, was that he did not want to direct. He had done some directing on *Mork and Mindy* towards the end of the run and harboured genuine ambitions in that direction. Now, he cannot see any circumstance in which he would get behind a camera.

'People say to me, "Why don't you direct?" ' he said recently. 'And I say, "It would be very difficult for me to say to someone, 'I'm sorry, you know that wasn't very good' " and then have them go "Well, what about *Popeye*?" ... I could never direct someone, I don't have the discipline.'

Since it was released in 1980, *Popeye* has become something of a Hollywood urban myth. The story is that the film was a complete disaster which lost millions of dollars for both studios. Some years after he had got over the trauma of the reaction to the film, Williams put the record straight: '... it wasn't that bad. There were some wonderful moments in *Popeye*,' he insists. 'Moments do not money make, but it did make some money because I got some cheques. And if I got money they must have made something. They must have made a lot of money, because before actors see any money, producers make a lot more.'

12

The Midas Curse

By the beginning of the Eighties Robin Williams was showing signs of running out of steam. He had been a sensation in the early days of *Mork and Mindy*, but he had been unable to translate that success into anything more meaningful. *Popeye*, while not a complete flop, had been nowhere near the career-making film everyone had expected. His next venture on to the big screen was more successful, but it was a qualified success.

Few movie débuts had been as anticipated as Robin Williams in *Popeye*. It seemed like the perfect combination, and the studios were bullish about his prospects. Once the box-office results were in, their enthusiasm waned somewhat and Williams found that the once plentiful supply of scripts was drying up. However, there was one among them which looked promising. John Irving's *The World According to Garp* was one of the most popular novels of the early Eighties. It was, as the title suggested, the story of a man's life and his view of the world.

T. S. Garp was raised by a formidable woman named Jenny Fields, who had wanted a child but not a husband. When she found herself nursing wounded soldiers the opportunity to solve her dilemma arrived in the form of Technical Sergeant Garp, a man with an unfortunate brain injury which had left him with a permanent erection. Jenny Fields took advantage of his condition and nine months later a son named T. S. Garp – after his 'father' – was born. Irving's rambling but fascinating novel is a story of life and love and loss as Garp grows up in a world full of women and becomes a successful writer himself.

It was a difficult novel to film, and once again the choice of director was not an obvious one. George Roy Hill was best known for films such as *Butch Cassidy and the Sundance Kid*, *The Sting* and *The Great Waldo Pepper*. These were all films which, in one way or another, celebrated maleness and male bonding. *Garp* on the other hand had a strongly feminist point of view. Williams was paid $300,000 to play the title role and found himself once again in the midst of an impressive cast. Glenn Close played his mother, John Lithgow was a transsexual former football star, Mary Beth Hurt played his wife, and Hume Cronyn and Jessica Tandy were his in-laws. Right from the start Williams was keen to play the role, sensing that it would provide him with the genuine dramatic challenge which Popeye had not presented. He also found that, unlike *Mork and Mindy*, this would require discipline, especially with a director who was not prone to giving Williams his head.

'I wasn't allowed to improvise,' says Williams. 'The first day I improvised George Roy Hill said, "Okay, that's a wrap." He made his point right away. Also he kind of forced me to stop. He'd say, "Okay, that's a joke. Let's go back to the next level and find out what's behind it." With comedy you can duck and dive out if it gets too serious. There you couldn't.'

The World According to Garp was a steep learning curve for Robin Williams, but he seems to have thrived on the challenge.

> Everything about *Popeye* and *Garp* is different [he says], starting with the directors. Altman and George Roy Hill represent two extremes. It was incredible to go from an Altman who gives you all that freedom to a Hill who says, 'You've got to do it this way.' They're like the yin and yang of the directing school. Hill knew exactly what he wanted . . . The roles themselves were opposites. *Garp* was like an oil drilling. I had to dig down and find things deep inside myself and bring them up. Heavy griefs and joys – births and deaths – *Garp* is an all-encompassing look at a man's life.

In the end Williams was pleased with his performance although, as he says now, he would play the role differently if he were playing it today with the benefit of being a parent himself. His performance as Garp is both funny and touching and, for audiences who only knew him from *Mork and Mindy*, a revelatory experience. It was the first time that audiences had seen a glimpse of the trained actor behind the manic performer. By and large they, and the critics, liked what they saw. Williams received a great deal of praise for a film which was generally admired by the critics but did only moderate box-office business. In the end, though, it was enough to re-establish Hollywood's faith in him and the scripts started to pick up again.

The World According to Garp was filmed during the final season of *Mork and Mindy* and released in July 1982, a month after the show had gone off the air. Williams filled in what was a fairly nervous period by going back on the road. A performance junkie, he sought solace in front of crowds, criss-crossing the country in a series of high-profile dates. For most of his life, whether as a lonely child in a huge mansion, or a shy bullied child at an intimidating boarding school, humour had been Robin Williams' sword and shield. It was his armour against the world, a way of being liked, and a way of dealing with his fear of being left on his own. Now he was finding that it was a double-edged sword.

'Humour is a dreadful curse,' says Eric Idle, 'and Robin was like Midas, being funny endlessly. Getting blasted was the only way he could stop.'

With the notable exception of those decent reviews he received for *The World According to Garp*, his film career had not panned out. His marriage was now in disarray, and he was becoming more and more reliant on vodka and cocaine.

His problems were largely self-inflicted and can be traced back to that very first series of *Mork and Mindy*. Williams has already alluded to the problems in the early days of his marriage, suggesting that Valerie Velardi was having some difficulty in riding the coat-tails of his success. In truth, if Velardi was having problems with anything it was with the way that Williams was handling his success. *Mork and Mindy* had made him a household name overnight, but it also made him a sex symbol. His little-boy-lost television persona, coupled with his athlete's physique and his devastating wit, made him something of a babe magnet. For someone to whom popularity had come relatively late in his life, the temptation must have been overpowering. One of his earliest magazine profiles, in *Playgirl* in March 1979, was already noting Williams' fondness for the perks of celebrity.

'He always grapples with Valerie when she shows up on the set,' wrote Richard J. Pietschmann, before noting, 'but he also continually grabs asses and squeezes tits and generally hugs and cuddles the best-looking women within range.'

Pietschmann also pointed out the relish with which Williams was responding to his new role as an 'alien sex symbol'. It wasn't long before others started to notice too. Williams had become a celebrity, which meant that, in their eyes, he was fair game for the gossip columnists and the supermarket tabloids. Less than a year after his marriage to Valerie Velardi the *New York Post* was suggesting that a divorce was in the pipeline.

The *National Enquirer*, which would become the bane of Williams' life, also suggested that he and Valerie and another woman were going out on triple dates. Williams was upset by the reports, according to *Mork and Mindy* co-star Pam Dawber quoted in the *New York Daily News*. On the other hand, she was also quoted as saying that he was not very secretive, suggesting that she too believed that he was the architect of his own misfortune.

One reason for Williams' behaviour may have been that he had deserted the one thing which had kept him reasonably sane up till now. He was no longer performing. Getting up on stage for Robin Williams was his entire *raison d'être*, and even when he had become famous with *Mork and Mindy* he continued to go back and perform at open mike nights at comedy hole-in-the-wall joints like the Holy City Zoo.

> It only sits 60 people, usually the same people [he explains]. I liked going in there late at night, after 12.30 when there's only about 12 people in there. Then it's really funny. There's something about it which strips away the pretensions. People still yell things at you and heckle you. They give you about five minutes grace. Then if you get them it's great, but after that five minutes you better have something. It's good, it really forces you to find stuff and tap into it.

Now Williams, who by the end of 1979 not only had a hit TV series but a hit album as well with his Grammy-winning *Reality . . . What a Concept*, appeared to be believing his own publicity. Far from finding something which would strip away the pretensions, he was now actively wallowing in them. He denies Pam Dawber's suggestion that he was making his behaviour too public, but he does admit that things got out of hand.

> Hollywood is so full of horseshit temptations. During the second year of the series, I kind of lost track of all kinds of stuff. I stopped performing. I mean, I did an album but when that was over, it was a kind of blaaah for a while. I lost track of everything, kind of . . . When things started really peaking you had friends you didn't know you had before. You'd be spending time at clubs all night long and then going to work the next day expecting people wouldn't notice and they did. You'd come in the next day and people would say, 'Oh, pardon me. Refried shit?'
>
> There was always someone somewhere to keep partying with. Hollywood is designed that way. And the temptations are so many and varied. There is everything . . . The deadly sins of Hollywood. They wait for everyone.

While Williams was out partying the nights away, his wife would eventually make her way back home to the heights of Topanga Canyon. Valerie Velardi is a hard-headed woman. She was not the sort to sit back and accept this kind of behaviour from her husband, but at the same time she was aware that she was dealing with precious cargo. Williams was bright, very intelligent and supremely talented. Yet in spite of being all those things, he was still not terribly mature emotionally. He was behaving like a kid locked in a toy store. Velardi said once that she knew that if she had simply drawn a line in the sand and told Williams that it would all have to stop and stop now, he would simply have walked out. She knew that if she was going to stand by her man then it would require something a little different. Living in Hollywood had already required several adjustments on Valerie Velardi's part. In the first place she had had to become used to being, as far as the Hollywood movers and shakers were concerned, a Hollywood wife.

> Robin and I would go to a party and separate, wander around, looking for a good time, and I would take up with somebody, maybe a woman or maybe a group who wouldn't be giving me the time of day. And all of a sudden they'd see a photographer taking a picture of Robin and me and it was 'What a wonderful dress', or 'What you said before was simply fascinating'.
>
> Now in the past, the way I would deal with that would be to say, 'I wasn't good enough for you then; why am I good enough for you now? Just because I'm screwing Robin Williams I'm hot to you now? I don't need this shit.' But instead of reacting like a shit, or someone who is hurt or rejected, I'd say, 'Okay, this is the life we're living – enjoy it, have a ball, but don't take it too seriously.'

But Williams was taking it seriously. He was a born-again party animal and the effects began to show, not least in the fact that his weight began to balloon up. There were also anxiety attacks on the set of *Mork and Mindy*, which suggests a Catch-22 scenario. Was he taking drugs because he was anxious, or was he suffering from cocaine-induced paranoia? Williams goes for the former.

> Do you think that drug abuse isn't old? [he asked a journalist recently]. If you look back at old newspaper headlines, it's old. People from the Twenties did all these things. Cocaine has been in Hollywood since the beginning of Hollywood. I think it's the pressure – some people snap. I used it to try and kind of numb out and forget, it was a reaction to sometimes try and escape from it all. I had a reverse metabolic reaction to cocaine, I would do it and

go catatonic. People think I must have been really wild; no, it was the exact opposite. It comes and goes because Hollywood is a high-pressure place. It isn't just the salaries, it's the nature of worrying about how you're doing. 'Am I still being creative?' It's also sometimes flirting with the dark side or whatever, chasing the dragon.

By his own admission Robin Williams was seriously messed up during this time of his life. Valerie Velardi, the woman he had often referred to as the stabilising influence on his life, did the best she could. She tried tough love by simply walking out and leaving him. There were a number of separations for about a month at a time when she had simply had enough. But she always came back, he was always pleased to see her, and before too long things were always back the way they had been. Another approach was called for. 'You can guide people,' Velardi says, 'you can make yourself interesting enough and important enough in your lover's life so that he'll always come back to you if you just keep growing along with it. If you just be part of their rhythm and give them a lot of freedom and be part of their growth instead of pulling them back from what is titillating and exciting. Let's face it, Robin is a stimulus junkie.'

Velardi's approach then was to accept Williams' womanising for what it was. She insists that he had a lot of female friends at the time but the relationships were nowhere as intense as people were speculating. Williams, according to his wife, loves women and loves their company. And, she says, that's mostly what it was about, simply spending time with friends who happened to be female. She never tried to stop him seeing female friends as long as he abided by one firm ground rule; no one would take her place.

It doesn't sit right [she said at the time], but under extraordinary circumstances, which we are under, if you don't make the necessary adjustments, then you can lose precious things. That's not to say that it gives us
the licence to go off and screw everything that's around. It's just the freedom
to at least feel like we're free individuals as opposed to being married and
locked in and 'You can't go out tonight because I know so-and-so is there,
and she's hot and pretty and I'm afraid you're gonna get involved with her'.
He's never going to get involved with anyone without me knowing about it.
And the other way doesn't work. You can't hold somebody in. They resent
you, hate you, and you become unattractive to them.

If I had jumped the gun and divorced him I would have lost the most
precious thing in my life and it would have curtailed our experience together,
which is a lot richer than anything he can get off the streets.

There were also times when Velardi would take matters into her own hands. The guiding and giving space would simply give way to a pre-emptive strike.

'She would march right up to some girl sitting at [Robin's] table and say, "Hello, I'm Valerie Williams, Robin's wife" ', claims Pam Dawber. 'Or call up a girl. Or have lunch with a girlfriend. And say, "You think he's gonna leave me for you? You're crazy". '

While Valerie was able to take matters into her own hands when it came to her husband's flirting and womanising, his substance abuse was an entirely different matter. There was no reasonable threat she could make to a line of cocaine or a pitcher of kamikazes – vodka and lime – which had become his drink of choice.

> I was 26 or 27 then [says Williams, trying to put it all into some kind of perspective], and then bang, there's all this money, and there are magazine covers. Between the drugs and the women and all that stuff, it's all coming at you and you're swallowed whole ... Even Gandhi would have been kind of hard pressed to handle it well ... the reason I did cocaine was so that I wouldn't have to talk to anybody ... For me, it was like a sedative, a way of pulling back from a world that I was afraid of.

The defining step for most addicts is the point where they accept the fact that they need help, the moment when they can realise for themselves that they have a problem. Williams, who could be so intuitive and aware in so many other areas, simply didn't see what was going on. Part of that was the drug culture which was pervasive in Hollywood at the time. Snorting cocaine was regarded in some quarters as almost a social skill and an outward symbol of your ability to compete in the hard world, play even harder, 24/7 lifestyle of contemporary Hollywood. Looking back, Williams recognises that what he needed was intervention.

'I think I was crying out for someone to say "Enough",' he admitted. 'In the end I had to make my own line. Anybody who finally kicks himself in the ass and wants to clean up makes his own line. You realise the final line is the edge.'

Williams' desire to get himself straight arose in the end from two disparate sources. A birth and a death.

13

Consequences

There was a nervous atmosphere on the set of *Mork and Mindy* on the afternoon of 5 March 1982. It wasn't just that the show was not doing well in the ratings and was only a matter of weeks away from being cancelled. There was something else, a sense of foreboding and deep concern about the star of the show. This time the concern was not about the harm he was doing himself; instead it was about the damage he might do himself. The comedian John Belushi had been found dead of a heroin and cocaine overdose at the Chateau Marmont hotel off Sunset Strip. He and Robin Williams were friends, and were related through their comedy and their fondness for recreational pharmaceuticals. Now that Belushi was dead, someone was going to have to break the news to Robin Williams.

> Somebody told me to tell him [says Pam Dawber], because they were afraid he would fall apart. You never knew how he was going to take something because he was so emotional. He was affected in the way, at first, that made it look as though he wasn't affected at all. He said, 'Wow, I was with him last night.' Then, as it absorbed, he became more and more devastated by it, because suddenly I think he began to see the parallels – just what fast living can do. And also, somebody the same age, somebody you just saw that night, to then suddenly be dead.

John Belushi was 33 years old when he died. He had risen to fame as one of the stars of the TV show *Saturday Night Live* and hit films such as

National Lampoon's Animal House. However, his prodigious talent was becoming increasingly overshadowed by his even more prodigious appetite for drugs. Belushi was capable of ingesting phenomenal amounts in his ever more desperate search for a high. On the night of his death he was contemplating what might be the ultimate creative achievement from his point of view: he was planning to inject himself on-screen with heroin for a part in a proposed movie. One of the reasons he was at Chateau Marmont that night was to seek the support of his friend and fellow Marmont resident Robert De Niro. Belushi felt De Niro was the greatest method actor who had ever lived and would undoubtedly have backed him up. Robin Williams was with Belushi briefly on the night he died. He spent no more than ten minutes in his friend's company – only long enough to do some drugs – and then left.

Even now Williams believes there was an element of conspiracy in his being there that night. It seems more likely that, in the absence of any obvious motive for involving him, he was there simply as a result of a misunderstanding.

I was only there for five or ten minutes [he says]. I saw him and split. He didn't want me there, really. He obviously had other things he was doing. I do think I was set up in some way to go over there. A guy at the Roxy said that John wanted me to stop by his bungalow. But when I went he wasn't looking for me. He wasn't even there. When he arrived he said 'What are you doing here?' and offered me a line of cocaine. I took it and then I drove home. If I had known what was going on, I would have stayed and tried to help. It wasn't like he was shooting up in front of me. The next day on the set of *Mork and Mindy,* Pam Dawber came up to me and said 'Your friend is dead.'

Williams and Belushi had first met about three years previously. They were not close, but in the three or four months before Belushi's death they had begun to see more of each other and were becoming closer. Given that they were both *habitués* of the celebrity drug scene, it was inevitable that their paths would cross in exclusive clubs or private lounges where the stars hung out at night.

'I admired the shit out of him,' says Williams, who probably secretly envied Belushi's uncompromising wild-man behaviour. 'I'd had a wonderful time with him. One time he took me to a heavy hard-core punk club, and I was scared shitless. People were slam dancing, which I had never seen before. It was like being on tour with Dante, if Dante was James Brown . . . I was like Beaver Cleaver in the Underworld.'

One of the things Williams most admired about Belushi was the fact that he had a constitution like an ox. He could put his body through the most terrible punishment and still emerge virtually unscathed. The idea that someone of Belushi's iron-clad constitution could succumb to an overdose must have given Williams pause for thought. In the end he dealt with Belushi's death in the only way he knew how: he went on-stage and performed.

The day after John Belushi died Robin Williams spent the afternoon speaking to a *Playboy* reporter as part of his first major interview with the magazine. This, incidentally, was also the interview in which he claimed that he had not got into hard drugs and never would, which implies a great deal of self-delusion either on the part of the interviewer or the interviewee. That night Williams went on-stage at The Comedy Store as a surprise guest and did an impromptu 45-minute set. 'It was good,' Williams recalled later to interviewer Lawrence Linderman, 'but there was a strange mood in the air. It was just kind of up and down.'

Williams never mentioned Belushi once during his set. Neither did any of the other comics at The Comedy Store that night. Williams believes it was partially out of respect for a dead colleague, but also no one particularly wanted to open a can of worms by talking about drug use, especially with so many reporters in the audience. Williams says he felt no guilt over John Belushi's death. He could not possibly have known how the evening was going to turn out and, even if he had, he did not know Belushi well enough to make any kind of satisfactory intervention.

But it still gnawed away at the back of his mind. If this could happen to Belushi, a man who was as strong as a bull and only a couple of years older than himself, then what did the future hold for Robin Williams? Not long after Belushi's death, Pam Dawber came across Williams standing quietly on the *Mork and Mindy* set. He was on his own and lost in thought. 'Don't you worry, Dawbs,' he told her quietly. 'It'll never happen to me.'

He was as good as his word. Within a year he was clean, sober, and a father. But there was still a lot of fall-out from his friendship with John Belushi to deal with before then. The police had been investigating the death of Belushi since the afternoon his body was found in the back bedroom of bungalow number three at the Chateau Marmont. The officers who were investigating the case, Detectives Russell Kuster and Addison Arce, guided by a coroner's verdict that Belushi had died of a drugs overdose, were inclined to believe that it was just another accidental death. They were going through the protocol of following all the required leads and wrapping up all the loose ends when the case was blown wide open by comments from an unlikely source. Cathy Smith, a friend of Belushi's who had infiltrated his inner circle because of her easy access to drugs, told the *National Enquirer* that she had been with Belushi on the night he died. She also told the newspaper that she had mixed the speed-ball – a mixture of cocaine and heroin – which had killed Belushi. Then, to cap it off, she named Robin Williams and Robert De Niro as having been with Belushi on the night he died.

The police were caught on the horns of a dilemma. No one really believed Smith's story, and the fact that she had received $15,000 for it didn't help her credibility much. But with Smith having gone public, her claims had to be investigated. Smith made her comments in a recorded interview with the *Enquirer,* and Addison Arce is one of the few people who have heard this tape. He is in no doubt that Smith was being set up.

By the time I got through listening to that tape it was obvious to me that they were getting her to say almost anything they wanted [he says]. It was almost like a controlled conversation where the interviewer would be providing 85 per cent or even 95 per cent of the information and she would just be sitting there saying 'That's right'. By the end of the conversation her voice was very slurred and her demeanour very casual. From that and the sucking noise during the interview it was obvious to me from working narcotics and being a policeman for so long that she was smoking a joint and enjoying a drink at the same time. It was a very relaxed atmosphere and they were having a conversation, but it was very definitely a controlled environment.

The *National Enquirer* had been the bane of Robin Williams' life for some time. They first crossed paths when Williams claims the paper tricked his mother into giving them an interview and supplying precious family photographs. These, according to Williams, were then used in a piece which suggested that he had grown up under the thumb of a bullying and tyrannical father. Now they had gone a step further and landed him in the middle of a homicide investigation. Perhaps this is what Williams suspected when he suggested that his presence at Belushi's bungalow had been a set-up? But is he suggesting that it was the *Enquirer* that set him up? Or that someone else set him up in the hope of selling the story to the *Enquirer*? We will never know.

Although the police did not necessarily believe the whole of Cathy Smith's story, there were parts which struck them as being plausible. According to Addison Arce, Smith described De Niro and Williams as attacking a bag of cocaine with straws 'like a Hoover vacuum cleaner'.

Williams' version was that he had called De Niro when he got to the
Chateau, but the actor had company and obviously did not want to be
disturbed. He never saw De Niro that night, but he did admit to doing
some cocaine in Belushi's room. The police were duty bound to investigate
now, if only to sort out what had happened leading up to the death
of John Belushi. Los Angeles Deputy District Attorney Mike Genelin
announced that the police were going to have to speak to both Williams
and De Niro. It is technically possible that, had they been with Belushi
that night, the two actors could have been charged under California's
felony murder laws. Since Belushi had died as a result of a felony being
committed, i.e. injecting drugs, then the person who had injected him
with those drugs could be guilty of second-degree murder. However, in
announcing that they wanted to speak to De Niro and Williams, Deputy
District Attorney Genelin made it plain that neither man was a suspect.
On her own admission, Smith had injected Belushi, who had something of
a phobia about needles. The police were chiefly concerned with obtaining
corroborative statements to piece together Belushi's final hours.

The investigation into Belushi's death brought on by Cathy Smith's
interview flared up in the summer of 1982. Neither De Niro nor Williams
was instantly available for questioning. De Niro had gone to Italy to make
a film, and his publicists made it perfectly plain that he would not be
returning to the United States for questioning. The LAPD, for its part,
would not authorise the expenditure for detectives to go to Italy to speak
to him. De Niro never spoke to the police and never gave any evidence
about Belushi's death other than to a Grand Jury, which he spoke to by
telephone some months later. Williams on the other hand did agree to
cooperate, but only up to a point. The investigation could not have come
at a worse time for him. He was in the midst of doing advance publicity
for *The World According to Garp*, the film which might establish him as a
serious actor, when he had to face up to being part of a police inquiry.
Indeed, when the story broke that the police were now treating Belushi's
death as homicide, Williams was in the middle of an interview for what
would be a cover story for *Rolling Stone*. One of his managers, David
Steinberg, went so far as to call the reporter later, asking for the tapes of
the interview to check for references to Belushi.

David Steinberg and the rest of Williams' management team eventually
struck a deal with the Police Department. Williams would be interviewed,
but only with his lawyers present and with the questions vetted in advance.
Detective Arce was not really expecting to find out anything significant
from the session, but once it had been effectively neutered the interview
became meaningless. 'I have no problems with attorneys being in an

interview,' he said later, 'but when they have me write the questions out beforehand then that's no interview.'

In the end, as expected, no charges were brought against Williams, nor were they ever likely to have been. The only one who needed to fear indictment was Cathy Smith, and on 15 March 1983 – just over a year after Belushi died – she was charged with murder in the second degree as well as other drugs offences. She was extradited from Canada and after being found guilty, served a short jail sentence.

The death of John Belushi was a salutary lesson not just for Robin Williams but for the whole of Hollywood. A great many stars began to see that cocaine and heroin were no longer high-priced fashion accessories, and large numbers began to clean up their act. Robin Williams was among them. It was David Steinberg and others close to him who finally gave him the intervention he desperately needed and persuaded him to seek treatment. But the response that he initially received when he tried to quit is an indication of the prevailing social climate in the film industry at the time.

> The weird thing about the drug period is that I didn't have to pay for it very often [he recalled several years later]. Most people give you cocaine when you're famous. It gives them a certain control over you; you are at least socially indebted to them. And it's also the old thing of perfect advertising. They can claim, 'I got Robin Williams fucked up.' 'You did. Lemme buy a gram then.' The more fucked up you get, the more they can work you around. You're being led around by your nostril. I went to one doctor and asked, 'Do I have a cocaine problem?' He said, 'How much do you do?' I said, 'Two grams a day.' He said, 'No, you don't have a problem.' I said 'Okay.'

Williams kicked drugs on his own. He didn't check into the Betty Ford Clinic or any other celebrity enclave. He was encouraged by his mother's belief in the Christian Scientist doctrine of self-healing and he was determined to end his drug addiction on his own. He dealt with his alcoholism likewise by handling it on his own.

> With alcohol it was decompression [he explains]. The same way I started drinking I stopped. You work your way down the ladder from Jack Daniels to mixed drinks to wine to wine coolers and finally to Perrier. With cocaine there is no way to decompress yourself. It took a few months . . . People come up to you with twitching Howdy Doody jaws and you think, 'Hmmmm, I looked like that.' You realise that if you saw by daylight the people that you

had been hanging out with at night, they'd scare the shit out of you. There are bugs that look better than that.

Along with kicking his drink and drugs addiction, Williams was especially keen to make a genuine attempt at rebuilding his relationship with Valerie. When that *Rolling Stone* article appeared in September 1982, Williams was already celebrating taking the first steps to getting himself clean and sober. He spoke of the strains on both of them of his becoming famous overnight; of going from being poor and newly married to being hugely successful and the centre of a huge national craze. He also spoke of his gratitude that they had survived.

'You go through this kind of phase ... and then you're through it,' he said, trying to be serious and articulate his feelings. 'It's like you go through one of those blizzards and you lose each other's hands for a while, and then you come through on the other side.'

Very soon he had another reason for staying straight. Williams and his wife admitted in the interview that they had been trying for a child. Not long afterwards Valerie discovered she was pregnant. This gave Williams added resolve.

'Zach was about to be born,' he said later, 'and I didn't want to miss it because I was coked up or drinking. It was hideous enough feeling hung over without a baby screaming. I mean there are times when you think God made babies cute so you don't eat them – imagine if you're loaded.'

14

Beautiful Boy

Possibly the single defining moment in a man's life is when he becomes a father. Suddenly, from being really accountable only for and to himself, he becomes responsible for the life and well-being of someone else. It is a challenging vocation to which all men react with varying degrees of success. Robin Williams was determined that the birth of Zachary Tim Williams was going to be the moment when his life turned around.

He had already kicked alcohol and cocaine, and he was now seriously getting back into shape. He had taken up running again, and a strenuous and dedicated fitness regime saw him back at something close to his fighting weight when his son was born. Williams had grown up more or less on his own, although he was never in any doubt that his parents loved him. He was determined that he would be around for Zachary more than his own father had been for him. However, it was also a good deal easier for Williams to take charge of his own life that it had been for his father.

He was also taking time to be a new dad, and in the process becoming much closer to his own father. All men ultimately become their fathers, but the process speeds up considerably when you have a child. Suddenly fatherhood is the one thing you have in common. You realise that the problems you are now facing with your child are no different from the ones your father faced with you. The birth of his grandchild brought Robert and Robin Williams much closer together. Williams had a new respect for his father; he began to realise just how difficult a job it is. There had never been any serious strain between father and son, but there were undoubtedly times of great distance, brought on by the gap in their ages if nothing else. Robert Williams could not have failed to notice his son's binges on booze and drugs, but neither he nor his wife would have been inclined to intervene. If Robin wanted help then he would need first to realise that he needed help. And when he finally took matters into his own hands and cleaned up his act, his parents would have been overjoyed.

The birth of Zachary was the beginning of a new era in Robin Williams' life. Almost from the moment when Zach was born, he and his father each saw the other in a different light. They were no longer father and son; they were simply fathers. Zach's birth sparked a *rapprochement* and an understanding between the two men which grew and deepened over the remaining years of Robert Williams' life. It was a source of great comfort and enjoyment for both men.

In career terms, Williams was still considering his options. *Mork and Mindy* was now vanished into the mists of time, and neither *Popeye* nor *The World According to Garp* had done what he had hoped. There was still live performing, and Williams continued to jump on and off 'Das Bus', as he called his tour coach, and entertain crowds large and small across the country. He was keen to continue his movie career, and the warm critical response for his performance in *The World According to Garp* allowed him to do that. The scripts which had tailed off after *Popeye* had started to pick up again and he was being offered some interesting roles. But he appeared determined to do things a little differently next time out.

'I'm just interested in learning what I can about movies,' he said at the time, 'because there are two possibilities. I can act in other people's films or I can eventually write and act in my own. I hope I can play a supporting actor in the next film I do, so that I can sit back and watch people work rather than take the burden of being a major character, as in *Popeye* and *Garp*.'

In the end Williams did sign up for another film not long after that, but things didn't turn out quite the way he planned. He would be part of an ensemble cast but not in a supporting role. He and Walter Matthau would be joint male leads in *The Survivors*, a black comedy from Michael Ritchie. Again this was an atypical role for Williams in the sense that there was nothing in the script which suggested that it could be the vehicle for his particular talents. Williams plays a middle-management executive who lives the ideal suburban life while harbouring dreams of being on the corporate fast track to the executive washroom. Summoned to a meeting one morning, Williams rushes in expecting promotion at the very least, only to find he is being fired. In a final indignity he is fired by his boss's parrot which has been trained to deliver the downsizing eulogy. As he leaves his former office, Williams stops for petrol at a nearby filling station which is owned by Matthau and inadvertently triggers an explosion which destroys the whole place and puts Matthau out of business. Williams and Matthau cross paths again at the unemployment office and ultimately, in a barely credible plot twist, they get mixed up with Jerry Reed as a hit man and find themselves doing battle with a crowd of angry survivalists.

Certainly the black humour of the early part of *The Survivors* would have appealed to Williams. Politically he would have been in tune with a timely script which focused on the consequences of nothing actually trickling down from Ronald Reagan's trickle-down Reaganomics. However, the second half of the film is totally wrong-headed and Williams' particular brand of humour seems ill-suited to a dark comedy which descends into broad farce. He tried his best, but at the end of the day his performance was rather like throwing a match into a box of fireworks; spectacular, entertaining and ultimately too volatile to be kept in such a restricting container. None of Robin Williams' first three films had come close to stretching him comedically or dramatically. That was partly the result of his inexperience in picking the right projects; it was also the fault of directors who did not appreciate his talents or know how to use them; but mostly it was the fault of a studio system which was resolutely trying to hammer a square peg into a round hole. What Robin Williams really needed was someone who understood what he could do and how best he could do it.

In Hollywood terms Paul Mazursky is almost a Renaissance man. He is best known as a director, but he is also an actor, a comedian, a scriptwriter and a producer. He began as a night-club comedian in his native New York before graduating to television as a writer for artists such as Danny Kaye and for television shows like *The Monkees*. By the end of the Sixties he had made his directing début with the then-controversial *Bob and Carol and Ted and Alice*. This was followed by a series of increasingly barbed studies of American society. Films such as *Blume in Love, Harry and Tonto* and *An Unmarried Woman* took a slightly skewed look at the American Dream. In the process they allowed Mazursky to build a reputation as one of the industry's most intelligent and literate directors, a genuine American *auteur*.

One of Mazursky's most perceptive looks at life in America came in 1984 when he made *Moscow on the Hudson*. It is the story of a Russian musician who defects on a visit to the United States; the actual defection takes place in Bloomingdale's – 'between Estée Lauder and Pierre Cardin'.

After being smuggled home by a security guard he marvels at life in the United States compared with the life he has left behind him. Then, after being mugged, he sees the other side of America – Mazursky shows the underbelly of the American Dream with crime, violence and poverty. Finally, however, the defector realises that, for all its faults, he is much better off in his new home. Although the film tends towards the sentimental too often for comfort, the central role of Vladimir the saxophonist could have been written for Robin Williams. For the first time in his film career, the actor also found a kindred spirit behind the camera. Paul Mazursky had been a stand-up comedian, he was one of Williams' gladiatorial fraternity, and he understood that Williams needed to be handled with care.

'At the time I knew Robin he was very manic,' recalled Mazursky some years later, suggesting that the toxin-free Williams hadn't quite found the calm that he was looking for. 'We went to several comedy clubs together and I once actually agreed to go on stage with him, but he was so funny I ran. On the set I always felt that what I had to work at was getting the tensions out, and I think we did it even though we had a couple of shouting matches at the beginning where I'd say "It's too much!" and he'd say "It's not anything!" I like the man very much. He's very sweet and he obviously wants to keep growing. He has a desperate need to be wonderful.'

If Williams did indeed have such a need, then he can thank Mazursky for allowing him to satiate his need on this film. Where Robert Altman had given him his head, and George Roy Hill had reined him in, Mazursky realised that Williams' artistic temperament had to be harnessed, not crushed. He needed direction, but he also needed to feel that he had an input into the creative process. The results are quite remarkable and, although it was not a huge commercial success, the film showed for the first time a glimpse of a maturing talent. As Vladimir the saxophonist, Williams submerged himself in a character for the first time. The accent, the mannerisms, the bewilderment of this stranger in a strange land were seamless. You could not tell where Williams stopped and Vladimir started and vice versa. Williams was not pretending to be someone else; he was playing a role. The strange alchemy between his Juilliard training and his mercurial comic gifts was showing signs of taking effect.

'I loved doing it,' said Williams of *Moscow on the Hudson*. 'Immersing yourself into another language and culture is wonderful. Oddly it was a little bit like Mork in that I was looking at American culture from the outside.'

Once again the reviews for *Moscow on the Hudson* were very good, maybe the best he had ever had, but once again the film failed to strike a chord with the people. It was at best a modest commercial success, meaning that he had now effectively struck out four times as a movie star. His career was not going as well as he or his managers had hoped. In addition his home life was rapidly declining into disarray. He and Valerie had come back together and Zach was the result of that. His birth, however, also threw into sharp focus the problems that still remained in the Williams marriage. Robin and Valerie were both devoted to Zach, they just weren't so sure they were still devoted to each other. Williams may have stopped drinking and doing coke, but he had not stopped his womanising. By the end of 1984 he had begun what would be a lengthy relationship with another woman. In addition he was spending more and more time performing. His comedy had always been his defence against the world; now it provided a hiding place. On the nights when he was performing on his concert tours he would finish his scheduled set and then the performance junkie would get into his car and prowl around looking for a fix. Eventually he would find another club, the smaller the better, and slip in quietly and do a late-night set. He got off on the buzz from the crowd when he stepped out of the shadows and into the limelight and they realised who it was. Some comedy fans effectively staked out certain of his favourite clubs in the seldom disappointed hope that he might turn up.

'As wonderful as he was, he was no prize package at that point,' recalled manager David Steinberg some ten years later. 'He was in a little trouble – there were four or five personalities trying to get out. The stage was the only place in his life where no one could fool with him.'

15

Enter Marsha

T he strain on Robin and Valerie Williams' marriage was beginning to tell. Williams had begun a relationship with Michelle 'Tish' Carter, a women he had met while she was working as a waitress at a night-club. He was deeply involved in this relationship and spending less and less time at home. The times he spent with Valerie could not have been happy ones. Even though she was unwilling to draw that line in the sand for her husband, it was becoming more and more unbearable.

'Neither of us was prepared for the sudden life shift,' she said later. 'He never stops performing or partying. And the women! Very attractive women throw themselves at men in his position. You'd have to be a saint to resist. But I have to admit, the other women were harder to take after I'd had a child.'

In the cold light of sobriety, both sides of the Williams marriage would have to admit that it was little more than a sham. They could rub along as best they could for the time being, but their marriage was holed below the waterline and sinking fast. And it appeared to be having an effect on Zachary. Both Robin and Valerie loved the boy dearly, but friends began to notice changes in his behaviour. When he was about 18 months old he started to have serious temper tantrums, and his nanny was unable to do anything about it. Privately friends felt that the nanny was not as sympathetic as she might have been to the little boy's needs.

While all this was going on, Marsha Garces was working as a waitress in San Francisco. Working at night helped put her through San Francisco State College by day, where she was studying fabrics and textiles as well as Mandarin Chinese. She had met Robin Williams at a party some 12 years previously but, given his lifestyle at that stage, that hardly put her in an exclusive club. It's debatable whether she made any impression on him at all in that first meeting, and even if she did it would be nothing like the effect she was about to have on him. Marsha Garces was the daughter of Leon Garces, a chef born in Cebu in the Philippines who had moved to the States, and his wife Ina, who was the daughter of Finnish immigrants who had settled in Owen, Wisconsin. When Leon and Ina got married they settled in Milwaukee where Marsha was born. She was the youngest of four children – one boy and three girls – and as the youngest she tended to spend a lot of time on her own. Going to school and mixing with other children did not help much.

'I grew up in a German community, where all the other kids were blond and we were dark, so I know what it feels like to be considered different,' she explains. 'I was different even from my brothers and sisters. They were very social, I was always by myself.'

As she was growing up she discovered a passion for art and design. She subsidised her art studies at the University of Wisconsin in Milwaukee by working as a waitress in several places throughout the city. The waitressing seemed to come naturally to her as she learned that she had the knack of putting people at their ease. In addition it didn't take up any of her daylight hours, which allowed her to continue with her studies. Eventually she grew tired of the Midwest and decided to move to California to continue her studies in San Francisco.

Marsha Garces is an attractive, dark-haired woman with deep, dark eyes. She has a ready smile and, as she found out, the ability to make people feel comfortable. She would not, however, have considered herself maternal. She had been married twice and had not felt the need or the urge to have any children. That would account for her surprise when she met a mutual friend in 1984, who told her about the Williams' problems with Zachary and their current nanny, and the friend suggested that Marsha would be an ideal replacement.

When she had been working in those restaurants Marsha had often joked, 'If I'm thirty and still slinging hash, drag me out of here.' She had not yet reached her landmark age, but it was looming on the horizon and maybe a change of vocation might not be a bad idea. She was duly interviewed and got the job, and made preparations to move out to the Williams ranch which sat in 600 acres of its own land in the Napa Valley. Williams had bought the original spread in Sonoma some years previously and had added to it over the years to guarantee almost total seclusion. It was bought in 1982 as a refuge from the madness of the film industry and his overnight fame. His friend Eric Idle had encouraged him by pointing out that he didn't need to talk into a microphone when he could smell a flower instead. The Sonoma estate – which Williams occasionally referred to as 'The Fuckin' Ranch' – was, literally, an attempt to stop and smell the roses. That aspect of the purchase hadn't worked out, but it was still ideal for Marsha Garces. There was enough room there to allow her to look after her new young charge, and she also had enough time and space to continue with the hand-dyed fabrics in which she was starting to specialise.

To begin with, Marsha had all the time and space in the world. She seldom saw Robin and Valerie as they went about their business wrapped up in their own lives. Zachary became the centre of her universe, and the woman who had not previously shown any maternal urges quickly discovered that this little boy hung the moon. The feeling was mutual. Zach stopped the tantrums and he and his new nanny formed a deep and abiding bond.

For Robin Williams things were going from bad to worse. His marriage was a disaster and his career seemed to be heading in the same direction. He had made another two feature films which were near total disasters. *The Best of Times* featured Williams opposite Kurt Russell as two former high-school football team-mates whose lives had been scarred by one defining game. Russell was the quarterback who had thrown the ball for what should have been the winning touchdown; Williams was the running back who had dropped the ball. Their team had lost the game, and both men, their ambition stunted by this catastrophic blow to their self-esteem, seemed destined to live out their lives in a small-town hell without ever reaching their full potential. Eventually Williams, who is by now a manager in the local bank, gets the idea that they should replay the game. If the result is different, then perhaps their lives might be different. *The Best of Times* was written by Ron Shelton, who has gone on to corner the market in sports movies such as *Bull Durham* and *White Men Can't Jump*, and directed by Roger Spottiswoode, who also went on to success, most notably with *Tomorrow Never Dies*. As well as Williams and Russell the cast also boasted Pamela Reed, Donald Moffat and M. Emmet Walsh. A lot of talent, to be sure, but none of it adequately harnessed in a film which, like Russell and Williams, never reached its full potential. *The Best of Times* barely got a cinema release and made its way quickly to the video shelves without causing much of a blip on the box-office radar.

The same fate befell Williams' next film, *Club Paradise*. Later, as he became more experienced, he would confess to not being an especially good judge of a script. The fact that he agreed to star in this film simply confirms that. On paper it should have been a box-office smash. The cast was virtually a Who's Who of American comedy in the Eighties. As well as Williams and *Saturday Night Live* alumni Rick Moranis – who had just starred in the smash *Ghostbusters* – and Brian Doyle-Murray, the comic talent also included Eugene Levy, Andrea Martin and Mary Gross. British model-turned-actress Twiggy provided the glamour, Jimmy Cliff provided the music, and Peter O'Toole provided a touch of class. The film was being directed by Harold Ramis, another *Ghostbusters* star who was also one of the hottest comedy directors around after the success of *Caddyshack* and *National Lampoon's Animal House*. Ramis had co-written the script with Brian Doyle-Murray, and the Hollywood insiders felt that the whole package was simply a licence to print money.

Williams played a Chicago fireman who was being invalided out of the job after a work-related accident. He decides to use his sizeable severance payment to live in the Caribbean and spend his days lying in the sun listening to the surf. But when he discovers that his chosen resort, Club Paradise, is under threat from ruthless developers, he gets involved in a scheme to attract tourists to the island to raise enough money to keep the resort going. In the end, however, *Club Paradise* the movie turned out to be as big a disaster as Club Paradise the resort. In subsequent interviews Williams has insisted that he did the film purely and simply for the money. He knew that there were problems with the script but he believed they could be fixed. It's worth remembering that this would be his sixth film and he had yet to have a box-office hit. His television and stand-up popularity had yet to translate on to the big screen and, given the talent attached to this one, this must have seemed like a golden opportunity for a much-needed hit. It's hardly surprising that he put aside his misgivings and decided to sign on.

'They said it would be a box-office smash – "a great combination of people", "we'll kick ass",' he recalled later. 'And then it was my ass that got kicked. That's when you get screwed. Jump in with your passion. Not as a whore.'

Williams and his loyal managers could not have been anything other than deeply concerned about where his career was going. But just at this low point, Williams came up with something which remains one of the hidden gems of his career. Abandoning films for the time being, he went back to television. His experience with ABC on *Mork and Mindy* had left him justifiably leery of the big networks, but this time he would be working for PBS, America's public broadcasting network. Williams was taking the lead in a TV version of Saul Bellow's *Seize the Day* – a phrase which would have echoes later in one of his most successful roles – as

part of the PBS Learning in Focus series. Williams played the central role
of Tommy Wilhelm who, to all intents and purposes, is a Jewish Willy
Loman. Tommy had wanted to be an entertainer, but his stern father,
played by Joseph Wiseman, wanted him to follow in his footsteps as a
doctor. Tommy had neither the ambition nor the aptitude for medicine
and in the end he became a salesman. Now, as he approaches forty, his
life is in complete disarray. Half of his territory – the better half – has
been taken away and given to the boss's son-in-law; he is juggling both
an ex-wife and a girlfriend and being crippled by alimony and support
payments; and the nest egg he had been saving has all been eaten away in
a series of bad investments. In desperation he approaches his father and
asks for help, only to have his own father turn his back on him and refuse
to bail him out. The film ends bleakly with Tommy sitting in the back of
a synagogue raving to himself on the verge of a complete mental collapse.

It is very easy to look at *Seize the Day* and read into it a correlation
between Tommy Wilhelm and his father and Robin Williams and his
own father. Unfortunately the comparisons don't really stand up. Robert
Williams may have been distant but he never once hardened his heart
against his son, even when he decided – as Tommy does – to go against
the family's chosen career path. Robert Williams had frequently been
there and ready to support his son whenever it was needed; it was merely
a point of pride on Robin Williams' part that he chose to make it on his
own. If the film relates to any aspect of Robin Williams' life then it is to
the state of his life at the time he was making it. This was a period where
Williams would later refer to himself as walking through his personal life
with all the certainty of a haemophiliac in a razor factory. Compared to
Williams' life at that point, Tommy Wilhelm didn't really have too much
to worry about. Nonetheless it is an extraordinary performance. Williams,
frankly, is too young to play Tommy, but although he had logged a lower
mileage, the panic in his eyes in this performance testifies to the fact that
they had all been hard miles. Williams was struggling to find a role which
showed off his comic skills but, almost as a by-product, he had found a
role which marked him as a serious actor of considerable promise. If he
was succeeding as an actor, however, he was failing miserably as a husband.
The time had come to do something about it.

Looking back on the events leading up to the end of his marriage,
Robin Williams is not especially proud of any of it. All things considered
his behaviour may be, in his own eyes, the most shameful thing he has
ever done. He continued to be completely self-absorbed. He continued
in his relationship with Tish Carter, and as far as he and Valerie were
concerned there was only one thing left to do.

In the beginning when I started doing stand-up in coffee-houses, I wasn't looking to be famous to be recognised [he says]. I just wanted to have a good time performing. Valerie helped in a lot of ways. We were working hard together and then this thing took off. Fame came, and that was strange to me ... and Valerie. It's a type of life that tends to tear people asunder. Hollywood is a weird place. The industry affected our relationship – strained it horribly. Finally it just became impossible for us to stay together.

Williams admits that he and Valerie had always had a tumultuous relationship. There was Latin blood in her, she was fiery and she would fight for her man when she had to. But with all the separations and the constant womanising they both realised it was a losing battle, especially when Valerie also started seeing another man.

There were things that were done that two people should never do to one another [says Williams]. I'd go off and run around because I didn't know what the fuck I wanted. I'd be a schmuck and she would respond in kind. And then we'd try to stop and deal with it and it wouldn't work. Finally I had to say, 'I can't do this to myself any more ... I'm tired of living this passive-aggressive shit.'

At the end of the day Robin and Valerie Williams had to consider the most important thing in each of their lives, Zach. 'Things ultimately went astray between me and Valerie,' says Williams. 'It was terribly painful but our marriage just was not functioning. The separation from her was difficult but it was also gentle. It was better to do that than to go at each other's throats.'

16

Growing Up

When Robin and Valerie Williams agreed to separate they were doing so as much in the best interests of their child as themselves. Williams moved out of the family home at Sonoma and into a beach house where he tried to get himself back together again. One of the important aspects of the separation was to make it as painless as possible for Zach. They arrived at a situation where, if Williams was on tour or on location, then the boy would stay with his mother. If Williams was in San Francisco, then he would have unhindered access to his son.

The split also had an effect on Marsha Garces. She had been feeling for some time that it was about time to move on anyway; she had held 15 jobs in as many years and was not really about making long-term career commitments to nannying. But she did love Zach and the boy was extremely fond of her. At the same time Williams was doing what he always did when he had a problem: he was exorcising them in public by going on tour. His working life was every bit as chaotic as his personal life, and what he really needed was someone to put things in order for him. He was looking around for an assistant at the same time as Marsha was looking to move on. As far as she was concerned, this would be an ideal way to take up a new challenge while keeping Zach in her life and she in his. So she became Robin Williams' secretary and personal assistant.

In the fullness of time and, as events unfolded, that simple action of changing careers would make Marsha Garces one of the most vilified women in show business. She was, according to the tabloids, 'the nanny who broke up Robin Williams' marriage'. It's a convenient label and, in newspaper terms, it's a sexy one too. But it doesn't bear closer scrutiny. For one thing, when she went to work for Robin Williams on his own, Marsha Garces was involved in her own long-term relationship and remained so for some time. Williams for his part was still involved with Tish Carter and, as David Steinberg had already hinted, given the shape he was in at that stage Williams was no catch for any woman. When Marsha Garces went to work for Robin Williams it was strictly business, nothing else. 'He was too screwed up and I wasn't interested in being sucked dry,' says Marsha of the early days of their professional relationship.

However, Marsha Garces quickly brought a sense of order to Williams' life. One of the first things he did when he started to get himself together was to go into therapy. Williams was still a fairly fragile individual. If he was to stay clean and sober then he would have to get through this crisis period in his life. One way of doing that was through a process of therapy which helped him discover more about his life.

'Therapy made me re-examine everything,' he admitted later. 'My life, how I related to people, how far I could push the "please like me" desire before there was nothing left of me to like. Therapy has helped me face my limitations, what I can and cannot do. And it's made me a much calmer and saner person.'

One of the people who undoubtedly forced Williams into therapy was Marsha Garces. From his earliest days as a little boy alone in a great big house Robin Williams has needed to be liked and feared being left alone. As a consequence of that he has required people to take charge of his life, to show him what needs to be done as opposed to what he wants to do. Someone needed to provide some no-nonsense assessment of where he was going with his life, and in this case it seems to have been Marsha.

'You've got two great careers,' she would tell him. 'You're really intelligent, you're healthy, you're strong, you're handsome, you have a great son – and you're totally depressed. You're an adult. Pull it together.'

And, slowly but surely, he did. Through the therapy he faced his anxieties and his fears. He was able to talk to someone seriously about the sort of things he used to hide from in his comedy.

For me, going through therapy and stuff [he admitted in a revealing interview with *Esquire* magazine], I'm just beginning to realise that it [childhood] wasn't always that happy. My childhood was kind of lonely. Quiet. My father was away, my mother was working, doing benefits. I was basically raised by this maid, and my mother would come in later, you know, and I knew her and she was wonderful and charming and witty. But I think maybe comedy was my way of connecting with my mother – 'I'll make Mommy laugh and that will be okay' ... Maybe it started off that I wanted the attention from my mother, but it was also that I could do something here. Comedy is something I was meant to do, whether it's that kind of divine purpose or not. I was meant to do this. I was not meant to sell insurance.

Williams then went on to talk candidly about his other greatest nightmare, being left by his parents:

The fear of abandonment – the oldest, the deepest, fear of all: 'I'm ditched. I'm history'. But ... you begin to know you'll survive. They [your parents] haven't been with you for a long time. You're okay. I can't deny the child inside me because obviously it's done kind of nice for me. And I love that. But to know what it comes from and let the genuine warmth grow ... that's what I see changing. Knowing that fame is obviously like a drug and recognising that, yeah, I kicked other drugs. And once you recognise that, you can get up and do what you want to do.

Williams is an intelligent man with a knowledge that verges on the intuitive rather than the learned. But for all of his remarkable intellect and prodigious mental acuity there was always a gap. There was a blind spot in terms of self-knowledge and it is this which therapy helped him address. He doubts he will ever attain inner peace, whatever that might be, and although he became a better person he is sensible enough to realise that even cleaned up he is not easy to live with.

'I'm no great shakes,' he says. 'It's the "love me" syndrome coupled with the "fuck you" syndrome. Like the great joke about the woman who comes up to the comic after the show and says, "God I really love what you do. I want to fuck your brains out!" And the comic says, "Did you see the first show or the second show?" '

Williams remains riddled with enough insecurities to stay as a great comedian while at the same time becoming a better person. There will always be an element of one hand reaching out to someone while the other hand pushes them away. But there is no doubt that the therapy changed his life. For one thing it helped him deal with the end of his relationship with Valerie without renewing his acquaintance with vodka and lime or cocaine.

It's not disappointing [he said of the failure of his marriage]. That's why therapy helps a lot. It forces you to look at your life and figure out what's functioning and what's not. You don't have to beat your brains against a wall if it's not working. That's why you choose to be separated rather than call each other an asshole every day. Ultimately things went astray. We changed, and then with me wandering off again a little bit, then coming back and saying, 'Wait, I need help' – it just got terribly painful.

Therapy also enabled Robin Williams to deal with his constant need to perform. He had always been there with a quip or a routine or a benefit show at the drop of a hat. As he parodied himself in the 'Mork Meets Robin Williams' episode of *Mork and Mindy* he was the comedian who couldn't say no. Now he was learning.

> The hardest word of all to say is 'no' [he admitted]. Bette Davis, back when we were doing the revival of *Laugh-In*, told me, 'The one word you'll need is "no".' The secret is to be able to turn things down, to not take on projects like *Club Paradise* or *The Best of Times* just because they say they want you to. If they can't get you, they'll get anybody, so wise up.

This desire to take just about anything for fear that he might not be offered anything else is at the heart of some miserable film choices at the start of Robin Williams' film career. Of the seven films he had done, two – *The World According to Garp* and *Moscow on the Hudson* – had been worth his while; Williams claimed at the time that these were the two films of which he felt most proud. One film, *Seize the Day*, was overly ambitious in that he was just too young for Tommy Wilhelm. But the other four were unmitigated disasters in almost every way.

Williams was also learning to say no in his personal life, and not just to drugs and drink. Ironically it was Valerie who first spotted this character flaw when they were first married and had tried to straighten it out. Now, with a combination of harsh experience, Marsha Garces and a good therapist, he was finally getting the message.

> People expect you to be constantly 'on' but you can't [Williams said]. You'd be drained like a car battery. You'd have to have two guys pull up with a truck and jump leads at your house every morning. You can't do it all the time. It's fun to perform, but if you have to do it all the time it's a drain. If you do it when you're ready for it then it's wonderful, but not all the time. It used to be in the old days I thought you could, but you can't. You have to take time, you have to recharge. I thought I had to be on all the time because I thought I had to keep performing, but you'll flame out. There's only so many times you can do that. It's like dry heaving. You're real drunk and you're leaning over the porcelain altar going 'There's nothing left', and your

body is going 'But there is'. At a certain point you run out of stuff. You have
to recharge or find another stimulus.

For Robin Williams the answer really came in finding another stimulus,
and in his case the stimulus was Marsha Garces. After about a year of
their professional relationship they began to realise that this was more
than an employer-employee thing. One of the turning-points came before
Williams' landmark 1986 concert at the Metropolitan Opera House in
New York; he was the first comedian to perform there.

'Robin was complaining, in a joking way, about the bimbettes who
knocked on his door at the hotel,' Marsha recalled. 'I asked him, "Why
are you so surprised? If I wasn't working with you and I didn't know how
screwed up you are, I'd be interested in you."'

One thing that therapy had not changed that much in Robin Williams
was the fear which still gripped him before he went on-stage. That night
at the Metropolitan Opera it would have been worse than usual. This was
a big gig. This was history in the making – and it was being filmed for
television and video. The potential to die a horrible comic death was
greater here than at any other time in his career. One of the little rituals
that Williams had fallen into over the past year was that just before he
would go on-stage Marsha, who was there for any last-minute panics,
would give him a hug. That hug would probably have been more welcome
at the Met than at any other time over the past year.

Marsha recalls: 'I told him, "You can do it. You're okay. I love you" –
which is what I say to my friends all the time.'

On the stage that night Williams gave one of the greatest stand-up
comedy performances of all time. It was lightning in a bottle and,
fortunately, it was captured on film. But at the moment of his triumph
he remembered what Marsha had told him as they waited in the wings.

'Marsha used to tell me I was a good person, and finally I believed it,'
he says.

This is what he needed. All his life he had wanted other people to like
him, but Marsha Garces convinced him that he had to like himself. By
doing that he no longer felt the need to be loved. Marsha Garces saved
Robin Williams' life, perhaps literally as well as figuratively.

She would just talk me down [says Williams of Garces' role when his
marriage was breaking up]. I was not suicidal but I was fucked up. My wife
was living with another man. I was just out of my fucking mind. I was very
indignant and very self-righteous and Marsha said, 'Listen, asshole, there's
no reason to be indignant, you were no prince and she was no saint' ...

I was living in a house on the beach and started to get my life together and I fell in love with Marsha. And that's why my life was saved by her and not ruined by her.

Friends of Williams very quickly noticed the difference that Marsha Garces had made in his life. 'Marsha is Robin's anchor,' claims Pam Dawber. 'She's reality. Ground zero. She's very sane and that's what he needs. She's incredibly loving too. She knows who is bad for him and who is good, and she helps keep the good relationships going.'

In the early days of their relationship there may have been an element of the Stockholm Syndrome, a psychological oddity where people in extreme conditions tend to fixate on others in the same situation – as when bonds form between hostages and their captors. Williams was certainly in a mess, and the fact that Garces was not prepared to indulge him could have helped create that circumstance. But there is no doubt that once they had acknowledged their feelings for each other, this quickly established itself as a deep, meaningful and sustaining love.

I moved out of the house and I was like goo. I was a babbling idiot [says Williams]. And then I became involved with Marsha. All of a sudden I started to calm down. I stopped running around with all this madness. I started to go, 'Wait, I can live a life. I don't have to live and die in my own sweat.' I slowly pulled myself up. I started to create and to work – kind of like the phoenix that rises out of its own ashes. Marsha is not someone who dragged somebody away. She's somebody who offered something, who said 'This is a way to live', and I went for it.

Am I going to run around now? [he continues rhetorically]. No. I'm at peace with myself. It's not something like 'I – am – very – happy', like I've got a dart in the back of my neck. But it's something like 'God, I don't want to blow this. This is wonderful stuff.'

17

'Goood Mooorning, Heraklion!'

In 1965, Robin Williams was 13 years old and enjoying life as much as any bright and studious pupil would at a private school in Detroit. Half a world away the 25-year-old Adrian Cronauer was coming to the end of his stint in the Air Force in Greece.

Cronauer was the son of a Pittsburgh machinist and a schoolteacher. He had always loved radio. As a small boy he would sit in his darkened bedroom long after lights out listening to his favourites on a jerry-rigged set of headphones when he was supposed to be asleep. At the age of 12 he auditioned for a gig as the piano player on a radio variety show called *Happy's Party*. He got the job and thus began a lifelong love affair with the communications business. By the time he was in high school he had graduated to working for the educational TV station in Pittsburgh where he was involved in the backroom staff of a show hosted by Fred Rogers. This was Rogers' first foray into television but Mr Rogers, as he would become known, and his fictional television neighbourhood went on to shape the minds of millions of young Americans over the next four decades as one of television's best-loved presenters.

It was inevitable that Cronauer would go on to try to make a living in broadcasting, which is why he spent four years as a broadcasting major at the American University in Washington. Cronauer started school in 1960 but it would be 25 years before he finally completed his degree. Cronauer was combining his classes with some real broadcasting work and as such he was officially only a part-time student. Someone from the college administration informed the draft board and, since he was not actually exempt from the draft on education grounds, Cronauer was contracted by the draft board and given a hard choice. It was actually more of a dilemma than a choice; he had thirty days to decide whether to enlist or be drafted. Since enlistment gave him some say in his future in the military, Cronauer signed on with the US Air Force.

Cronauer had been passed 1-A by the draft board and had put in his application for flight training to be a pilot. But, to his horror, when he went to Texas for basic training he found that instead of releasing them at the end of three years, they were holding on to pilots. Figuring he could be in the Air Force until he was 30, Cronauer quickly cancelled his application and looked around for something else instead.

'They said, "What can we do with you?" I told them, "Here are my credentials. I majored in broadcasting, I've been a disc jockey, I've worked in television." And they said, "Oh, all right, we'll make you a radio and television production specialist".'

As a television and radio specialist, Cronauer's first job was to supervise the making of instructional films on how to prepare aircraft engines and launch missiles. Eventually he was sent to Crete in the Greek islands, where he ended up as the presenter of an early morning radio show at the US Air Force base on Heraklion. It was there, in the autumn of 1963, that he coined what would become his trademark phrase when he first uttered the deathless words 'Goood mooorning, Heraklion'.

'As a catchphrase it has more of a clang than a ring to it,' he admits.

Cronauer served at Heraklion for about a year and a half which was bringing him ever closer to the end of his three-year hitch. He would have to make a decision about his future and make it quickly.

When my enlistment was coming to an end in Crete [he explains], the normal procedure would be to rotate back to the United States, and that would mean going back to another educational television facility and I didn't want to do that. I wanted to see a little bit more of the world. I had only a year left of my enlistment and there were only two places I could go that were one-year tours, Korea or Vietnam. I chose Vietnam. There was not that much fighting going on over there. We were still an advisory mission and at that time the American contingent was still very small. They were living in hotels in downtown Saigon. All the fighting was being done by Vietnamese out in rice paddies and the boondocks, and the Americans were sitting back in their hotels in a cheerleading position. I could see no problems in going to Vietnam. About four weeks after I had turned in my paperwork, by which time it was too late to retract it, we got word that the Viet Cong had blown up the radio station in Saigon.

So Cronauer was now going into a war zone, and one with an ever-increasing American presence. The Gulf of Tonkin incident at the end of 1964, in which the Americans accused North Vietnamese gunboats of attacking American ships on the Gulf, allowed President Lyndon Johnson to step up America's involvement in the war. In the space of a single year, 1965, American troop numbers almost doubled from just over 55,000 men to 100,000. Adrian Cronauer arrived in Vietnam just as the escalation was beginning and quickly found himself wrapped up in the siege mentality. He would present his morning *Dawn Buster* show with a loaded ·45 on the studio desk, and he was expected to use it if the situation arose.

> The first week I was there, I walked down the street and saw a little old lady with a basket over her arm [says Cronauer]. I said to myself, 'She's the one. She's got the grenade that's going to get me.' I immediately crossed the street only to find there was another little old lady with another basket on that side too. You quickly develop a fatalistic attitude. If the grenade or the bullet is going to get me then it has my name on it. It's not until about a month before you are due to rotate out that you start looking for the little old ladies with the baskets again.

Adrian Cronauer was something of a jack of all trades at the Armed Forces Radio station in Saigon. He presented the early morning show, where of course his signature call sign had now become 'Goood mooorning, Vietnam'. He was also, in the early days, the station's news director and latterly the production manager for the station.

> I grew up in Pittsburgh, and there was a morning man there by the name of Reeves Cordick and he sort of owned morning drive-time radio. My conception of what a good morning show should sound like was pretty much what Cordick did, so I deliberately fashioned and modelled my show on that. But since I was also the production manager I tried to make the station sound very much like Stateside radio. I expanded the range of top 40 music, we had Number One Hits and Golden Oldies and all these sorts of features. We also had on-air promotions and mock contests just to try to make it sound as much as possible like a Stateside station.

With thousands of raw recruits arriving every week, Cronauer's efforts at bringing a little slice of Americana to the Far East were much appreciated by the troops. Though, he concedes, they occasionally had a strange way of showing their appreciation.

I was told that after a while, especially when they were out in the field, the troops had their own particular way of responding [he recalls]. When I would start my show by shouting 'Goood mooorning, Vietnam', they would usually respond by shouting in unison 'Get fucked, Cronauer'. I'm told that on at least one occasion when I yelled it, a guy picked up his M-16 and blew his radio away. I guess he was having a particularly bad day.

Cronauer served his 12-month tour of duty without major incident. He was never wounded but he insists, quite properly, that there is no one who served in Vietnam who doesn't bear some sort of scar. When he was finished with Vietnam he was finished with the Air Force, and after his discharge he went back to his first love, broadcasting. His first job was as a television anchor man in Lima, Ohio. Eighteen months later he went on to be programme director of a small TV station in Roanoke in Virginia. He liked Virginia and based himself there for almost eight years, including a stint working as a management consultant in San Francisco, and then going back to run a radio station in Virginia. Nothing apparently seemed to satisfy him during an increasingly peripatetic existence which also included starting up and then selling a successful advertising agency, and spending seven years in New York making commercials, teaching and working part-time at WQXR, a station for which he had always dreamed of working.

There is no doubt, though, that while he was criss-crossing the country in a number of well-paid and successful jobs, a large part of Adrian Cronauer was still in Vietnam. He was increasingly upset at the way the troops in South East Asia were being portrayed at home. He was particularly incensed at the ease with which people in the United States were able to believe the troops in Vietnam were little more than a bunch of drug-taking, baby-killing rapists. He was also angry, like so many veterans, that they had been forced to slink home with their tails between their legs and made to feel ashamed for doing nothing more than serving their country.

One of Cronauer's closest friends in Saigon was Ben Moses. Moses had a position in military intelligence but he was also a disc jockey who would later go on to be an Emmy-award-winning television producer. He and Cronauer had kept in touch over the intervening years and together in the late Seventies they hit on the idea of turning their Vietnam experiences into something more meaningful to a wider audience. It was Cronauer's idea to try to come up with an allegorical story about the effect of Vietnam on one man, reflecting the effect of the war on the United States as a whole.

I served in Vietnam through 1965 and that was the year in which America
became involved in the war in a major way [explains Cronauer]. I watched
Saigon go in a single year from being this sleepy little French colonial
town – the Paris of the Orient – to a nightmare because of this massive
influx of troops and equipment and money. By the time I left, the black
market was flourishing, the economy was in ruins, the traffic was
unmanageable and the whole place was totally different from when I
arrived there.

Cronauer and Moses originally tried to get their idea off the ground in
1979 as a television sitcom, hoping it might combine the popularity of two
other hit shows, *M*A*S*H* and *WKRP in Cincinnati*. Not surprisingly,
television executives were less than thrilled with the concept. They had
difficulty in visualising any scenario in which the words 'comedy' and
'Vietnam' could reasonably coexist. To the average American, comedy in
Vietnam meant Bob Hope entertaining the troops on a USO tour. Doors
were politely but firmly shut in their faces, but Moses and Cronauer kept
plugging away. Eventually they decided to try for a television movie rather
than a weekly sitcom, and Moses wrote a script about an essentially
fictional character who just happened to be called Adrian Cronauer. On
the basis that no one had seemed to find Vietnam remotely funny, there
was more drama in this version and fewer laughs. The TV movie brought
largely the same response as the TV sitcom and it rattled around various
companies and numerous executives for four years. It eventually made
its way to the desk of Larry Brezner in the hope that it might be suitable
for one of his clients. Unlike many others Brezner could see the potential
in the script. He optioned it almost immediately and then passed it on to
writer Mitch Markowitz in order to punch it up and make it funnier.
Markowitz had written for *M*A*S*H*, as well as the ground-breaking cult
comedy *Mary Hartman, Mary Hartman*. He was completely in tune with
the ideas that Moses and Cronauer were trying to get across and had
exactly the right sensibility to bring out the laughs without sacrificing the
drama.

Larry Brezner was Robin Williams' personal manager. It is by no means
certain that when he came across the script he saw it as the perfect vehicle
for his client, but both men must have known that after seven films
without a substantial hit – and including the disastrous *Club Paradise* –
there were not going to be many more opportunities for stardom. Williams happened by Brezner's office one day and, looking through a pile
of material, he came across Markowitz's script. Williams often describes

himself as a poor judge of material, but after reading this one he decided it was for him.

For once, his instincts were spot on. Whether they knew it or not at the time, Brezner and Williams had just found the perfect role.

18

From the Delta to the DMZ

Larry Brezner was convinced that *Good Morning Vietnam,* as Moses and Cronauer's project was now known, would be a hit. There were others, however, who did not share his feeling. Paramount Pictures, for example, were interested but only if they were prepared to turn the movie into a broad, farcical, low comedy – a cross between *National Lampoon's Animal House* and *Stripes.* Brezner was adamant that the script should retain Cronauer's original allegorical notion of a man changed by the circumstances he faces in Vietnam, reflecting the changes faced by America in the same period. Eventually Paramount and Brezner disagreed so comprehensively that the studio put the script into turnaround. This is a fairly common occurrence in Hollywood and basically means that the producer has a certain amount of time to find someone else who will make the project and be prepared to reimburse the original studio for the money they had invested in developing it.

If Brezner was worried about the script languishing in Development Hell for any length of time he need not have been. Barely 24 hours after being put into turnaround *Good Morning Vietnam* was picked up by Jeffrey Katzenberg, the chairman of Walt Disney Studios. Katzenberg was known in the industry as 'the Golden Retriever' for his ability to sniff out commercial prospects, and his instincts once again had not let him down. He saw *Good Morning Vietnam* as a perfect project for Disney's Touchstone Pictures, the division which had been set up some three years earlier to allow Disney to escape from the strait-jacket of its family image and make slightly more adult pictures.

With the script having found a secure home, Brezner and Markowitz went to work on making sure that it would fit Robin Williams like a glove. None of his previous seven pictures had been so immaculately or carefully hand-tooled to suit the actor's needs. Whether they said it or not, everyone connected with the picture knew that this time they were going for all the marbles; this was the movie which would either make Robin Williams a star, or send him back to television. 'If this isn't a breakthrough,' joked Williams, 'then we've made a very expensive travel film.'

Good Morning Vietnam was still essentially a film about Adrian Cronauer, but the more it progressed the more it became about someone who was Cronauer in name only. In the film Cronauer arrives in Saigon from Greece in 1965 and quickly becomes a forces favourite with his madcap comedy and his unconventional methods. Before Cronauer, Armed Forces Radio consisted of Ray Connif music and bland announcements about avoiding foot rot and razor burns. Cronauer, in the movie at least, turned it into the bastard child of Howard Stern and Wolfman Jack with James Brown music and *risqué* stand-up routines. The Armed Forces Radio authorities in the shape of Bruno Kirby and the late J. T. Walsh don't take kindly to Cronauer's flouting of their regulations and his, in their eyes, mockery of their conventions. Cronauer is also pursuing an unrequited love affair with Trinh, a Vietnamese girl, in the process becoming very friendly with her brother, Tuan. It is Tuan who urges Cronauer to leave a favourite GI bar only seconds before it is blown up, and it is he who goes into the jungle to rescue Cronauer when he has fallen victim to a Viet Cong ambush. When his superiors discover that Tuan is in fact a wanted Viet Cong terrorist, they finally have the means to get rid of Cronauer. Five months into his tour Cronauer is manoeuvred into an honourable discharge and sent back to the United States.

'Larry Brezner played a very active role in developing the script,' recalls the real Adrian Cronauer. 'His first idea was that every good film has to be a love story and it doesn't have to be a traditional boy-girl love story.'

The example that Brezner quoted to Cronauer was the hit comedy *Arthur*, in which Dudley Moore played a drunken millionaire playboy who falls in love with shopgirl Liza Minnelli. But, as Brezner pointed out, the real love story in *Arthur* is not between Moore and Minnelli. Instead it is between Moore and his faithful butler played by John Gielgud, who has looked after Arthur all of his life and has become something of a surrogate father.

In *Good Morning Vietnam* [Cronauer explains], Brezner felt that although the sex interest was between Robin Williams and the girl, the real love story was between Williams and her brother. That was one of his foundations. The script went through about five different versions – in one version they had me captured by the Viet Cong and put in a bamboo cage, in another I got married to the Vietnamese girl – and I was able to get hold of a copy of each version. Each time I got one I would sit down and write page after page of suggestions for additions and deletions. Some of them they accepted and some of them they ignored.

In the main Larry Brezner was generally very receptive to his notes, but Cronauer maintains that he found a real problem with Barry Levinson, who had been signed on to direct the film. With so much attention being lavished on the script, it was equally important that just as much care be taken in the choice of the director. Everyone agreed that Levinson was the right man for the job. Levinson, as it happened, had been a broadcaster in his youth and he had also been a successful comedy writer. He had a reputation as an actor's director. In films like the classic *Diner* and *Tin Men* he had taken a cast of quality actors and encouraged them to improvise and given them the freedom to find their roles within the confines of the script. Levinson would be perfect for handling someone like Robin Williams, who thrived on freedom but also needed to be told when he had gone too far.

He puts up road cones [Williams says, describing Levinson's technique]. It's a bit like going to driving school. It's not like hitting a wall, you know when you run over it that you've gone too far, but there's no real harm done. So you know what the limits are and that's nice. The good part for me was the stuff that was done when I was out of the radio studio, Barry took all the pressure off me. He told me there were times when I didn't have to be funny. He told me, 'Just play off people. If you're quiet, then that's good.' That was very freeing, because the tendency is 'I have to find a joke here', but then you realise you don't have to. It's all right. That gives it another side completely, which helps.

While Robin Williams' fictional Adrian Cronauer was finding Levinson a joy to work with, the real Adrian Cronauer was less impressed:

Barry Levinson was a strange person to deal with. I don't know what his problem was, but he became very much afraid of me. I had a deal where I would play a small cameo role in the movie, from the very beginning that had been my arrangement with Larry Brezner, but Levinson would have none of it. I don't know what his feelings were about it, I can't even speculate.

Robin Williams
as Mork (1979)
in what he assumed
was traditional
Earth garb.

Williams in his
Orkan space suit in
the early days of
Mork & Mindy.
He started out with
a guest appearance
on *Happy Days* in
1978 and ended up
with a show which
ran for 91 episodes
from 1979 to 1983.

Party animal. Robin Williams and first wife Valerie were among the favoured who were allowed past the velvet rope and given free rein at New York's chic Studio 54 (1979).

Williams underwent daily torture in his full Popeye make-up in 1980. The latex forearms were so tight they frequently cut off the circulation.

Old friends. Robin Williams and Christopher Reeve after a performance of Reeve's *The Fifth of July* in 1981. The friendship would be tested by adversity over the years but never broken. When Reeve met with his tragic accident Williams was at his bed-side making him laugh.

As asylum seeker Vladimir Ivanoff in *Moscow on the Hudson* (1984). Williams gave some hint of his potential as an actor. The fact that the film was directed by former comedian Paul Mazursky helped.

By deciding in 1986 to play Tommy Wilhelm in a PBS adaptation of *Seize the Day* Robin Williams went back to his dramatic roots. Despite being a shade young for the role it remains an impressive performance as a man at the end of his tether.

A star is born. After a string of cinematic failures Williams scored a smash hit and his first Best Actor nomination as DJ Adrian Cronauer in *Good Morning Vietnam* (1987).

Robin Williams and Steve Martin as Estragon and Vladimir in the controversial Lincoln Center production of *Waiting for Godot* in 1988.

Despite the personal problems which still beset him in 1987, everything was forgotten when Williams took the stage for his stand-up routine that December.

As well as turning his life around (in 1988), Marsha Garces Williams became Robin Williams' good right arm in terms of his career choices. It was she who found and produced *Mrs Doubtfire*.

Carpe diem. Robin Williams as teacher John Keating and some of his young charges in *Dead Poets' Society* (1989). The script originally called for Williams to die at the end but this idea was junked by director Peter Weir.

Would you buy a used car from this man? Robin Williams as Joey O'Brien in *Cadillac Man,* (1989) a film which – much like Joey's cars – never quite lived up to its promise.

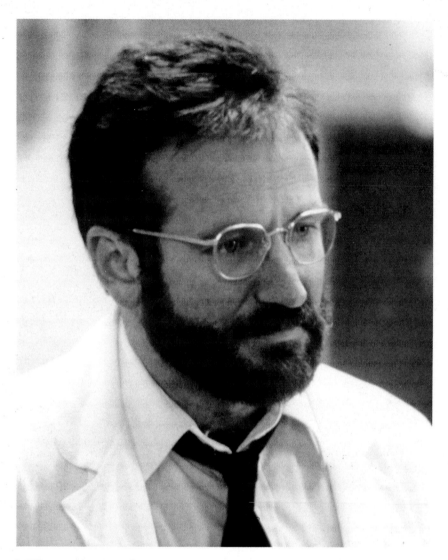

Williams was so moved when he read the script for *Awakenings* (1990) on a plane that he burst into tears. Playing Dr Malcolm Sayer, the fictional Oliver Sacks, lead to a long-lasting friendship and mutual admiration between Williams and Sacks.

Always the bridesmaid, never the bride. His performance as Parry in *The Fisher King* (1991) brought Williams a third Best Actor nomination but once again he came away empty-handed on Oscar night.

Williams had been making a mini-career out of playing lost boys when Steven Spielberg persuaded him to play the ultimate lost boy – Peter Pan – in *Hook* (1991). Despite a hostile reception in Hollywood the film turned into one of Williams biggest hits.

Williams and Steven Spielberg have been close friends for years. When Spielberg was feeling depressed during the shooting of *Schindler's List* he would spend hours on the phone being cheered up by Williams.

It got to the point where I couldn't find out what was going on. I could get
no feedback whatsoever once they had started shooting. It got to the point
where I had almost to threaten to go public with my dissatisfaction.

From Cronauer's point of view you can understand his frustration,
especially at being denied the opportunity to appear in the movie in
however small a role. It would have been a nice gesture to have him in the
movie, especially with Ben Moses getting a screen credit as co-producer.
His frustration was made all the more acute because he considered himself
a fan of Levinson's previous work. But, from Levinson's point of view,
you can also appreciate that from the moment the cameras start turning
it is his picture. Film-making is a collaborative process, to be sure, but
there can be only one vision and that has to belong to the director.
Levinson has made no public comments about Cronauer other than to
say that he didn't find him funny either in person or on the tapes of
shows. That being the case, he presumably felt that Cronauer had little to
contribute, which makes Levinson guilty of gracelessness rather than
actual malice.

Cronauer himself admits that there is a school of thought articulated
by John Grisham, another lawyer who has done well out of Hollywood,
which says that if you have a property which is being turned into a film
then you should take the money and – not walk – run away without
looking back. Instead of perhaps wisely following the Grisham dictum,
Cronauer became so concerned about the lack of information coming
from the set that he eventually insisted on a moral turpitude clause being
introduced into his contract to control the way he would be portrayed in
the film. He was anxious that he did not turn out to be a murderer, or a
drug addict, or a baby-killer. This appears to be something of an over-
reaction. Even though the film was being made for Disney's adult arm
Touchstone Pictures, Robin Williams' film career was not yet in such dire
straits that it would require such a radical change of image.

Williams and Cronauer never met at any stage during shooting or in
the pre-production process. The official version is that Williams is such a
gifted and intuitive mimic that the film-makers wanted the two men kept
apart so that Williams did not end up imitating Cronauer on-screen.

That's the story I usually see [says Cronauer], but I don't believe that was
true. Something else was going on there and I have yet to figure out what it
was. At one point my wife and I went to Hollywood to see a rough cut of
the film and we had dinner with Barry Levinson and his wife. I could say
charitably that the man is very shy, but there was no rapport, no attempt to

talk to me about the film in any way, shape or form. My wife and I talked about this. I cannot understand what he was afraid of, or what he was worried that I could do to hurt him or his film.

Regardless of what Barry Levinson might have felt about Adrian Cronauer, there was another fear behind the scenes at *Good Morning Vietnam*, and it was a very genuine one. Was Robin Williams still funny? His previous seven films had been box-office disasters. Two of them – *Garp* and *Moscow on the Hudson* – had brought warm reviews for Williams, but there were no queues stretching round the block. Williams was 35 when he made *Good Morning Vietnam* – ten years older than Cronauer had been when he was in Saigon – and his off-screen life was in tatters. He had kicked his cocaine habit but his marriage had broken down. As well as being emotionally torn by the end of his relationship with Valerie Velardi, he was also distraught about his relationship with his son, Zach. The boy was four years old now and Williams was desperately beating himself up about what kind of father he would be to his son. Was Zach destined to grow up the same way he did, with a loving father who was unable to communicate that affection? Williams was in the process of turning his life around. He was in therapy for the first time in his life, but still there was a genuine concern that he might have lost his gift for mayhem and anarchy.

'When he said "That's it, enough",' according to his friend and manager Larry Brezner, 'there was a fear he'd lose his edge, but he's as free as ever he was.'

A lot of that freedom was brought about by the direct influence of Marsha Garces. When they were on location in Thailand she seldom left Williams' side. She was there for whatever he needed. She went over lines with him, she provided massages to ease his tensions, she found books about 1965 and went over them with him, they even wrote some of his dialogue together. 'She was the hardest working person on the set,' says producer Mark Johnson. 'She was there for him 24 hours a day. She truly loves him.'

Undoubtedly Levinson's careful direction also played a great part in making sure that Williams not only had not lost his edge, but was able to take his craft up another level. There is in fact a lot less comedy than people remember in *Good Morning Vietnam*. The first half of the film deals with Williams' microphone mania, with the audio meters pinning themselves into the red zone as he bawls out Cronauer's trademark greeting. But the second half of the film, in the aftermath of the restaurant bombing, concentrates more on the human drama of Cronauer's relationship with Tuan and Trinh. There is very little comedy in this section of the film, and Williams is required to give a real performance as Cronauer changes and loses his innocence. Levinson's assurance that it was all right to be quiet removed from Williams the fear of silence which had been a weakness of some of his earlier work, on the stage as well as in films. Levinson gave Williams a safe place to express emotion. Undoubtedly Williams was able to draw on the turmoil of his personal life to portray some sense of Cronauer's loss and betrayal and disillusionment. But he was also, perhaps for the first time, able to do what he had originally been trained to do. Williams was an actor who became a comedian and this was the perfect vehicle.

> This combined two worlds that I'd kept separate [he explains]. One was stand-up comedy, the other was acting. Maybe there was a little bit left over from my Juilliard training – 'I'll be an actor, but I'm weak so I'll talk about my genitals'. So I combined the two and became an actor talking about my genitals. I was putting the two together because I had played characters like that in *Moscow on the Hudson* and *Garp*, or in *Seize the Day* where I played a guy having a nervous breakdown. In this one I thought I would try to put them together. The character is basically 98 per cent me. There is a slight veneer of a character but I can't say I studied immensely. It's me.

Williams' injection of himself into the Adrian Cronauer character extended to rewriting most of Cronauer's monologues. These captured for the first time on-screen the freewheeling word-associative adrenalin rush of Williams' stand-up performances. For the first time in the cinema, there was the realisation of the promise that had been shown in *Mork and Mindy*. The notion of eavesdropping on a performance was accentuated by Levinson's decision frequently not to tell Williams when the cameras were rolling. The results are some scenes of glorious spontaneity.

> They had it all written out but it wasn't very good [Williams admits], it was mostly a lot of jokes about food. So we said 'Okay, thank you' and threw it out. We came in with different character ideas like the military intelligence man who's not too tightly wrapped – this guy's coming in on one engine to begin with. We did them all. We would try things and Barry was so good because he would just tell us to try something else. Or he would throw in an idea because he's a comic himself. It's great, he really understands.

Levinson took an active part in the rewrites – by his estimate they discarded or changed about 40 per cent of the script – and his own comedy background made it very easy for him to understand his star. Like Paul Mazursky in *Moscow on the Hudson*, there was no one better equipped at that point to direct Robin Williams.

> Working with Robin on his routines was a little like playing football when we were kids [explains Levinson]. We used to say, 'Why don't you get over here? You there. Okay, let's go.' Robin would do a take and I would say, 'I like that thing about so-and-so. I don't think that bit works, but this bit is quite good. What about that thing you talked about the other day about the nudist monk? Let's give that a try.' Then he'd go and do another take, we'd go over it again and say, 'This is good, save this. Drop that. Add this. I think we're in fine shape. Let's see if you've got other ideas.' Then another idea would emerge that wasn't really developed; we'd talk about it and explore it a little more, and then start shooting again. We shot very fast, a lot of footage, and basically hammered out that whole section of the movie.

The use of the comic characters on air is one of the few similarities between Williams' interpretation and the real Adrian Cronauer. Cronauer's *Dawn Buster* show featured large helpings of comedy, but he's the first to admit that it was very different from Robin Williams' madcap monologues.

> What Robin Williams was doing wasn't really accurate – it was more 1988 radio than 1965 – but it was good [says Cronauer]. He was essentially doing Robin Williams with music. I did comedy but it was more situational comedy with pre-recorded material. We had characters like Sergeant Bassett who was a kind of Gyro Gearloose guy who was always coming up with weird inventions, and Boris the keeper of the Vault of Dusty Discs. He spoke like Boris Karloff and he always wanted me to play *Monster Mash*. And then there was a woman with a sultry voice who became the AFRS Friendly Thermometer. She was essentially just a seductive voice who came in to tell everybody how hot she was that day. The troops loved it, it was the theatre of the mind, which is a lot of fun.

Cronauer concedes that in terms of the resemblance to what actually happened to him in Saigon, *Good Morning Vietnam* is about 45 per cent accurate. For one thing he served his full 12-month tour of duty and wasn't bounced out of the country after five months. He did teach an English class to the Vietnamese but he had, for example, no Viet Cong friends, nor did he have a romantic relationship, unrequited or otherwise, with any Vietnamese girls. He did try to push the envelope in terms of breaking down the restrictions of military censorship of the news but again his confrontations were nowhere near as intense as Williams' battles. 'If I had done everything Robin Williams does in this film I'd have been court-martialled on the spot. I'd probably still be in Leavenworth,' says Cronauer.

The one dramatic incident in the film which is drawn from Cronauer's real-life experience is the bombing of Jimmy Wah's, the fictional GI bar in Saigon. The death of two soldiers in the blast is the catalyst, in the film at least, for an escalation in the conflict and a hardening of attitudes on both sides. It is also the beginning of the movie Cronauer's dis-illusionment with the military. In the film Williams escapes death by seconds when Tuan, who planted the bomb, warns him to get out. The sequence is based on the real-life bombing of the Mekong Floating res-taurant, a popular haunt for American servicemen. Cronauer had left the restaurant only moments before it was blown apart by the Viet Cong using claymore mines. At that stage he was the news director on the station and he argued the case for broadcasting the news of the bombing. But in real life at least he lost.

Robin Williams finally met the man he had been playing in the movie when *Good Morning Vietnam* premièred in New York in December 1987. 'As I recall,' says Cronauer, 'when we were introduced we shook hands and he said "It's nice to meet you" and I said "It's nice to meet me too" and we both laughed at that. We never developed a real relationship. We still exchange Christmas cards but it's not like we're bowling buddies.'

The real Adrian Cronauer is now a successful media lawyer in Wash-ington DC. There is perhaps a certain irony in the fact that he is and always has been a card-carrying Republican. He is still keenly involved in Veterans politics and was co-chairman of the Veterans for Dole group in the last US election. He also recorded a national TV commercial for the George Bush campaign in 1992 which effectively accused Bill Clinton of lying about his military service record. Quite a contrast to Williams himself, whose political leanings lie in the opposite direction, and who portrayed Cronauer as a man who gave the impression that he would be quite happy to leave the studio and join an anti-war demonstration.

The real Adrian Cronauer doesn't really have a problem with his screen characterisation. 'I have always been something of an iconoclast,' he explains. 'A lot of people have seen the movie and said to me, "Well you must be anti-military." That's not the case. What I am is anti-stupidity, and Lord knows in the military you encounter a whole lot of stupidity.'

Good Morning Vietnam has certainly been a positive factor for me in my life [says Cronauer, looking back on the experience]. The film came along at the right time because I was in the process of going to law school. I was going to the University of Pennsylvania, which is a fairly expensive school, and I planned to come out of three years in law school with a personal debt the size of a small South American country. Instead I came out in the black, which for a new lawyer is about the best feeling you can get with your clothes on. I have also become kind of an icon to many veterans. When the film came out my wife and I discussed this and she said, 'Adrian, you have to realise that you are now Adrian Cronauer Vietnam disc jockey' – and she was right. Of all the names that people remember from Vietnam there is probably General Westmoreland, William Calley of My Lai, Ron Kovic from *Born on the Fourth of July* – and me! And of those names I probably have the most positive image. So I have had a chance to get out and talk to a lot of the veterans.

I have also been told by many veterans that they think it's the first film that has shown Vietnam veterans as they really are, rather than as murderers and rapists and baby-killers, or dope addicts and psychotics. It has happened maybe a couple of dozen times or more that a man will come up to me and shake my hand and say quietly, 'Thank you for helping me get through that.' I never realised at the time how great an impact Armed Forces Radio had.

The impact that the film really had on the men and women who fought in Vietnam was forcibly brought home to Adrian Cronauer a few years after the film came out when he went along as a guest speaker at a veterans' reunion.

A lady came over and said her husband really wanted to meet me. The man was crippled and couldn't make it over, so I had to go and see him. I went over and he had arm braces on, and he was wearing his black beret and some of the military regalia. He started telling me how he was a lieutenant in charge of a platoon which was being shipped out into the field and they were in their truck when I came along in a jeep. I stopped and talked to the troops and entertained them for a while. And he wanted me to know how much that meant to his troops, and he was crying while he was telling me this. The problem is, that never happened. That was only in the film.

I talked with a friend who was a military psychologist who wasn't surprised to hear that. This man was suffering from Post Traumatic Stress Syndrome and had undergone some experiences that were so traumatic that he picked up the story of the film and substituted that for something that he couldn't deal with. Too often the media portrayed Americans in Vietnam as monsters and I really wanted this film to redress the balance.

For once, even if it is after the event, Adrian Cronauer and Barry Levinson are in complete agreement. 'What little political reaction there was to the film was very good,' says the director. 'I spoke to a number of veterans who felt it said a lot without actually showing the fighting. I think that because there was humour in the film and no graphic violence, the political implications were probably overlooked by some who simply saw it as a diversion.'

19

A Death in the Family

On the morning of Sunday, 18 October 1987 Robert F. Williams died. He was 81 years old and had been suffering from cancer for some time. He died peacefully in his sleep at the family home in Tiburon, where he and his wife had settled after their nomadic but comfortable existence throughout the Midwest with the Ford Company. Robin Williams was not with him when he died, but he was nearby at his own home in San Francisco. The death of his father was a devastating blow for Williams. It came in a year when his marriage was ending, his career was on the line, and his relationship with his own son was in some doubt. The death of Robert Williams was all the more affecting because it came at a point when father and son had finally begun to get to know one another.

It would be a misconception to see Robert Williams as a cold and distant father, perhaps not unlike the father figure Jonathan Hyde would play some years later in *Jumanji*. Robert Williams was a man of his time and a product of the work ethic of the Twenties and Thirties. The prime motivation in his life was providing for both his families. He was a hard worker and by all accounts good at his job. If his job took him away from home a lot, then it was not through desire but necessity. Similarly, if the family had to move from time to time, it was not always because they wanted to.

Robert Williams was a senior executive in the motor industry. He was by any consideration a captain of industry and thus a powerful man of influence and standing. Had he been alive in the Nineties, there is little doubt that he would have been one of Tom Wolfe's 'Masters of the Universe'.

There is also little doubt that Robert Williams loved his son, he just wasn't always there to show it. Robin Williams had frequently described his father as an elegant and sophisticated man with a very dry sense of humour. It is from his father, he claims, that he gets his love of theatre. Williams and his mother used to affectionately refer to Williams Senior as 'Lord Posh' as well as 'Lord Stokesbury', so urbane and sophisticated was his manner. Again as a product of his times, and through having been in his late forties when his youngest son was born, Robert Williams may have had difficulty in displaying his emotions, but all the evidence suggests he loved his son and was proud of him.

When his son announced that he was turning his back on his father's chosen career in the diplomatic corps for what amounted to a life as a vagabond player, Robert Williams did not behave like a dictatorial autocrat. He was pragmatic, as you would expect from a man in his position. His response was not to put any barriers in his son's way, but simply to cut his losses and bring him to a less expensive school closer to home. Likewise, when Williams then announced that he was going to New York to try to make a go of life as a performer, his father's only response was a perfectly sensible one. He merely suggested that his son acquire a back-up trade for when times would inevitably get tough. These are not the actions of a man who does not love his son.

Once Robin Williams became a father himself, he found that he could appreciate and understand the difficulties that his own father had gone through. By all accounts Robert Williams was the perfect grandfather for Zachary, and the support of both grandparents would have been invaluable to the boy during a difficult period. The little boy spent many weekends with his grandparents in Tiburon.

'It's a wonderful feeling when your father becomes not a god but a man to you,' says Williams. 'When he comes down from the mountain and you see he's this man with weaknesses, and you love him as this whole being, not this figurehead.' And father and son were now beginning to reach the stage where they were finally able to display their feelings for one another.

My father loved boats [Williams recalled recently], and once for Fathers' Day I gave him a beautiful hand-made model of a whaling boat. He was just totally stunned by that because it was something that he really loved and it really touched him. And that was at the point also where I was getting to know him as a person. I had probably just started to make it and have a

career, and when I gave him that gift it was something very special for both
of us.

The news of his father's death was broken to Robin Williams in a telephone
call from his mother. She simply called him and told him without fuss or
histrionics that his father was dead. Some months later, after *Good
Morning Vietnam* had been a certified hit, Williams spoke frankly and
movingly to *Rolling Stone* magazine about his father.

> I got to know another side [of him] in the last few years [he told writer Bill
> Zehme]. I saw that he was funkier, that he had a dark side that made the
> other side work. He was much older than me; he died at 81. Up until four
> or five years ago I kept distance out of respect. Then we made a connection
> ... He'd had operations and chemotherapy. It's weird. Everyone thinks of
> their dad as invincible, and in the end here's this little tiny creature almost
> all bone. You have to say goodbye to him as this very frail being.
>
> At least he was at home and died very peacefully in his sleep. My mother
> thought he was still asleep. She came downstairs and kept trying to shake
> him. She called me that morning and said, 'Robin, your father's dead.' She
> was a little in shock but she sounded happy in a certain way, if only because
> he went without pain.

You could argue that Robin Williams' life has been dominated by women.
Whether it was Valerie Velardi, Marsha Garces, Tish Carter or his own
mother, women have been the dominant and defining force in his life.
But the relationship between a man and his father transcends those
definitions.

'When I started to talk to my father,' he recalled, 'it was like *The Wizard
of Oz* where you look behind the curtain and see the man for what he is.
There was this little man behind the curtain going, "Take care of your
mother and I love you and I've been worried about certain things. And
I'm afraid but I'm not afraid." It's an amazing combination of exhilaration
and sadness at the same time because the god turns into a man.'

Williams was speaking here as a father himself and, more importantly,
a father who was facing the possibility of losing his son. With his marriage
to Valerie on the rocks, the question of custody of Zach, who was now
five, would loom large in his future. When he spoke of his hopes and fears
for his son, there is an obvious echo of what he felt he had learned from
his childhood relationship with his own father.

'I've learned to have the security not to worry that he will love me,' said
Williams, 'as long as I keep the connection strong enough. I've learned

not to try and force the love. You can't. All you can do is try and set up a world for him that's safe and stable enough to make him happy.'

Williams was very concerned that the separation from his wife should have as little effect on his son as possible. He was adamant that, wherever possible, Zachary would be kept out of the public eye, so he could grow up and have a life of his own.

'He's more comfortable with it now,' he says of Zach's attitude to the estrangement. 'He understands it ... we have a good custody arrangement, so he comes and goes freely. He knows exactly how many days he's here and how many days he's there. Children at his age don't want to deal with the anger and volatility or whatever would develop. As long as things are peaceable, he's fine switching back and forth.'

Robin Williams had one final act to perform for his father. Robert Williams was a lifelong lover of water and boats, so, not long after the services, there was one last remembrance. Robin Williams and his two half-brothers – Todd, who was now a wine distributor, and Lauren, a high-school physics teacher – met to scatter their father's ashes in San Francisco Bay.

It was sad but also cathartic and wonderful in the sense that it brought my two half-brothers and me closer together [Williams told Bill Zehme]. It kind of melded us closer as a family than we've ever been before. We've always been very separate.

That day we gathered right on the sea in front of where my parents live. It was funny. At one point I had poured the ashes out, and they're floating off into the mist, seagulls flying overhead. A truly serene moment. Then I looked into the urn and said to my brother, 'There's still some ashes left, Todd. What do I do?' He said, 'It's Dad – he's holding on!' I thought, 'Yeah, you're right. He's hanging on.' He was an amazing man who had the courage not to impose limitations on his sons, to literally say, 'I see you have something you want to do – do it.'

20

Waitin'

G*ood Morning Vietnam* opened in December 1987 just over two months after Robert Williams' death. Almost immediately the film proved that everyone from Adrian Cronauer through Jeffrey Katzenberg through Larry Brezner and ultimately through to Robin Williams himself had been absolutely right. The film was a huge commercial success and Robin Williams received some of the best reviews of his career. The critics believed that he had found the right role at last and the public seemed to agree. In three weeks of limited release – where it was playing on only four screens in the whole country – it was making $1 million a week. On its first weekend on wide release it grossed $12 million which is an impressive sum now, but in 1988 was a huge opening. By the end of its run the film had grossed $123.9 million in the United States alone – a figure roughly equivalent to the combined grosses of his first seven films. But later, when he was promoting the film in Europe, Williams revealed that he had had some misgivings about whether or not the audience would take to it. He had been genuinely concerned that young audiences in the latter part of 1987 and the early part of 1988 would not get references to 1965.

'That's why a lot of the jokes and references are about television like Gomer Pyle and Elvis,' said Williams, explaining the gamble. 'You tried to find some kind of broad reference. I worried that too many people would see it and wonder, "What the hell is he talking about?" But it worked. I've seen the film with all sorts of audiences and it does work. Maybe it just sounds funny.'

The timing of the release of *Good Morning Vietnam* was crucial. Putting out a movie about the trauma of Vietnam at Christmas may not have seemed on the surface to be the ideal marketing move. Other films like the James Brooks television satire *Broadcast News* or the Steven Spielberg-produced comedy adventure **batteries not included* may have seemed like surer commercial bets. But Disney felt that they had a potential Oscar candidate on their hands with *Good Morning Vietnam*, and the limited pre-Christmas release was designed to ensure that it would qualify for the following year's Academy Awards.

The closing date for qualification for the Oscars is the end of the calendar year, midnight on 31 December to be precise. To be eligible for an Academy Award a film has to have played at least one full week on at least one screen in Los Angeles, so the four-screen limited release in December was enough to fulfil the criteria. The ballot papers and a list of eligible films are sent to the 5000-odd members of the Academy of Motion Picture Arts and Sciences in January. After the usual intensive lobbying and advertising campaigns the nominations are announced in mid-February, and the awards themselves are handed out on or about the last Monday in March. Buoyed up by a groundswell of critical acclaim and box-office receipts, Robin Williams found himself nominated for an Academy Award for the first time. The other nominees were Michael Douglas – also a first-time nominee – for *Wall Street*, William Hurt for *Broadcast News*, Marcello Mastroianni for *Dark Eyes* and Oscar veteran Jack Nicholson for *Ironweed*. The competition was tough. Hurt, for example, was enjoying a run of three successive Best Actor nominations. Nicholson, on the other hand, was the nominations kingpin, his nod for *Ironweed* being his ninth Oscar nomination. Douglas, who had previously picked up an Oscar as a producer for *One Flew Over the Cuckoo's Nest*, was making his début as a nominee and also had in his favour the phenomenal success of *Fatal Attraction* which had been released in the same year.

Three-time nominee Mastrioanni was the obvious outsider of the quintet. His nomination was as much in recognition of his long and distinguished career as for his performance in *Dark Eyes*, a charming period comedy in which he played an Italian aristocrat. Leaving him out of the equation, Williams then became the longest-odds candidate for a number of reasons. First there was the fact that *Good Morning Vietnam* had not received nominations for either Best Picture or Best Director, which are generally seen as prerequisites for success. But most importantly, as Barry Levinson pointed out, a lot of people read the film the wrong way. Despite its considerable dramatic content it was marketed as a comedy and was perceived as a comedy. By extension Williams, although he had shown considerable subtlety as an actor in his performance, was still seen as a comedian. Oscar has not been kind to comedy over the years. Only horror movies have fared more poorly in terms of the statuettes they've been awarded. In the 70-year history of the Academy Awards only four men have won Best Actor Oscars for what might be termed comic performances: James Stewart in *The Philadelphia Story*, Lee Marvin for *Cat Ballou*, Richard Dreyfuss for *The Goodbye Girl* and Jack Nicholson for *As Good As It Gets*. All four of these wins were by straight actors in comic roles. No established comedian has ever won a Best Actor Oscar and that includes the comedy greats like Chaplin and Keaton. What's worse in the case of Robin Williams was that he was seen as a television comedian and therefore in the eyes of the Academy something of an *arriviste*. The Academy had been happy to turn to Williams a couple of years earlier when he replaced long-time Oscar night compère Johnny Carson in a bid to boost flagging TV ratings, but it was not yet ready to give him the coveted statuette.

In the end the Best Actor contest came down to a straight fight between Douglas and Hurt. It was Douglas who took away the prize for his performance as *über*-speculator Gordon Gekko, whose 'greed is good' mantra symbolised the mood of the post-Reagan Eighties. Douglas, incidentally, like Williams, was in a film with no nominations for Best Picture or Best Director, proving if nothing else that occasionally nothing is certain when it comes to the Oscars. What probably tipped the scales for him and against Hurt was the full trophy cabinet syndrome. Hurt already had one Best Actor Oscar for *Kiss of the Spider Woman*, and two statuettes in three years would have been just too much.

Williams however at least had the consolation of winning a Golden Globe from the Hollywood Foreign Press Association as Best Actor in a Musical or Comedy. It was his second Golden Globe; he had won for *Mork and Mindy* some years earlier. All told it wasn't a bad spell for Robin Williams in terms of awards. He also picked up an Emmy for Best Individual Performance in a Variety or Music Programme. The show in question was *ABC Presents a Royal Gala*, a benefit concert which had been staged in England in front of Prince Charles and Princess Diana. Although Williams was delighted to receive the honour, the Emmy brought back memories of one of the worst nights of his life.

'I was getting ready for The Prince's Trust concert and I went to a club in Windsor and I just blanked,' he recalls. 'It was like one of those old movies from the Fifties where they show the comic on-stage, and the lights are in your face, and I just opened my mouth and nothing came out.'

For someone like Williams, whose act is based on fear of so many different types, being confronted with any comedian's greatest fear must have been a terrifying moment. His act used to include a routine in which he pretended to be a comedian dying on-stage in a puddle of flop sweat. It was certainly a defining moment for Williams to go through it for real at such a stage in his career. Even ten years later he can recall the experience almost unbidden as one of the most salutary nights of his career.

> It really scared me and the next night I did the show and it was better. It's good to have one of those nights once in a while because it just scares you and it sobers you up real quick. I kept looking up to see if Prince Charles was laughing and they said he was so I thought 'Good, I can come back.' It was one of those nights where I could see the first ten rows of attitude going 'Who are you?'

There's no doubt that the sight of Williams in what he describes as 'full-tilt bozo' mode must have been curious to say the least to a typical British charity audience who had paid large amounts of money to be entertained by a man who appeared to be having a psychotic episode on-stage. For his part the culture shock for Williams must have been just as great. He wasn't in the Holy City Zoo now, and not even a little pre-show encouragement from Princess Diana could make him any more relaxed.

> Meeting the Princess was amazing [he admitted some years later]. She's exquisite. I knew he would have a certain presence, but with her you go 'Wow'. She's obviously been trained to do certain things, one of which is the look. She'll look at you, then turn away, then look at you again. It's beyond coquette. Before the show she asked me, 'Do you know what you're going to do tonight?' I said, 'I really don't know, but after you see it, I don't think you'll want me back.' She said, 'Oh, don't tell me that.' And she gave me one of those looks.
>
> At one point [says Williams recalling the performance itself], I came off the stage and into the audience. I said to one lady, 'Look at those jewels. You could wear them or feed Thailand.' And she looked at me and said, 'Yes. Yes, I could.' So I thought, 'Right, I'm going back up on to the stage.'

It was certainly safer on-stage for Williams, and with the security of the footlights between him and the audience he went on to give a devastating performance which was justly recognised with the Emmy award.

Although he had made his name as a comedian, first in stand-up and then in *Mork and Mindy*, it is important to remember that comedy was not Robin Williams' chosen field. He was a comedian by inclination but originally set out to be an actor as an avocation. Juilliard does not produce stand-up comedians as a matter of course. Williams had been classically trained and now in the early part of 1988 he was inclined to put his training to the test.

When he had finished *Good Morning Vietnam*, Williams had no other film projects in mind. Both he and his manager Larry Brezner were waiting for the reaction to the Vietnam movie before deciding on their next move. Brezner was keen to develop Williams into a fully-fledged movie star, the sort of bankable actor whose name was enough to raise finance for a picture and guarantee a good opening weekend. Williams on the other hand was keen to find projects which interested him in their own right and was less concerned with their overall effect on his career. However, both men were of the same mind when Williams decided he would make his stage début in a production of *Waiting for Godot* at the Lincoln Center in New York. The production was being put together by director Mike Nichols. With cinema hits such as *The Graduate* to his credit, as well as some landmark satirical performances with Elaine May, Nichols is one of America's most intelligent, literate and respected directors. He had held a number of readings of Beckett's play in the autumn of 1997 with a hand-picked group of actors. By the end of this unconventional auditioning process he had narrowed his choices for the four principals down to Robin Williams, Steve Martin, F. Murray Abraham and Bill Irwin. Rehearsals were to be held in May 1988, and the play would open for an eight-week run starting in mid-June. Having settled on their proposed cast, Nichols and Gregory Mosher, the artistic director of Lincoln Center, flew to Paris for discussions with Beckett himself, who approved their choice of cast.

'We're going to do a musical version called *Waitin'*,' Williams joked, trying to make light of his first foray into legitimate theatre. But even though he joked in public, he was well aware of the size of the challenge which faced him and the risks he was preparing to take. 'It's wonderful stuff,' he continued. 'Beckett is like Pinter on valium. You do it, because the experience itself will change you.'

Williams was at a stage in his life where he not only needed change, he actively sought it out and embraced it. Having the courage to go on-stage as an actor was only part of it. His relationship with Marsha Garces was getting stronger and closer. He and Valerie had made public the news of their split. He was now living with Marsha and the stability he was beginning to find in his domestic life was being reflected in a greater willingness to stretch himself in his creative life. Scheduling problems meant that *Waiting for Godot*, which was not being done as any kind of musical, would not now be able to go ahead until the autumn of 1988. Williams and Garces moved from San Francisco to the Upper West Side of New York for most of the year, with Zach making frequent visits.

The production was formally announced in the Lincoln Center's newsletter to its members in September. The play would be staged at the Mitzi E. Newhouse Theater from 11 October until 27 November. The seven-week run was predicated on the availability of the five cast members – Nichols had added young Lukas Haas to his original quartet – and the small 299-seat auditorium instantly made this the hottest ticket in town. The Lincoln Center correctly anticipated that demand would be huge. There were not even enough tickets to satisfy their own members who would have the chance to buy them before the general public. To ensure as much fair play as possible an independent accounting firm was brought in to supervise a ballot of members to make sure that the tickets were distributed as fairly as possible. In a bid to play down accusations of élitism Mosher and Bernard Gersten, executive producer of Lincoln Center Theater, let it be known that they planned to make a TV film version of the production so that as many people as possible could see this stellar production. That never materialised, but there is at least a record of it on video in the New York Public Library for the Performing Arts.

Waiting for Godot was first performed in Paris on 5 January 1953. Beckett described it as a 'tragicomedy in two acts'. Its central characters are two tramps – Vladimir and Estragon – who wait on a deserted country road for a mysterious character called Godot. Their wait is long and to pass the time they hold rambling discussions on their own lives and the nature of life in general. In each of the two acts they meet an overbearing man named Pozzo, and Lucky, his improbably named slave. Each of the two acts ends with a young boy coming on-stage to tell them that Godot will not be here tonight but will certainly meet them if only they will come again tomorrow.

Waiting for Godot had enjoyed a chequered reputation in its 35 years; at one point it had been censored in England. But it had endured to become a classic and this Lincoln Center production was the first major New York revival of the play in more than ten years.

Nichols had chosen his cast with care. Steve Martin would be Vladimir, Robin Williams was Estragon, F. Murray Abraham played Pozzo, with Bill Irwin as Lucky. The young Haas appeared at the end of each act to announce the unfortunate delay of the eponymous Godot. In terms of billing the cast was listed in alphabetical order which put Abraham first and made Robin Williams last on the bill. Few theatrical events had been more keenly anticipated and, not surprisingly, there was not a seat to be had for the entire run.

The play begins with a darkened stage. Then with a drum roll and a clash of cymbals the lights come up to reveal a tramp struggling with an ill-fitting boot. This is Estragon, played by Williams. His costume looks like an explosion in a charity shop. A battered bowler hat lends a forlorn dignity to a blue-grey ruffled shirt with a huge wing collar, a hooded sweat top with cut-off sleeves, flared trousers which fit where they touch and are held up tentatively with an old piece of string. A swarthy growth of unshaven stubble gives him the look of an Emmett Kelly clown. After much struggling with the boot he is joined by Steve Martin as Vladimir, who cuts a slightly more presentable figure but not by much. Together they debate, bicker and squabble about their miserable lives as they wait for Godot. They are joined periodically by Pozzo, a man of self-styled wealth and taste who lives to abuse his mute slave Lucky. After a while Pozzo and Lucky go on their way and eventually the boy arrives to announce that Godot will not be coming. The second act more or less mirrors the first, except for some great tragedy having befallen Pozzo, who has been blinded between the two acts.

Williams' great genital dilemma quickly manifests itself in the performance. Should he be a straight actor like they told him in Juilliard, or should he talk about his genitals? There is very little actual discussion of his genitals in the play but, in the first half in particular, there is much fumbling and manipulation of them by Williams. He seems to lack the will, if not the desire, to make this final leap into straight acting. There is always something going on to remind the audience that they're watching Robin Williams and not Estragon. Whether it's pantomimed foot odour, inappropriate motor car noises, comic business with carrots, or a variety of accents including John Wayne and Gabby Hayes, Williams seems reluctant to subsume himself to the text. To be fair, he is not alone in this. Steve Martin similarly brings too much of his screen baggage to his role as Estragon, who might as well be playing in *The Jerk* or *The Man with Two Brains*. Only fitfully do they appear as anything other than Robin Williams and Steve Martin, and they are aided and abetted by an audience which seems to see its function as a sitcom laugh track, chiming in at every bit of business.

Neither Williams nor Steve Martin seems terribly concerned about serving Beckett's text, and director Mike Nichols must also bear some degree of responsibility. One of the *coups de théâtre* in Godot comes when Lucky finally speaks. Having been mute throughout, he has one magnificent stream-of-consciousness soliloquy which is a test of any actor's ability. It's not just a question of remembering the words, which spew out like a burst water main, it's capturing the sense of Lucky's frustration as an intelligent man trapped in this lumbering body and used for brute labour. It is a pivotal moment in the play and in most productions the speech is generally accompanied by a respectful silence from whoever is playing Vladimir and Estragon. Beckett's stage directions are normally quite explicit and they do not leave a lot of room for interpretation. In this production, however, the opening of Bill Irwin's soliloquy as Lucky is the cue for Martin and Williams to mime, caper and play shamelessly to the audience throughout his speech. Whether it is funny is neither here nor there, the effect is to distance the audience from the world of Beckett and make them aware they are doing nothing more than watching the Steve and Robin show.

Waiting for Godot was a sell-out, as expected, but its critical reception was less than rapturous. And criticism came from an unexpected quarter in a scathing letter from the playwright himself. The letter was the result of correspondence between Beckett and producer-director Jack Garfein, described by the *New York Post* as a long-time friend of Beckett. Garfein had sent Beckett copies of the reviews and also, apparently, a copy of the programme for the production. Beckett was in a nursing home in Paris receiving physiotherapy for his arthritis. This, coupled with the fact that he was now 82, meant it would have been almost impossible for him to travel to New York. Had he done so he might not have liked what he saw. In his letter to Garfein, reprinted in the *Post*, Beckett was scathing about the production. 'I deplore the liberties taken in N.Y. *Godot*, with text and on stage,' he wrote.

Beckett's reaction meant that any proposed television version of this particular production was dead in the water. He was unlikely to give his permission if he felt so strongly about this version. A Lincoln Center spokesman later admitted that they did not have the television rights, nor did they ever have them. Another spokesman, however, suggested that Gregory Mosher's original comments regarding a TV version had been made in good faith, although they were also aware that it would soften the criticism about no one being able to see the play. Garfein insisted that he was about to stage his own version of the play and that he also had Beckett's permission to film it, but as yet there is no sign of the film.

Williams did not react well to the criticism of the production and his performance. In the first place he criticised the exclusivity of the event by blaming the Lincoln Center subscription audience. 'They came because it was an event, the thing to do,' he said with uncharacteristic bitterness.

'We put our ass out and got kicked for it,' he would reflect some years later. 'Some nights I would improvise a bit and the hard-core Beckett fans got pissed off. We played it as a comedy team; it wasn't existential. Like these two guys from vaudeville who would go into routines that would fall apart into angst. Basically it's Laurel and Hardy, which is how Beckett had staged it in Germany.'

Beckett's own reaction to the Lincoln Center production suggests that he and Williams differ more in their interpretation of the piece than Williams thinks. Critics generally shared Beckett's view about the changes which had been made to the text. Williams lambasted them, accusing them of double standards in their treatment of the play. These were the ones, according to Williams, who 'used to despise Beckett and now hold him godlike'.

But he insisted that, even if he had been bloodied by the criticism, he would remain unbowed. He said that he would love to do another play in New York, possibly doing *Godot* again. He also pointed out that as you get older you learn how to play what he calls the 'frightening silences'.

I thought, 'Wouldn't it be great to do *Godot* again?' [he said recently]. Except this time I would be Lucky, the one who has the big long speech, the five-minute monologue. *Godot* is one of the great pieces of writing of the twentieth century. It has great comic and tragic moments. It has everything you could ever want in a play. I would love to do that again.

Williams would mature as an actor over the years. He would learn to use the stillness of the silences instead of being intimidated by them. He would no longer feel it necessary to leap in and fill the void with noise. But he has never acted again on the stage from that day to this.

21

Dances with Lepers

It was Andy Warhol who said that one day everyone would be famous for 15 minutes. As far as a great many people were concerned, Robin Williams had pretty well used up his quarter of an hour almost ten years ago when *Mork and Mindy* became a hit. Now *Good Morning Vietnam* had made him a household name all over again and removed him from the province of the terminally hip and addicts of retro-television. Williams is in no doubt about what might have happened had *Good Morning Vietnam* gone the way of most of his other movies. On one occasion just before the film was released he was doing another night at the Holy City Zoo when he started being heckled by someone about his performance in *Popeye*.

'No ... no more *Popeye*,' Williams told him. 'But I have a new movie that just might work. If not I'll be off somewhere shouting "Show me a vowel". There's a scary thought.'

The prospect of a career as a perennial game-show celebrity guest might have been genuinely terrifying to Williams. But he had given some serious thought to what might have happened if, instead of being hailed by *Time* magazine as 'the best military comedy since *M*A*S*H*, *Good Morning Vietnam* had joined his other films in going down the box-office drain.

'You're not hosed totally,' he recalled. 'You simply slip down the comedy food chain of that list of people who get scripts ... It all kind of works that way. If this film had failed I'd go down another couple of notches. So you have to work your way back up again or do character parts – or you fall back and punt,' he said, reverting to an analogy from his brief and spectacularly unsuccessful football career. 'Now with this I knew I had the open fields to run through. The radio broadcasts obviously afforded me the freedom to improvise, yet the story had dramatic elements which provided some interesting turns.'

He had, he said – joining the consensus – found the right role at last. But he also conceded that not finding the right role up till now had been as much his fault as anyone else's.

> It was part ego, part stubbornness in trying to do something unexpected. Then there were other times when I took on slight projects thinking 'I can fix this'. I got suckered into a couple of films like that – *The Best of Times*, *Club Paradise* – I thought, 'Well, they'll give me the freedom to do my thing', but it turned out they didn't. Also for the first time I didn't have any fear or tension. Barry Levinson kind of took away the onus of being 'on' . . . I would ease into a scene and it helped me a lot. I started to relax.

In becoming famous all over again, Robin Williams once again came to the attention of the American media. Up until *Good Morning Vietnam* his marital situation was not really of interest to anyone. With the exception of the odd burst of notoriety such as the Belushi investigation, Robin Williams did not tend to register in the celebrity radar. However, once he had a $100-million-grossing movie, a Golden Globe award and an Oscar nomination, he became fair game for America's growing celebrity media circus. Williams' relationship with the media had been somewhat ambivalent. He was, in the main, accessible to the mainstream media and he plainly had his favourites, opening his heart to *Rolling Stone* on a number of occasions. As for the *National Enquirer* he had been having a running feud with the paper since the days of *Mork and Mindy*.

> My mother is so naïve about certain things [he explained, outlining the origins of his antipathy]. The *National Enquirer* called her and said, 'We're doing a story and we'd like to have some photos.' She gave them some photos of my father and me and some school photos. They used these pictures to imply that my father was this tyrant and I came from this horrible existence and that's why I was funny . . . She [his mother] felt used, and she was.

People magazine, however, sat somewhere between the *Enquirer* and *Rolling Stone*. It dealt in celebrity tittle-tattle but in such a way that it had become the defining force of American popular culture in the late

Seventies and Eighties. You knew you had arrived when you made the cover of *People* magazine. Indeed it was *People* that was among the first to recognise Williams' potential back in 1978 on that first series of *Mork and Mindy*, referring to his 'brilliantly sophisticated mixture of wisecracks, double-talk and improvisations' which it said made the show 'sizzle'. Now that Williams had finally fulfilled the potential they had highlighted a decade earlier they were planning another cover story for their 22 February 1988 issue.

Celebrity profiling in the Nineties has become something of a domesticated animal. Contemporary stars frequently insist on choosing the journalist, vetting the questions, controlling the access and often getting approval on the finished article before they will consent to a few moments of their time. Ten years ago this practice was in its infancy and Williams was certainly not powerful enough to put too many preconditions on his interview. Indeed it was quite the opposite. He was intelligent enough to know that the events of his recent past were potentially the stuff that tabloid dreams were made of. So, he reasoned, rather than try to hide it, he would be honest about it. When he spoke to journalist Brad Darrach, Williams tried to explain that there were certain things that he did not want to talk about. But, as he later explained to *Playboy* magazine, it all went horribly wrong.

> I was trying to tidy up the last ends of my first marriage and get on with my life with Marsha [he told *Playboy* Contributing Editor Lawrence Grobel]. I didn't want to talk about that, because I was trying to be respectful of my first marriage and end it decently. And then it just exploded. But I was so angry and horrified that the interview turned this way, it was like being mugged. At the end they said, 'We have to ask you certain questions or you don't get the cover.' Fuck it, I don't need a cover that badly. I sat down and talked to the reporter very personally and said, 'This is what's up. This is the truth.' And they didn't put any of it in. They made it seem exactly what they wanted to do from the very beginning: Marsha broke up the marriage. Which is total horseshit.

Once again the last remnants of Williams' naïveté had been his undoing. He chose what he felt was the intelligent approach to the *People* journalists. Unfortunately it wasn't the smart approach. The smart approach would have been to volunteer nothing, indeed to turn down the interview in the first place. Instead Williams was, in journalistic parlance, 'stitched up' with a front page which has now become notorious. The headline read: 'Robin Williams. Public triumph, private anguish'.

If that wasn't enough, the rest of the cover – which contained only one small posed shot of Williams plus another, not terribly flattering shot of Williams and Garces – went on to say: '*Good Morning Vietnam* has made the comic genius into a movie star at last, but his life is a minefield. Having beaten alcohol and drugs, he's now entangled in a love affair with his son's nanny that has left his wife embittered – and Zachary, 4, in the middle. It's the emotional challenge of his life. "I'll do anything," he says, "to keep my son from harm".'

It was a remarkable piece of journalism which attempted to sensationalise a situation that had all but been resolved. Two years previously it might have been a story, now it was simply rehashing old events. However, as far as the majority of the *People* readership and, by extension, most of America were concerned it was news to them. Williams suddenly became some kind of coke-snorting booze-hound all over again, while Marsha – described as 'sloe-eyed, elegantly slender' – was one step removed from a man-eating home-wrecker. *People* made great play out of her refusal to be interviewed and quoted 'friends' in filling in her background details as sketchily as possible. Similar 'friends' and 'close observers' were used to put Valerie Velardi's side of the story. Unfortunately a great deal of the innuendo thrown around by the story did not quite square with the quotes from Valerie herself in the same article.

'Robin has been conducting himself very well,' she offered generously. 'We're acting together in Zach's interest. We separated to re-examine our lives. It's a time for personal growth for both of us. I see another man but I live alone, and I like it that way.'

Given that the paragraph which follows those quotes begins 'Who's kidding who?' in the voice of the journalist, this certainly seems to have been one of those articles where the angle has been decided before the interview and nothing anyone says subsequently will change that. Like Valerie Velardi, Robin Williams admitted that his prime concern in this unfortunate saga was his son.

> He's just wonderful [he enthused]. The most sobering and wonderful thing in my life. Blond. Valerie's blue eyes. My chin. Full lips. He looks like an Aryan poster child ... He's amazingly adaptive and we all try very hard to make the new arrangement work. We all love Zachary and Zachary loves us all. Also we're all in therapy, and that's helped a lot – Jesus, I should get a discount. Valerie and I have a good understanding too. The separation was difficult, but it was also gentle. Better to do that than to go at each other's throats ... I'll do anything to keep my son from harm. What I'm trying to do now is to work with Valerie to transform our marriage into a relationship

in which we share Zachary and do all we can to make him happy. I expect my involvement with Valerie will go on until I die.

Although Valerie Velardi would talk about the state of their relationship now and the fact that she was seeing another man, she would offer no comment about Marsha Garces. 'You're not gonna get that out of me in 100 years,' she 'blurted', according to *People*. But on the other hand what did they really expect her to say? She is hardly going to be silly enough to humiliate publicly the woman who still meant so much to her son. That's not to say that Williams was unaware of how his wife – they were only separated and not yet divorced – felt about the new love of his life.

> The problem is intensified because Zachary loves Marsha and Marsha loves the child [he said]. So for Valerie, along with the feeling that Marsha took *me* away, there's the threat that Marsha might replace *her* in Zach's affections. That won't happen. Valerie is a very good mother. Nothing could shake his love for her. And I won't give her unnecessary pain. A relationship as long and close as ours can't be brushed aside. Besides we've got to work together for Zach. He's fine except when things get tense. He doesn't want tension … To live in this grey area is hard for everyone concerned. People have to get on with their lives.

Through all of the quotes from Robin Williams which appear in the article you can plainly see his sub-text. He is trying to do the decent thing by Valerie, by Marsha, by Zach, and even by *People* itself in attempting to lay all his cards on the table. Unfortunately his candour came back to bite him. The villain of this piece was very definitely Marsha Garces as far as *People* was concerned. Williams did not immediately condemn the article at the time. He felt it was better to allow things hopefully to blow over. That, he admitted later, was a mistake. He should have offered a more immediate and more robust defence, because without it what he came to call 'the nanny thing' would haunt them both for years.

People magazine also suffered as a consequence. Williams was and is a popular man in Hollywood, with lots of friends. His experience encouraged them to be a lot more careful in future, and ironically it was pieces like this article which helped usher in the more restrictive climate for entertainment journalists in the years to come.

'They went from being a magazine people wanted to do to a magazine people were wary of,' claims Williams. 'It was really a hatchet job, a set-up, an ambush. A very low blow. And it cost them. Celebrities got very worried. It was like "Why should I do a story with you?".'

The incident with *People* magazine and his frequent battles with the *National Enquirer* have inevitably coloured Robin Williams' relations with the press. These days he generally only does interviews when he has something to promote, and even then he is selective. On a recent visit to Britain, for example, his people insisted that he would not talk to any tabloid newspapers and only broadsheets were given access.

'It is a dance,' he admitted of the relationship between the famous and the press. 'It's like two lepers doing a tango – "Uh-oh, you walked away with an arm". It's difficult with journalists because they come in thinking, "Well I've got to find something", and we know. It's like a Bergman film where you are playing Parcheesi with Death.'

22

Oh Captain, My Captain

The cover story on the February 1988 issue of *People* magazine may not have done Robin Williams' public image many favours. On the other hand, even while he was railing at being set up by *People*, privately Williams and his handlers must have been breathing a sigh of relief. They would have been relieved because of the story that *People* missed, a scandal which was potentially more damaging to Williams than the tawdry claims that he had ditched his wife in favour of his child's nanny.

On Tuesday, 26 April 1988 a lawsuit was filed against Robin Williams in the San Francisco Superior Court. The suit was filed by Tish Carter and sought $6 million in damages after claiming that Robin Williams had infected her with herpes. Although the suit was filed in the San Francisco Superior Court some two months after the *People* story, it had been active for almost two years. It was originally filed in another court in 1986, and if *People* had found out about that, all the box-office magic in the world would have made it difficult for Williams to recover from the double whammy.

According to Carter's lawyer, Adolph B. Canelo, she met the comedian in December 1984 while she was working as a cocktail waitress at the Improv comedy club in Los Angeles. This would have been right in the middle of Williams' period of serious womanising. Williams has never denied having a relationship with Carter and, although a gagging order forbids him from talking about it directly, he has strongly indicated that it was this relationship which ultimately led to the breakdown of his marriage to Valerie Velardi. It's alleged that Williams and Carter had their affair from December 1984 until November 1985. According to her lawsuit she discovered on 20 November 1985 that she had been infected with the incurable, sexually transmitted disease herpes. She claimed that she told Williams, and that he told her on the same day that he had been infected since high school. Through Canelo, Carter then brought an action against Williams. It was originally filed in a small court in Stanislaus County, in California, with the express purpose of avoiding publicity while negotiations went on with Williams and his legal team. However, when those negotiations came to nothing, Canelo transferred the action from Stanislaus County to the San Francisco Superior Court, where it could not help but attract publicity.

As filed in the Superior Court, the suit charged Williams with being negligent and also responsible for the negligent infliction of mental suffering, and with fraud because he failed to tell Carter that he had herpes. The suit went on to say that Williams ought to have known that since herpes is a sexually transmitted disease it would be 'most likely' that Carter would be infected. As a consequence of that the suit alleged she would 'suffer a great deal of pain, worry and embarrassment not only after she first learned of the disease but for the rest of her life'.

According to Canelo, apart from denying that he had herpes, there had been little response from Williams' legal team. That appeared to be the general tactic of the Williams camp about the whole Carter business. They had made no comment to the media and were obviously taking the view that this was just one of the many nuisance suits that a man in Williams' position would get in the course of his career. However, the fact that this was originally filed in 1986, when Williams' career was in a trough, should perhaps have alerted them to the possibility that this was not necessarily a fame-inspired get-rich-quick scheme. Once the case was filed in the Superior Court it was only a matter of time before it came to the attention of the media. And so it did, although some treated it differently from others. The *San Francisco Chronicle* contained a relatively sober and straightforward account of the action on an inside page; the *National Enquirer*, renewing their battle with their old foe, splashed it across the front page with what appeared to be undisguised glee. Now that it was out in the open, Williams could no longer afford to play a waiting game. He had tried that before over the break-up of his marriage and found himself and his new love pilloried. This time he would have to take the offensive.

Robin Williams' legal affairs have been handled for many years by Gerald Margolis who, at the time of the action, was a partner in the Los

Angeles firm of Margolis, Ryan, Burrill, Besser. This was an extremely high-profile law firm which specialised in entertainment law and, as well as Williams, also represented big names such as Eric Clapton, Mick Jagger, Keith Richards and Paul Simon. In San Francisco, the showbiz responsibilities of Margolis, Ryan, Burrill, Besser, were generally looked after by Phil Ryan, another partner in the firm. As a consequence it was Ryan who looked after the Carter case for Williams. Ironically, as well as looking after Williams, Ryan was also Valerie Velardi's personal attorney, although he would not be involved in their divorce proceedings.

Ryan had built up a reputation for himself in the Bay Area for being almost as flamboyant as some of the people he represents. His standard fee for a civil action then was $250 an hour, and he generally indulged in what might safely be described as a rock-and-roll lifestyle. A self-described 'loudmouth trial attorney', he was the sort of flamboyant character who used rock videos as evidence, did not shrink from holding full-scale press conferences, and on one occasion, when defending a client accused of murder, handed out carnations to supporters going into court. But his extravagance could not disguise a shrewd legal mind and an uncompromising approach on behalf of those who engaged his services. The break-up of the cult Seventies band Jefferson Starship is a perfect example of how effective Ryan can be. When Paul Kantner, one of the founders of Jefferson Airplane – as the band was originally called – wanted to leave in 1984, it was Ryan who handled an increasingly acrimonious split. But when co-founder Grace Slick decided she too wanted to leave the band in 1988, the first person she turned to was Ryan, even though he had 'screwed her over' in the original action.

'Entertainers are strange beasts,' Robin Williams told the *San Francisco Chronicle* over lunch with a reporter, Phil Ryan and Marsha Garces. 'Most of the world looks at you like "Eeeech". But he [Ryan] understands. You need someone like that to kind of wade through the diverse things that happen.'

In acting for Williams, Ryan quickly found himself not so much wading as wallowing hip-deep in the Carter case. Rather than take the approach favoured by many celebrities and simply offer some cash to make it go away, Ryan was favouring a full-frontal approach in Williams' defence. That lunch was only the first step in a high-profile campaign to protect his client's interests. The first thing he did was to tell Williams not to utter a word about the case and, to this day, he has followed his lawyer's instructions. Any comment about Tish Carter would come from Phil Ryan; and come they did.

'We have examined Miss Carter's medical records,' he informed the

Chronicle, 'and they indicate she does not have herpes. She does have warts, however,' he added archly, 'and Mr Williams has no pet frogs ... Miss Carter seems to think there is public interest in her genital history. We don't think there is, just as there's no interest in Robin's. Or mine for that matter.'

But there was more to Phil Ryan than a few arch dismissals of Carter's claims. He was immediately going for the jugular by announcing that he would be filing a cross-complaint against Carter. Ryan gave only a few hints of what he might be claiming, but the details were finally revealed on Thursday, 6 October 1988, when he filed a complaint on behalf of Robin Williams in the San Francisco Superior Court. Basically Ryan was claiming that Carter had lied in an attempted extortion scam against his client to get money and a car.

Williams, according to the lawsuit, was claiming that Carter had used 'duress, coercion and fraud' to coax money from him since 1985. The *San Francisco Chronicle* went on to publish more details of Williams' complaint. 'Carter,' it alleged, 'intentionally and with extraordinary malice, made these representations to Williams, threatening damage to his public persona and damage to his family life in order to extort money and property from him.'

The suit also alleged that Carter began plotting against Williams after he had told her at the start of their relationship that he had herpes. She claimed to have contracted the disease in 1985, although Williams' suit said two herpes tests in 1986 proved negative. When Williams tried to break off the relationship, he claimed, Carter then told him she was pregnant and demanded $20,000 and a new car. She also threatened to go public with her allegations. Williams' lawsuit charged her with extortion, conspiracy and international infliction of emotional distress. It was also asking for an unspecified amount in damages.

Plainly this was a case which was going to run and run, and it would be several years yet before it would be finally resolved. In the meantime, while the drama was being played out by various teams of lawyers in San Francisco court rooms, Williams was on-stage in New York completing his run in *Waiting for Godot*. And immediately afterwards he was due to start work on another film.

Williams and Brezner had thought long and hard about the follow-up to *Good Morning Vietnam* and there were a number of possibilities in the pipeline. Far and away the most intriguing was the chance to play The Joker in *Batman*. Bob Kane's comic-book creation was finally being given the treatment he deserved with a big-budget screen version directed by Tim Burton, whose dark vision was closer to the comic book's sensibilities than anything before or since. *Batman* was being produced by Jon Peters and Peter Guber, and Burton ran into some problems with his casting choices. It seems that while Burton was keen on Williams for a role which probably more than any other would have given free rein to his manic abilities, Guber and Peters were more concerned with the star power of Jack Nicholson. In the end the producers prevailed and Nicholson got the role which eventually netted him a pay-day reported to be around $50 million once his cut of the box-office and merchandising revenues were taken into account.

Looking back on the *Batman* experience, Williams feels that perhaps he was a little naïve. He felt that his name had been used to get Nicholson interested and then he had been dumped once Nicholson bit.

What they do a lot of times, they bait people [he explained]. They'll say, 'Robin might do this, are you in or out?' A lot of things are word of mouth and a lot of people are offered something and then immediately it's taken away and given to somebody else . . . He [Nicholson] had been offered it six months before and then it was given to me. I replied, but they said I was too late. They said they'd gone to Jack over the weekend because I didn't reply soon enough. I said, 'You gave me till Monday, I replied before the deadline.' But it was just to get Jack off the pot.

His relationship with Marsha Garces had changed Williams' attitude to his profession; although he was angry about the *Batman* episode he could be sanguine at the same time. He had also learned a deal of humility and was now pursuing parts that he wanted and was not above auditioning to get them.

'I'm not going to play that game of "What do you mean audition? I'm Robin Williams",' he says. 'Fuck it. I'll go read. It's worth it to try. And it felt better to read with somebody than to get hired and not have the chemistry work out. It's sobering, too, because some of the parts have fallen through.'

One of the parts which did fall through was in *Midnight Run* in which Robert De Niro was to play a bounty hunter trying to bring back a Mob book-keeper. This would be the part which would spark something of a box-office renaissance for De Niro, but to begin with the studios were concerned about his pulling power. Ned Tanen, who was head of Paramount at the time, was looking for some box-office insurance. At one point they considered rewriting the book-keeper's role for Cher, who had just won an Oscar for *Moonstruck*. And one of those who actively campaigned for the role was Williams, who was keen to work alongside his friend De Niro.

> I met with them [De Niro and director Martin Brest] three or four times and it got real close [says Williams]. It was almost there and then they went with somebody else. The character was supposed to be an accountant for the Mafia. Charles Grodin got the part. I was craving it. I thought 'I can be as funny', but they wanted someone obviously more in type. And in the end he was better for it. But it was rough for me. I had to remind myself: 'Okay, come on, you've got other things.'

One of those other things turned out to be a man who was quickly turning into a fertile source for Robin Williams' films. Dustin Hoffman had passed on *Popeye* and *The World According to Garp*, and now he was about to pass on another film. Like the first two, *Dead Poets Society* ended up starring Robin Williams.

'I should be just hanging out by his house,' Williams jokes. ' "What did you pass on? Yeah? OK, that sounds good. What else?".'

Dead Poets Society was an original screenplay by Tom Schulman which was being directed by the Australian Peter Weir, who had carved out a Hollywood reputation with his success with the Harrison Ford film *Witness*. It is the story of John Keating, an English teacher at a select private school who believes that poetry is a living, breathing thing. His unusual methods earn the displeasure of the teaching establishment and some of the parents, but they touch the hearts of some of his young charges. In the end, when he leaves the school, he has changed their lives for ever. While *Good Morning Vietnam* had given him the opportunity to combine comedy and drama, this was an out-and-out dramatic role. Once he saw the screenplay Williams knew that he had to do *Dead Poets Society*.

'It talks about something of the heart and pursuing that which is a dream – and in some cases to a tragic end,' he explains. 'Originally my character was supposed to have leukaemia, which would have been *Dead Poets Love Story*. Then Peter Weir said, "Let's lose that. Focus on the boys." Lose the melodrama and it becomes much simpler and much better.'

Williams responds to good direction. Whether it was from John Houseman back in Juilliard or Barry Levinson on *Good Morning Vietnam*, Williams can see and recognise someone who is trying to help his performance. One of his greatest strengths is his intelligence, and he was smart enough here to see that Peter Weir was stretching him dramatically like no one else before. To find the character of John Keating, Williams drew from two sources. The first was one of his own teachers at Detroit Country Day School, John Campbell, whom he describes as a 'radical of the highest order, a crusader of conscience'.

'John Campbell is an abrasive man,' says Williams. 'He was my wrestling coach, a history teacher who basically said history would make a great farce, and that most wars would be hilarious except that massive numbers of people die from the madness.'

You can see why Campbell would appeal to Williams in the process of building John Keating's character. But the other guiding influence on Robin Williams' performance was much more profound. It came from his own father.

> They were yin and yang, my parents [Williams explains]. My mother is this outrageous character who is so sweet and basically believes in the goodness of people. And Dad had seen the nasty side of people. He had been in combat. She told me, 'There are no boundaries.' And he gave me this depth that helps with acting and even with comedy, saying, 'Fuck it. Do you believe in this? Do you really want to talk about it? Do it. Don't be frightened off.' Somewhere in his early life he had to give up certain things, certain dreams. And when I found mine he was deeply pleased.

Williams acknowledges that his father had worked hard in an industry which could be as thankless and heedless as the film industry. He also suggests it was his father who recognised those parallels. But Robert Williams had also seen that although his son's life was in transition, he was slowly becoming the master of his own fate.

> He was this wonderful elegant man who thought the world was going to hell in a hand basket [says Robin Williams]. It was basically 'You can't trust them. Watch out for them. They'll nail ya. Everybody's out to nail ya' . . . I realise that what he gave me is what's been working now in some of these dramatic movies. He had a great stillness and power to him, a great kind of . . . I can only use the word depth. He knew exactly what and where he'd been, who he was and why he did certain things. He was never pushed along. If things weren't done the way he felt was right, he left. That's coming into play now when I do movies like *Dead Poets Society*. I find myself thinking, 'That's for you, Pop.'

23

A Little Spark of Madness

R obin Williams felt Marsha Garces' influence most keenly in his private life. There was no more drinking, no more drugs, and no more womanising. What there was, was peace and quiet and time to take a breath. Even for his fans, however, the influence of Marsha Garces on Robin Williams could be keenly felt in his performance. Williams' comedy before and after Marsha came into his life was like chalk and cheese.

Most of America knew Williams as Mork from Ork, but it was not long after the initial impact of the success of that series that millions got to see the other side of Williams. The comedy special *Robin Williams: Off the Wall* was recorded at the Roxy in Los Angeles to be screened by the cable station HBO in 1978. This was a period when, by his own admission, Williams was drinking and using drugs, and the resulting performance is at times astonishing, and at other points simply painful. *Off the Wall* is a picture of a man on the edge; a man who cannot control his boundless energy.

Williams begins by surveying the celebrity-studded audience. Those out front included friends and colleagues such as Henry Winkler, John Ritter, Tony Danza and JoAnne Worley. 'Everyone I know is here,' quips an incredulous Williams. 'Some people I've slept with twice.'

He then proceeds to launch into an increasingly frenetic routine. Early in the show he takes leave of the stage and clambers hand over hand into the balcony where he does a *faux* Charles Laughton schtick from *The Hunchback of Notre Dame*. Back down on the stage much of the humour is drug-laced and drug-influenced. Describing himself as 'George Jessel on acid', Williams unveils the eclectic range of comic characters which vie for attention in his magpie mind as he prowls the stage sucking in stimuli from an eager crowd. He moves in the blink of an eye from an old blind bluesman to televangelist the Reverend Ernest Lee Sincere. In between we have the six-year-old Little Billy performing the by now famous 'Death of a Sperm' ballet and Williams as children's TV host Mr Rogers microwaving a hamster to teach children about the horrors of radiation. This is Williams using his famous duck and cover technique of comedy. It is brilliant, manic and entirely illusory.

Unlike most comedians his routine is not a revelatory process; we learn nothing about Robin Williams in the course of the show. In fact the opposite holds true, in that we are so bombarded by images that we leave the show even more confused about who Williams is than we were when we sat down.

There are, however, one or two moments of clarity in the obfuscatory hilarity. Williams starts into one of his other stock routines, the one about the comedian dying on-stage. This time it looks uncomfortably real. After about half an hour of his act Williams' wheels are spinning to the point where he comes close to being too hip for the room. By the time he gets to the dying comic, the audience are not quite sure what to make of it. There is the strong sense that as Williams makes comments about 'a gentle rose, dying here like me', he's getting uncomfortably close to the real thing. There is just a momentary glimpse of fear in his eyes, and the audience are just at the point where they are beginning to laugh because of who he is rather than what he's saying. At the last minute, like a pitcher at the bottom of the eighth inning, Williams makes a brilliant save and regains the day and with it the audience.

There are moments, too, when Williams goes into what he describes as 'Zen-lock', a period of total comedic freedom, a point where he is almost not in charge of what is going on around him. One such moment comes near the end when Williams leaves the stage and wanders among the audience in a spoof-Shakespearean soliloquy. In the middle of the monologue he wonders aloud whether it is 'nobler to suffer the slings and arrows or do some crazy shit on TV at eight o'clock'. Bearing in mind that the HBO show was recorded at the end of the first series of *Mork and Mindy*, it's pretty obvious that the disillusionment had set in at a fairly early stage. Then towards the last few minutes of the show Williams gets back on stage and adopts a variation of his Grandpa Funk persona; the old man who feeds heroin to pigeons because it keeps them coming back. This time Grandpa Funk is Williams himself looking back from the future to his own career. It's a painful little routine which shows signs of an extremely bleak worldview.

'We're only given a little spark of madness,' says Williams/Grandpa Funk. 'If you lose that you're nothing.'

After introducing Nicky Lenin, the Soviet Union's only entertainer, for an encore, Williams leaves the stage to tumultuous applause. The cameras follow him backstage where he collapses into a chair in a kind of post-orgasmic state, exhausted but satisfied and a little dislocated from the real world.

Off the Wall is rather like a distillation of everything that Robin Williams had been up to that point. The routines are brilliant but entirely fuelled by fear, a fear of rejection which had dogged him since childhood. This is the performance of a man who desperately needs and wants to be liked. This is Robin Williams, performance junkie par excellence.

Four years later Williams committed another stand-up routine for posterity with the release of *An Evening with Robin Williams.* This concert was recorded in the Great American Music Hall in his adoptive home town San Francisco, with Lovin' Spoonful founder John Sebastian providing a musical warm-up. If *Off the Wall* was a portrait of a man on the edge, *An Evening with Robin Williams* was an uncomfortable look at a man clawing his way back from the abyss. This was Williams after John Belushi had died and, more importantly, after Zachary had been born. There was much less drug humour here now; experience had taught him that it was no longer that funny. Williams appears on-stage like a man with every nerve-ending laid bare and twitching. Some of the routines – grabbing a camera from an audience member and taking a picture of his own penis, or heckling a woman who has the misfortune to require a bathroom break – are uncharacteristically cruel for a man who has never turned on his audience like some of his fellow Kalashnikov comedians. Williams here is nowhere near as innovative as he falls back on tried and trusted material. The penis jokes which are a staple of his act come thick and fast. A police siren sounds outside and he quips 'Here comes my ride', a line he has been using for 15 years now. It's like watching a drowning man swimming for shore: you don't necessarily enjoy the spectacle, but you can't help hoping that he reaches dry land.

An Evening with Robin Williams is a performance for a man in transition both in terms of his life and in terms of his material. The comedians Williams envies, such as Richard Pryor and Sam Kinnison, are those who are able to take their lives and turn them into comedy. Those for whom comedy is a catharsis. For the first time in his career Williams was starting to do that. *An Evening with Robin Williams* contains an early routine about childbirth and Zachary which he would hone and develop over the years. He acknowledged that it was a major change in direction.

> I need to work more on that [he said of incorporating personal material into his act], and if you do that it makes your work richer. That's one part that I think that I'll grow into. That'll give it a depth. If I look at the other stuff there is an energy and a mind, but it's still kind of flying all over the place. To have that thing that Richard Pryor has always had, it's so real that it's scary, that type of thing where you are not just opening a vein, you're basically pulling veins out of your arms. Scary stuff.

But Williams was able to deal with it and to incorporate it into his act. The quintessential Robin Williams stand-up performances came on the weekend of 9 and 10 August 1986, when Williams became the first solo comedian to perform at the Metropolitan Opera House in New York. The concerts were preserved and edited into a TV special which was later released on video. *Robin Williams: An Evening at the Met* is a remarkable piece of work – both on video and on live CD – which finally presents the sharpest comic mind of his generation functioning at the peak of its ability. This was Williams clean and sober and, thanks to Marsha Garces who was a vitally important part of his life at this stage, able to confront his life through his art. The man who had been not waving but possibly drowning in *An Evening with Robin Williams* had finally made it back to shore.

Taken as individual routines, *An Evening at the Met* is a very funny series of musings on drink, drugs, law enforcement, Ronald Reagan, penis jokes (again!), lust, sexual prowess and just about anything else that comes to mind. Taken as a whole, however, this is a very different Robin Williams performance. For one thing it is very tightly structured. There is still room for him to suck up all the creative energy in the room, but nothing is going to deflect him from where he is going. Hecklers are dealt with crisply and effectively as he heads for his pre-determined goal. Instead of the Williams who prowled the stage at the Roxy like a caged animal or who went through a fair approximation of a psychotic episode at the Great American Music Hall, this is a man in command of the medium. He strides around the stage at the Met with confidence and poise and delivers a routine which is almost a meditation on his life thus far.

We begin with alcohol and his confessional account of the fact that he is a recovering alcoholic – 'I'm the same asshole, I just have fewer dents in my car'. He knew he had an alcohol problem when he was found 'nude on the hood of my car with my keys in my ass'. After acknowledging that

alcohol is designed to 'bring out the asshole in everybody' he heads off
for more of his personal purgatory. From alcohol he moves on to cocaine –
'anything that makes you paranoid and impotent, gimme more of that' –
and acknowledges how drugs almost destroyed him.

'Freebasing,' he says derisively. 'It's not free, it costs you your home. It
should be called homebasing.'

Nothing is spared. After the drink and the drugs come the women, as
he moves on to the period when he was 'driven to find Miss Right, or at
least Miss Right-Now'. None of this is delivered in a remotely mawkish or
maudlin manner. This is great material and he is in devastating form, so
much so that anyone who didn't know Williams' background would
simply see it as a trenchant commentary on contemporary mores. It is
painful, but only if you know where he's been. Williams' comedic Stations
of the Cross eventually take him through his Good Friday and into his
Easter Sunday in the form of his son Zachary. Time and again he rails at
the problems of parenthood, but each time he stops himself short with
the phrase 'They handed me my son', and his voice softens and his eyes
widen with wonder each time he says it. Eventually Williams uses his
incredible mimetic skills to 'become' his son as he and Zach wander off
the stage together.

The concert at the Met was and remains a high point in Robin Williams'
career. This was still before *Good Morning Vietnam* and all of the success
which would follow that, but it is a landmark in Williams' career in that
it marks the first time that he was able to put it all together. For the first
time, with Marsha's help, the fear had gone. He would still be scared
before a performance but that was only stage-fright, not the paralysing
primal fear he had felt before. That concert at the Met heralded a genuine
purple patch in Robin Williams' comedy career. This was a period in
which he could take the time to go on the road and play to thousands of
people at a single venue. This was the last period in his life in which he
could do that before he was swallowed up completely by his film career.

The men who had the dubious task of opening for Robin Williams on
that tour were an incredibly gifted comedy juggling act called the Raspyni
Brothers. Choosing an opening act for a comic is a very difficult decision.
Williams had tended to use musicians before. John Sebastian had opened
for him, and his opener of choice at that stage was San Francisco jazzman
and vocalist extraordinaire Bobby McFerrin. However, the idea of going
on the road did not appeal to McFerrin, so Williams needed a new opener.
Billy Crystal suggested a comedy juggling act he had seen on *The Tonight
Show*, and so the Raspyni Brothers – alias Barry Friedman and Dan
Holzman – were hired on his recommendation. All things considered,

they were perfect; funny enough to get the crowd laughing, but with an act that was sufficiently different from Williams' not to steal any of his thunder.

'Robin is definitely the best stand-up I have ever seen, out of all of them,' says Holzman. 'Billy Crystal is very good because he could do all these character pieces, very structured, a bit like watching a play. But Robin is the only one who I could stay and watch every night because he was always different.'

Holzman and Friedman are in a perfect position to judge Williams at this stage of his career. They have opened for a Who's Who of contemporary American comedians including Billy Crystal, Dana Carvey, Dennis Miller, Garry Shandling and David Brenner. Friedman shares his partner's endorsement of Williams as the best of the best.

> He has a huge library of material, so that when something did come up he had a good line or a good quip ready for it [says Friedman]. 'Like other comedians he has his standard things, but probably from his training at Juilliard, he has the ability to make it sound like he had never said it before. In comedy the beginning and the end are the most important parts of the act. They're bookmarks and the bit in the middle kind of takes care of itself. But Robin would close with something one night and the next night you'd see him open with it. We've worked with a lot of styles and some you can set your watch by. Dennis Miller, for example, is very scripted. But Robin can just go off at a tangent.
>
> Robin also has the ability to move you. That stuff about his kid at The Met moves you to tears. With other comedians, such as Howie Mandel, you get a lot of bathroom jokes but you don't expect them to touch you emotionally. Robin and Billy were the two who could do that.

Williams also honed his talent for improvisation on that tour, which took in a lot of college and university campuses. One of the few things he insisted on was that there should be a box of toys on stage every night. He also insisted that the choice of toys or props be entirely up to the concert organisers.

> That would be his encore [recalls Holzman]. He would just go over to the box and take something out and riff on it. Some comedians do that with their own boxes of props – Carrot Top for example always knows what's in there, that's the point of his act – but Robin never knew until he got there. It was just great to watch. I don't know anyone else who would take that kind of risk. He was also one of the few comedians you could interact with.

The relationship between a comic and his warm-up is a kind of strange one, it is basically employer-employee. A lot of them don't watch your show, they don't want anything to do with you. But every night we could hear Robin laughing backstage. It was great to hear that laugh. It was louder than anyone else.

He also liked to do our opening announcement for us, he would use a different comedy voice each time. Garry Shandling used to do that too. A lot of other guys take their role of being a celebrity a bit too seriously, but Robin was a lot of fun.

On one occasion, Williams took his status as the star of the show so lightly that he held up proceedings until the Raspynis could get there.

We were flying on Eastern Airlines into Miami for a show on Superbowl Weekend [remembers Barry Friedman]. The show was at eight but the plane was delayed and we didn't touch down until eight. We were changing into our stage clothes in the limo at the same time that we were on the phone to Robin, and he was just so cool about the whole thing. We could hear the stage manager in the background saying, 'Can we start, can we start?' and Robin was saying, 'Let's just talk a little while and calm these guys down.' Then he went out and did a whole routine about how bad Eastern Airlines were.

He was also very relaxed with his fans [remembers Dan Holzman]. One time in Oregon this girl came up to him and she was so excited to meet him that she was in tears, she was freaking out. His reaction was so genuine. He couldn't understand why she would respond like that, as far as he was concerned he was just a guy. He was so gentle with her when he could just have blown her off completely – I've seen some guys do that. Another time we were driving between gigs and we stopped at a fast food joint. Robin went in and everyone kind of freaked out. The manager came over and apologised but Robin said, 'Let me eat my meal, and then we can play around.' After he had finished his meal he stood up and did about 15 or 20 minutes, he fooled around with the drive-in speaker, he did all this stuff just for the benefit of the folk in the restaurant. It was very cool.

I think some people have a persona and they are not the people you think they are, but I think one of the reasons Robin is so popular is that people sense he has a good heart.

The most obvious public demonstration of Robin Williams' good-heartedness also came in the middle of this incredibly fertile comedic spell. In 1986, along with his good friends Billy Crystal and Whoopi Goldberg, Williams founded the American version of Comic Relief. This triumvirate of talent acts as the backbone for a series of live concerts and television specials which are designed to raise funds for the homeless in America. The first of those benefits – a live three-hour show screened on HBO on 29 March 1986 – raised $2.5 million. It's hardly surprising that Williams, who was raised in a spirit of radicalism by his father, who had found out at first hand what an unfair place the world could be, should have become involved in something like Comic Relief. That initial spirit was further fostered by his Juilliard mentor John Houseman, who felt that activism and drama went hand in hand. Now Williams felt confident enough to play a leading role in helping people who were being dealt seconds by the system.

> What's changed for me [he says] is that rather than just sit and criticise, you say OK, what can you actually do to start wading into it and make it work, instead of just saying 'You're wrong. That sucks. They're ripping us off'. Now we have to fight from our local community up and work on schools and for the homeless. All that's left now in a lot of our schools is reading, writing and arithmetic, everything else is considered ketchup ... We're raising a nation of overweight, unintelligent people. The cities have broken down, the educational systems suffer cutbacks. The reality is we're broke.

In the dozen or so years since that first Comic Relief event Williams has done his bit to address himself to the issues rather than just shouting about them. In the first ten years of its operating Comic Relief raised more than $35 million for charitable works.

24

Do You Take This Woman

On 30 April 1989 Robin Williams and Marsha Garces were married. The divorce settlement had taken three years to finalise and had come through at the start of the month. A few weeks later, at a quiet ceremony in Lake Tahoe, Williams married the woman who had been his redemption.

It was a small gathering with a wedding party of barely 30 guests. Those present on that day were among the most important people in Robin Williams' life. Apart from his immediate family the guests included fellow comedians Billy Crystal and Bobcat Goldthwait and their wives, Barry Levinson and his wife, as well as *Good Morning Vietnam* producer Mark Johnson and his wife. The wedding was the culmination of what had been a hectic and turbulent period in Robin Williams' life. There were still some outstanding issues – not least the Tish Carter lawsuit – but he could now move on.

Williams had been working fairly constantly for the past 18 months. After shooting *Good Morning Vietnam*, there had been a series of concert dates, there had been meetings over other roles, and finally there was the filming of *Dead Poets Society*. The shooting of Peter Weir's movie overlapped with the end of the run of *Waiting for Godot*. This meant that Williams was filming a movie in Delaware while he was also on-stage every night in New York, some 150 miles to the south. It was tough, but with some creative scheduling he was able to emerge relatively unscathed. By the time filming ended in January 1989, however, Williams and Marsha Garces had been away from home for a total of five months. They were both keen to get back to San Francisco. They wanted to spend some quality time with Zach for one thing, and Williams wanted to stay in touch with his recently widowed mother. But there was another pressing reason for their return to California.

Marsha Garces was pregnant. By the time *Dead Poets Society* was finished she was three months gone. That, however, did not prevent her from performing her usual tasks in supporting Williams in whatever he needed. By the time the couple were finally married, Marsha was almost six months pregnant. This was the ultimate declaration of Williams' commitment to this woman. He had put his old ways behind him and was now ready to start family life all over again. Valerie Velardi for her part was also building a new life for herself; she had had a baby early the previous year. For Williams it was a case of having his mid-life crisis a little early; whereas most men wait until their forties, he had his in his thirties.

'I guess I've been going through a mid-life crisis for about five or six years,' he admitted. 'When's it supposed to hit, forty? I think I got laid enough. Sport-fucking I explored. That's done, thank you. That was nuts. That was totally the opposite of intimacy.'

With Marsha it seemed he had found everything he never knew he was looking for: strength, stability, intimacy, and the space to get to know himself. This seemed to be the real thing. But perhaps he had already had the real thing in his marriage to Valerie Velardi and just wasn't aware of it.

'I don't know,' he told *Esquire* magazine in June 1989, just a few weeks after he had remarried. 'Part of me says no and part of me says maybe. Obviously it's like asking an amnesiac what happened. I don't know. That's something that'll take years to work out in therapy. Now, I know I have the real thing.'

Three months after they were married Marsha Williams gave birth to a baby girl. They decided to call her Zelda, but not for what might appear to be the obvious reasons. 'Most people think we named her after Zelda Fitzgerald,' Williams explains, 'But my son named her – after a character in a Nintendo game. He has a very fertile imagination.'

However, Williams did promise Marsha that if there were any more children there would be 'no more Z's'. While *Dead Poets Society* was in post-production and being readied for an end-of-year release to qualify for hoped-for Oscar nominations, Williams retreated to the Bay Area to spend time with his new family. They divided their time between a spacious apartment in San Francisco and the ranch in Sonoma. Both Williams and his wife decided that they no longer wanted to live in Los

Angeles, which had too many unpleasant associations with Williams'
past.

'LA is like Disneyland staged by Dante,' says Williams. 'I lived there
when I was doing *Mork and Mindy* and I was so paranoid about my
career. In San Francisco, variety is a spice of life, it's not a magazine.'

When he went on retreat in San Francisco, Williams could indulge in
two of his favourite pastimes: reading science fiction and playing with his
children. The houses boast a room full of computers and electronic games,
and Williams and Zachary fight for equal time on the consoles. When
they're not playing computer games, they prefer to watch television
together.

'Our favourites are *Sesame Street* and those old Warner Brothers cartoons,' Williams revealed. 'Sometimes while Zach and I are watching
them, I do wacky voices, the same way I do in my act. And Zach will say,
"Daddy, don't use that voice. Just be Daddy." And that's just what I want
to do. Just be Daddy.'

While Williams was dividing his time being Daddy between San Francisco and Sonoma, the buzz was gathering in Hollywood about *Dead
Poets Society*. The film in which his John Keating would exhort his young
charges with the words 'Carpe diem' ('Seize the day') was gathering all
sorts of praise. Williams had established himself as what he had always
intended to be, a dramatic actor. The box-office results were quite remarkable. In the United States the film took a fraction under $96 million, not
as much as *Good Morning Vietnam* but, bearing in mind that this was
aimed at an older, more discerning audience, still a remarkable figure.
Audiences were riveted, and moved to tears by the ending of the film, in
which Keating leaves the school as the boys stand on their desks in tribute
to the man who has changed their lives. The response overseas was even
better than in the domestic market. Commercially the film took $140
million internationally, and overseas audiences were similarly moved by
the story. In Japan, for example, the house lights remained down for five
minutes after the film ended, to allow the emotional patrons time to
compose themselves and regain face before leaving the cinema.

With this kind of response another Oscar nomination seemed a decent
prospect. And indeed when the nominations were announced Williams
found himself nominated in the Best Actor category for his second film
in succession. This time Williams was nominated with a clutch of Best
Actor débutants. His fellow nominees were Kenneth Branagh for *Henry
V*, Tom Cruise for *Born on the Fourth of July*, Daniel Day-Lewis for *My
Left Foot* and Morgan Freeman for *Driving Miss Daisy*. The tipsters seemed
to be fairly evenly split about who might win the award. A case could be

made for each of them, it seemed, although there was intense lobbying for Cruise as a disabled Vietnam veteran. Unfortunately for Williams, the one thing that all the pundits did seem to agree on was that he was once again the outsider of the bunch. Despite the quality of his performance, his background in television and especially comedy was once again working against him. It is, it seems, easier for the proverbial camel to pass through the eye of a needle than for a comic to win a Best Actor award. There was much talk before the event of split votes and candidates emerging through the gap. *Driving Miss Daisy* had most nominations and it was felt that Freeman might win on the momentum of what many thought might be a clean sweep for the movie. On the other hand Spike Lee's *Do the Right Thing*, which presented a much more uncompromising view of black life in America, had been completely overlooked by the Academy. As a consequence there was something of a backlash building against *Driving Miss Daisy* with its somewhat more sentimental view of race relations in the South.

Williams remained remarkably calm throughout. While other nominees fretted nervously in their rooms, Williams enjoyed a relaxed eve-of-awards dinner at the Bel Air hotel in Los Angeles with his best friend Billy Crystal, who would be hosting the event. In the end the Oscar went to Daniel Day-Lewis for his portrayal of disabled writer Christy Brown in *My Left Foot*. It was a remarkable performance and it once again confirmed the Academy's fondness for honouring actors playing characters who overcome devastating adversity. In the end *Dead Poets Society* won only one Oscar, for Tom Schulman's script. Williams had been passed over again, but this time he could be more sanguine about events. He had discovered there were more important things in life than Academy Awards.

The final postscript to the *Dead Poets Society* saga came more than a year later when John Campbell, the man on whom Williams had based his performance, was fired from Detroit Country Day School. The circumstances of his dismissal were uncannily similar to those of John Keating's in the film. Campbell, who was then 55 and had been at the school for almost 30 years, had been on probation for several years. After he had been dismissed the school headmaster Gerald Hansen claimed that Campbell 'had not satisfactorily demonstrated a willingness to adhere to all the academic and professional standards of the school'.

Campbell, it seemed, was keen that his students simply teach themselves. On one notable occasion he insisted that anyone could teach history. To prove his point he went out into the street, stopped the first car he found, and asked the driver to come in and take the class. When asked later how the class had gone, Campbell said he didn't know, he had left. The fact that he made such an indelible mark on obviously bright students, such as Robin Williams, testified to Campbell's ability. He also had the support of the PTA, who claimed he was 'one of the few who doesn't bore parents at Faculty Night'. But in the end it was all too much for the school administration and they got rid of him.

John Campbell saw *Dead Poets Society* and enjoyed it. Like Adrian Cronauer before him, he didn't think that Robin Williams' portrayal was terribly accurate. Unlike Cronauer, however, Campbell felt his former pupil had erred on the side of caution.

'Actually Robin Williams wasn't as radical a teacher as I am,' Campbell insists. 'He tells the students to rip out the pages in their books. I tell them to throw the whole thing in the garbage.'

25

The Thief of Bad Gags?

The folklorist and philosopher Joseph Campbell suggests that there are only seven basic stories. No matter what they are, everything else is simply a permutation of one or more of these seven elements. By extension there are probably no more than seven different jokes in the sense that whatever the gag is and whoever is telling it, it can be boiled down to easily classifiable basic components. One of the things which makes Robin Williams such a great comedian is his ability to recognise this. His steel-trap mind can take almost any scenario and instantly turn it into a joke by almost intuitively adapting it to the basic format.

But in the summer of 1989 there were suggestions that perhaps there was a little less to Williams than met the eye. It seemed to begin in an issue of *GQ* magazine which more or less accused Williams of stealing material. According to *GQ*, 'his [Williams'] reputation for taking jokes and quickly making them his own is unequalled'. These were serious charges, and Williams' friends sprang quickly to his defence. Whoopi Goldberg, for example, claimed that Williams was not doing anything different from any other comedian: 'They made it sound as if Robin were taking their [other comics'] livelihoods away,' she said. 'Comics do this all the time. Someone says a great line and it stays with you and you use it. We had "Make my day". Everybody was using it. Is that theft?'

Daniel Holzman of the Raspyni Brothers agrees with Goldberg, but suggests that it is Williams' own skill which is at the heart of the criticism: 'The bigger your library, the more chance there is of some comics thinking that your library and their library are kind of intersecting,' he explains.

'It's hard because you have to have so much material in your head that you're not sure whether you said it first or whether someone else said it first.'

The allegations eventually became a joke in themselves. Comics would point out that Lindy's famous diner in Times Square in New York, which has sandwiches named after famous comedians, has introduced a 'Robin Williams'. It's just two slices of bread – you have to steal the meat. Joking or not, Williams certainly took the allegations seriously and they began to affect him. He began to wonder whether he had in fact stolen material, and endured long bouts of self-doubt about just how original he was. Was this really all him, or was his undoubted mimetic ability simply soaking up other people's material and reprocessing it as his own? For a while Williams admits he even believed it. On his own admission, when you spend up to eight hours a day listening to comedy, some of it is bound to rub off. In Williams' case it was the nature of his celebrity which got him into difficulty.

'I hung out in clubs eight hours a night, improvising with people, playing with them, doing routines,' he explains. 'And I heard some lines once in a while and I used some lines on talk shows accidentally. That's what got me this reputation.'

Williams was simply doing what every other observational comedian was doing. His life and his surroundings, and that includes lines from other comedians, were informing his art. However, where another comic could use material he had heard elsewhere in front of an audience of a few hundred and no one would be the wiser, when Williams appeared on Johnny Carson or David Letterman he was repeating lines in front of audiences numbering millions. As a mark of common decency, Williams was genuinely and sincerely apologetic whenever he discovered he had used someone else's material inadvertently. So apologetic, in fact, that he would willingly pay them for the line. But even this had to stop.

'I started getting tired of just paying, of being the chump,' he says. 'I said, "Hey, wait a minute. It's not true." People were accusing me of stealing stuff that was basically from my own life. And then I went, "Wait, this is nuts. I didn't take that. That's about my mother."'

Williams admits that one of his most famously quoted lines, about cocaine, is not original. 'A drunken guy came up to me on the street years ago,' he recalls, 'and he said, "Robin, here's something for you. Cocaine is God's way of saying you're making too much fucking money." A lot of times people come up and tell you this stuff. And you have to be careful. Did they hear this somewhere else?'

The most absurd point in the whole situation came at a time when

THE THIEF OF BAD GAGS?

Williams was accused of stealing material from a comedian he hadn't seen perform in two years. At the time Williams said this would be genuinely worth *National Enquirer's* interest in him as the world's first psychic thief. Eventually Williams realised that he was as much sinned against as sinning. People were shamelessly lifting his material and he was supposed to be flattered, but if he used a line from someone else then it was comic larceny. After a time he came to terms with it, but it has left him more cautious. Those late-night sets which he so much used to enjoy performing would now be done a little differently. He would build precautions into his approach.

> I don't want to take anyone else's time [he explains]. I got tired of other comics giving me looks like, 'What the fuck are you doing here?' . . . It's just hard to find the clubs right now because they are so jammed. You don't want to bump anybody. If I go on any place it's usually in the middle of the week, late at night, unannounced. When no one else is there, so no one can say 'You took my line'.

While this comic storm in a teacup was raging around him, Robin Williams was getting on with his film career. After taking some much-needed time off to get married and get adjusted to his new family, he was eager to get back into the fray. He had shown in *Good Morning Vietnam* that he could do screen comedy and in *Dead Poets Society* that he could do straight drama. For his next project he was going to mix them in a drama which bordered on black farce. In *Cadillac Man*, Williams was once again teamed up with an Australian director, as he had been in *Dead Poets*. The film was directed by Roger Donaldson, who was rapidly acquiring a solid commercial reputation after his successes with *No Way Out* and *Cocktail*. *Cadillac Man* must have been an appealing project on paper for Williams, who could reasonably have expected to provide another showcase for his full dramatic and comedic range.

Williams plays Joey O'Brien, a used-car salesman who is almost at the end of his rope. Life in Queens is one long hustle for Joey as he desperately attempts to keep his life together. He is under pressure from his ex-wife for more money, his teenage daughter is running wild, he has two mistresses whose names he can't remember, and he owes $20,000 to a local gangster. On top of all that, his boss is finally on to him and if he doesn't meet his quota of selling twenty cars in a single day then he is going to lose his job. This however is the least of his worries because gun-toting Tim Robbins has just ridden his motorcycle through the window of the car showroom. His wife, the showroom receptionist, is having an affair with one of the salesmen and he is going to hold everyone hostage until he finds out who it is. Ironically, in this instance, Joey is not the philanderer. But he pretends to be, in order to use his negotiating skills to the utmost to try to get everyone out alive.

Cadillac Man never quite lives up to the promise of its sales pitch, which was basically *Good Morning Vietnam* in a car showroom. Williams has one or two good moments. There is a gloriously sleazy opening in which he tries to peddle used cars to a stalled funeral cortège – the funeral director could certainly use a new hearse, and while he's at it perhaps the widow might like a luxury car as a tribute to the dear departed? Williams also excels in another delightfully frantic moment when he tries to juggle four customers at once as his time runs out to hit his quota. But for all Williams' skill, the material was just too thin to stretch him. Tim Robbins, however, who underplays gloriously while Williams tries to spin meta-phorical plates, steals the film from under him.

Cadillac Man failed to strike a chord with the movie-going public. It's debatable whether it was a summer movie, and certainly in the summer of 1990 it got lost in the shuffle and was swamped by predictable hits such as *Die Hard 2*, *Total Recall* and *Dick Tracy*. Hopes that it might emerge as the sleeper hit of the summer were dashed when the previously un-heralded *Ghost* proved to be a runaway success, breaking the $100 million barrier and leaving *Cadillac Man* to gather an unspectacular $27 million. But whatever disappointments Williams had over *Cadillac Man*, they would be short-lived. He was now about to embark on one of the most spectacularly successful periods of his career.

Dr Oliver Sacks is a neurological genius and acclaimed author of best-selling books such as *The Man Who Mistook His Wife for a Hat*. In the late Sixties he was responsible for ground-breaking work on a group of patients at the Beth Abraham Hospital in the Bronx in New York. These patients were survivors of the epidemic of sleeping sickness, encaphilitis lethargica, which had swept America after the First World War. Between 1916 and 1927 the disease struck down 5 million people. More than 1.5 million people died; others were attacked by a form of Parkinsonism which left them frozen, often in grotesque positions. It was some of these patients, who had effectively been locked away from public view, that inspired Dr Sacks to try to revive them after he had arrived at the hospital in 1966. By using trial and error with doses of a new wonder drug L-DOPA, Sacks was able to restore them to useful and constructive life. The drug, however, was not always successful and one of Sacks' greatest triumphs and disasters was Leonard L, a young man who awoke from his vegetative state to enjoy the world around him, only to lapse back after a relatively short time. The story of Sacks and his patients had already been told before in a British television documentary, as well as a Harold Pinter play called *A Kind of Alaska*. There had been some interest from Hollywood in a film, but Sacks had always resisted.

> I got approached by Hollywood in 1979 and the two would-be producers Walter Parkes and Larry Lasker came to the hospital in 1980 [explains Sacks]. Leonard L was alive then, a lot of the patients were alive. We talked about things and I was surprised by their interest. I was excited. I was intrigued. I was piqued. I was challenged. I was frightened. I was conflicted. I think one has to be. I didn't know how things would come out. I was very frightened of some exploitative film, but they seemed very good people who had an essential feeling of respect for the patients and the phenomena. I think that feeling of respect seemed to me a guarantee that if a film were made it would be a decent one. Then years passed and I didn't think a film would ever be made, not much happened until 1987 when a script suddenly arrived.

Despite the best efforts of Parkes and Lasker the script was gathering no interest whatsoever at Fox until it was found by director Penny Marshall. After her phenomenal success with *Big*, Marshall could have her pick of projects. Once she found the Oliver Sacks script she took it to Columbia who acquired it on her behalf and started to develop it. *Awakenings*, as the script was now called, concentrated on the relationship between Oliver Sacks and Leonard L. Marshall was hugely enthusiastic about the project and she very quickly brought it to the attention of Robert De Niro. The two had almost worked together in *Big* and, although she was keen for him to play the doctor, De Niro was equally keen to play the role of Leonard L. While she was casting around, Marshall went to see *Dead Poets Society* and was hugely impressed with Robin Williams' performance. She recommended it to De Niro, who agreed with her, and Williams was duly sent a script.

> I happened to read it on a plane [Williams recalls], and I was quite moved – to the point where a stewardess thought there was something wrong with me. It decimated me ... It's weird because when you first read it you think, 'How will this play?' Because it's basically internal; a man going through all these realisations and putting together a medical puzzle. And then after that to read Oliver's book and go, 'My God, it's all true.' It reads like Greek drama. It's something like Sisyphus. To rise and then fall, the human struggle of it all.

Williams immersed himself in the study of Oliver Sacks. He spent time with him, he spent time with his patients, he absorbed everything there was to know about him. This concerned Penny Marshall, who was worried that Williams was actually impersonating Oliver Sacks rather than playing a character. This was solved by a small but significant change; the character's name was altered to Dr Malcolm Sayer.

'It freed both him and me simultaneously, it relaxed a certain stand-off,' says Williams of the change. 'Oliver had been coming to the set all the time to help us, and for him it was like walking into a three-dimensional mirror.'

Sacks, for his part, found the whole experience of becoming a character in a film about his own life as amusing as it was bemusing.

The portrayer portrayed, the discloser disclosed [he smiles ironically]. I had it coming to me. I objected violently when I saw that I was a character in the script. 'I'm not a character,' I said. 'I'm the author, get me out of here.' They said, 'No, you have to be a character.'

I was very closely involved in the patients' lives and they were part of my life, I still feel very strongly for them. I still have their charts out, I never put their charts away. On the other hand I didn't entirely like the idea of 'the doctor's story', which they wanted to do and to have a sort of symmetry. But I suppose there was something in it and I do recognise some resemblance between the shy, bumbling, awkward, diffident, but sort of quite tenacious and tough-minded young Dr Sayer and myself of thirty years ago.

The phrase I used to describe Robin was 'a younger identical twin'. That was very uncanny. I didn't really feel as though I was being observed by him. We did things together and went around together, but he not only picked up my gestures and mannerisms such as they are – one isn't conscious of them, only other people have gestures and mannerisms. I've had to give most of them up because people feel I'm imitating Robin. But, more, he would sort of pick up opinions, interests, aspirations, really a whole identity. It was really extraordinary, I've never had an experience like this – a sort of mimesis, a sort of genius. Then there was more distance and he developed the character differently.

Sacks, a great bear of a man, was also amused by Williams' description of him as 'part Schweitzer – part Schwarzenegger'. But the two men formed a close and abiding friendship during that four-month shoot in often difficult conditions in New York. They remain friends still and frequently correspond or get together when their schedules allow. Science is one of Williams' great enthusiasms and he admits to being in awe of men like

Oliver Sacks. He has a passion for Einstein in particular, and one of his proudest possessions is Einstein's autograph. For Williams there are clear parallels between great science and great comedy.

> I love the idea that most of them will admit their major discoveries are accidents [says Williams of the scientists he admires]. They find out that something will trigger that one random association that allows the rest of the discovery. That, to me, is astonishing. It's the ultimate improvisation. When they find that thing, you see, the majority of them will say it was an accident or they had a dream. If you think of Einstein they would say it's his wife, there is a theory that it was actually his first wife who came up with the theory of relativity. And they have that child-like quality. When you see these interviews their eyes light up and they look like kids because they are talking about that which they find the joy in and it's incredible. My favourite scientist to see and see lecture is Richard Feynman. Here's this brilliant man, but he makes science so accessible, it's wonderful.

For Williams the experience of working with long-time friend Robert De Niro was as exhilarating as working with Oliver Sacks. The two had almost worked together before in *Midnight Run*, but this time it had come off and Williams suspected he would have to be on the top of his game.

> It's like hang-gliding nude over the grand canyon [says Williams of working with De Niro]. It can be kind of frightening sometimes. That kind of thing when you go 'Oh my God, it's him' ... But after a couple of weeks I finally went 'Oh stop – don't carry that whole thing'. You've got to work with the man, not the myth ... There's a wonderful thing in this movie that I don't think I've seen him do before – a kind of innocence. A shyness that people don't expect, and then he smiles and he's got this wonderful warmth, because normally he's playing very scary guys.

Warmth or not, there were still persistent reports from the set of *Awakenings* that Williams had lost his temper and broken De Niro's nose. Both actors, and director Penny Marshall, were keen to play down any talk of ill-feeling. The official version is that the two men were rehearsing a scene and Williams' elbow flew up and hit De Niro on the nose. The blow was such that the noise of De Niro's nose breaking was apparently picked up by the sound recordist on the soundtrack. De Niro, ever the trouper, did nine more takes with an increasingly stunned Williams before he decided to let wiser counsel prevail and went to a nearby hospital to have it checked. Ironically, De Niro says Williams actually did him a favour.

He had broken his nose some years ago, and he claims Williams' blow straightened it out again.

There's no doubt that, given his bulk and his weight and his athletic prowess, Williams probably could break a man's nose should he so desire. But it seems much too far out of character to have been deliberate. In fact, according to Penny Marshall, De Niro laughed so long and hard at Williams' pre-take routines that she was worried that he would look far too healthy for his scenes as the pallid Leonard.

'It was in various press accounts that I got angry and broke his nose,' Williams acknowledges. 'If that was true I don't think I'd be here saying "Let's talk". At least not with my own teeth.'

26

A Chink in the Armour

A *wakenings* was a solid commercial success for Robin Williams. It took just over $52 million domestically and more than made up for the box-office disappointment of *Cadillac Man*. Having won back-to-back Oscar nominations with *Good Morning Vietnam* and *Dead Poets Society* he could count himself unlucky not to have made it three out of four nominations with *Awakenings*. But for a quirk of billing he might yet have been wondering whether he should be preparing an acceptance speech for Oscar night. Although Williams has the larger role as Dr Sayer, there is no doubt that De Niro's supporting role as Leonard is the showier. Perhaps also thanks to De Niro's greater clout, he was the one who was first-billed and he was the one who ended up with the Academy Award nomination. In the end he would lose out to Jeremy Irons in *Reversal of Fortune*, and *Awakenings* itself would lose out to *Dances With Wolves* in the Best Picture race.

In any event by the time the 1991 Academy Awards were being played out in Los Angeles, Williams was hard at work on another film. He had worked for director Terry Gilliam some years before in Gilliam's magnificent folly *The Adventures of Baron Munchausen*. Although he is American born, Gilliam had spent a large part of his working life in Britain as a ground-breaking animator and founder-member of the Monty Python team. *Munchausen* was a distillation of all of his comic fantasies, but it proved so ruinously expensive that hardly anyone saw his delirious vision of the classic folk tales. Williams was roped in for an unbilled cameo in the 1988 movie as the disembodied head of the King of the Moon. Three years later Gilliam was back behind the camera for the first time since *Munchausen* with *The Fisher King*. There was no doubt in his mind that, once again, he wanted to work with Williams.

'The thing with Robin is, he has the ability to go from manic to mad to tender and vulnerable,' says Gilliam. 'He's the most unique mind on the planet. There's nobody like him out there.'

Gilliam's assessment of Williams may be exaggerated, but in terms of *The Fisher King* it is entirely accurate. It is debatable whether any other actor could have tackled the incredibly difficult role of Parry. The film is essentially a story of redemption. Jeff Bridges is a New York shock jock whose cavalier on-air manner is the fuse which ignites a gunman's murderous rampage in a quiet restaurant. The ensuing controversy ruins Bridges' career, and we find him all but down and out on the streets of New York. He is about to be set on fire by a street gang when he is rescued by a rag-tag man dressed in what approximates to a junkyard's version of a suit of armour. This is Parry, a former professor of medieval history. His wife was killed in the restaurant shooting and he has subsequently become unhinged by the tragedy. Feeling grateful and at the same time responsible, Bridges buys into Parry's quest for the Holy Grail in a final resolution which leaves both men changed and renewed by their adventure together.

For Williams it would be one of the most challenging roles of his career to date as well as one which he admitted he was only just beginning to feel sufficiently confident to tackle. In one location interview he conceded that ten years previously he would never have even come close to nailing Parry's character. Whatever characterisation he might have attempted then would have been largely comedic and taken the film in an entirely different direction. But for Williams *The Fisher King* was an important film to do; it was a film which spoke to him as an actor but also as an activist.

'*Fisher King* I did,' he recalls, 'because it's about bottom-line compassion, about redemption, about not taking people on initial value but looking deeper. It's about dependency and strange relationships that come and go.'

Williams was also enthusiastic about the film because the tragic circumstances in which Parry finds himself through no fault of his own are exactly the conditions which encouraged Williams to help set up Comic Relief.

'Laughing is better than a diatribe,' he explains. 'With comedy you can pull people in and say "Look at some of the things in the fun house mirror, but (really) look at them." That's what *The Fisher King* does –

starts out oh-wow funny and strange, but behind all that is a horrible vision Parry cannot deal with.'

The demands placed on him by Gilliam were considerable. As well as reacting to Bridges and other members of the cast such as Mercedes Ruehl and Amanda Plummer, Williams also had to convey Parry's own private madness. This was the vision he referred to as Parry is pursued by a knight in blood-red armour mounted upon a fearsome charger which is more monster than horse. 'Terry shoots stuff that has a half-life,' says Williams. 'You walk out and then it hits you ... Red knights. Sixty-foot samurais. Icarus. Simple things. He creates images that are shot into your skull.'

Although Gilliam and Williams had formed something of a mutual admiration society, there were some people connected with *The Fisher King* who were less certain. Jeff Bridges, for example, was not sure that Williams would be able to do anything other than go for the laugh. In the end he was delighted to find that Williams could not only handle the serious side of playing Parry but also keep the company in stitches during the lengthy down time in a long and tedious shoot. Screenwriter Richard LaGravenese was similarly surprised by the depth of emotion which Williams put into his pain-wracked performance.

Williams, however, had been working hard at his craft and was working hard at letting his defences down and simply being himself in front of the camera. It was a process, he claimed, which had been going on since *The World According to Garp*. 'For the first time I actually got comfortable even to be – and this sounds like a strange thing to say – to be myself. To be able to stop, relate, listen. To be interesting without doing all kinds of business ... It was [hard]. I'd built a whole thing and then I was asked to give it up, to work without the armour.'

For Terry Gilliam, *The Fisher King* was a difficult film. He was going into the movie with the reputation of an extravagant spendthrift, and if he wasn't exactly drinking in the last chance saloon he could certainly hear the tinkling of the victrola behind the bat-wing doors. It was also a hard movie to shoot, many of the sequences involved long night shoots and there was always the potential to go over-budget on a film where every dollar he spent would be scrutinised. But, in these difficult circumstances, Gilliam found Williams to be head and shoulders above almost any other actor he had worked with.

Robin sensed the weariness,' says Gilliam, recalling one particular night-time sequence, 'and suddenly went into a breathtaking 20-minute show. It was so specific. He knew every member of the crew. He knew their peculiarities, he had details and it was one of the great shows of our time. Afterwards everyone was just flying. We got back to work and zapped right through the evening. It was exactly what we needed.'

When *The Fisher King* was finished, Williams maintained what was becoming a prodigious work rate. He agreed to take one of two small cameo roles – the other was played by Andy Garcia – in *Dead Again*, a thriller from actor-director Kenneth Branagh. This, for the first time, gave him the chance to play a less than savoury character – a doctor who had been struck off for misconduct.

> It was a great experience [he said]. Sometimes when you come in and do a role where you are unbilled, or barely billed, you're not under the same pressure ... I just want to keep playing different characters to change the perception of just being 'the manic'. In *Dead Again* I played a slightly evil character. I think the job for me is to keep pushing the boundaries so I don't get labelled as one particular thing, that 'manic' thing. I'll save that for the performance, for the stand-up, when I'm in public.

While Williams was forging ahead in his professional life, matters were coming to a head in his private life. Tish Carter's lawsuit had been rumbling on for the better part of five years now and had recently been joined by his own countersuit. Williams' lawyer Phil Ryan had also filed a motion to dismiss Carter's suit, and it was this motion which was to be considered by the San Francisco Superior Court in September 1991. But Ryan was not finding things going quite the way he wanted. Instead of the summary dismissal he would doubtless have been expecting, Judge William Cahill further delayed his ruling. At a hearing on 10 September he decided that it could not be as simple as deciding which of the parties was in the wrong. Judge Cahill decided that first of all he would have to make up his mind on whether Williams actually had any legal duty to warn Carter that he was suffering from a sexually transmitted disease. Both sides were given a further five days to present their opinions on this issue and Judge Cahill tentatively set a trial date of 13 January 1992.

Judge Cahill's apparently simple ruling had now raised the stakes immeasurably in the Williams case. Instead of being a glorified ex-lovers' spat – albeit a high-profile one – the case was now beginning to take on a seriously precedential aspect.

It was now felt in some quarters that this had all the makings of a landmark case. If Judge Cahill ruled that Williams did indeed have a legal duty to inform Carter of any sexual diseases he may or may not have had, then the consequences could be awesome. In theory such a ruling would mean that anyone who failed to tell a partner of a potentially sexually transmitted disease could then be held liable if the partner then contracted an illness. Carter did eventually concede in pre-trial motions that she had never asked Williams whether he had any sexually transmitted disease, but with the wheels of justice grinding inexorably on, this was of little consequence.

The Williams legal team redoubled their efforts to have the case thrown out but there was more bad news when Judge Cahill finally delivered his ruling on 8 November 1991. The judge had decided that there were no grounds on which to dismiss the case. In a four-page written judgement he argued that only a trial would be able to ascertain whether Carter had asked Williams whether he had herpes, and whether Williams was obliged to warn her of any disease he might have had. The trial date remained set for 13 January, but Ryan was now promising to take Judge Cahill's ruling to the Court of Appeal.

Both sets of lawyers were adamant now that there would be no compromise. A settlement conference had been pencilled in for early December but no one was even remotely optimistic of any settlement being reached. Adolph Canelo, who was acting for Carter, said they had gone through settlement negotiations before which had amounted to nothing, and he saw no reason why this should be any different. Ryan for his part continued to insist that there would be no settlement because his client was not going to be extorted.

By going to the Court of Appeal, Phil Ryan succeeded only in dragging out the litigation further. The original trial date of 13 January 1992 came and went, and a few weeks later – on 21 February – the state Supreme Court finally handed down its ruling in which it refused to block the trial. Only one of the Supreme Court judges felt that Judge Cahill's ruling required to be reviewed. This meant that, the original ruling standing, a trial could now go ahead in late summer.

The trial in fact was due to take place in San Francisco Superior Court in the first week of August 1992. But, just six days before the case was due to go before the judge and jury, there was a surprising resolution. Williams quietly, and without fuss, settled out of court. In addition to the settlement, Williams and Carter also reached a confidential agreement in his countersuit that she had tried to extort money and a car from him. Williams, who is subject to a gagging order, has made no direct comment on the case since. Whether he settled because her case had merit or because he simply had become tired of it and wanted to make it go away, no one but he, and his legal team, will know.

Even after the settlement his lawyers were still referring to the suit as 'nothing but extortion'. And one of Williams' legal team gave the *New*

York Daily News a blunt but succinct explanation for why the case had been settled. 'At the last minute he got cold feet,' said the unnamed lawyer. 'He didn't want his reputation sullied by a money-grabbing attention seeker.'

27

Think Happy Thoughts

Los Angeles is one of the world's greatest tourist destinations for movie fans. Every year millions of them flock to Hollywood to visit theme parks such as Disneyland, or Universal Studios, or to stroll down the Walk of Fame on Hollywood Boulevard or simply to fit their own hands and feet into the cement imprints enshrined in the forecourt of the Chinese Theater. But in the summer of 1991, the biggest movie attraction in Hollywood was also the most exclusive. Nine stages at Columbia Studios at Culver City had been taken over by Steven Spielberg for his new film *Hook*. The film was a modernistic retelling of J. M. Barrie's *Peter Pan*, and Spielberg had spent $8 million on recreating Neverland here on what was once the old MGM back lot. Stage 30 – once the domain of Esther Williams – and stage 27 – where *The Bounty* once sailed – had been taken over by the giant tangle of tree houses which was home to the Lost Boys. Stage 15 was taken over by Pirate Town, complete with saloons and bawdy houses. But dominating all of this was *The Jolly Roger*, the 70-foot pirate galleon which was the flagship of Captain Hook.

Although it was in theory the most exclusive attraction in town, it may not have seemed so in practice. Day in and day out there was a constant stream of VIP visitors, often with their children, to look at the marvels Spielberg was creating. The list included Demi Moore, Tom Cruise, Whoopi Goldberg, Warren Beatty – who was filming *Bugsy* next door – Michelle Pfeiffer, Bruce Willis, Mel Gibson, Prince – before he became The Artist Formerly Known As Prince – and real royalty in the shape of Queen Noor of Jordan. As budgets spiralled and schedules lengthened,

Spielberg continued to receive his visitors with good grace, but no one was really surprised when he decided that his next film, *Jurassic Park*, would be shot on a closed set.

Hook is the story of Peter Pan as an adult. He has grown up and left Neverland and the Lost Boys and become a corporate lawyer going by the name of Peter Banning. Meanwhile his old nemesis Captain Hook has grown bored and tired of having no one to fight, so he comes to London to steal Peter Pan's children. Peter has become materialistic and inattentive, especially to his son. Hook attempts to seduce the boy away by becoming the father he has never had. Peter follows Hook to Neverland, but it is only by embracing his true heritage that he can hope to win the day and save his children.

The original idea came from the son of screenwriter Jim Hart who, while out in the family car one day, asked what if Peter Pan had grown up. Hart was intrigued by the idea and began to develop it, and in August 1990 TriStar Pictures announced plans for *Hook*, as Hart's script became known. Steven Spielberg, who had long wanted to make a live-action Peter Pan film, possibly with Michael Jackson, would direct. Dustin Hoffman would take the title role and Robin Williams would play Peter. *Hook*, which was due to start shooting in January 1991, was one of two projects that Williams had agreed to do as he was completing filming on *The Fisher King*; the other was *Toys*, with Barry Levinson, which he would begin once he had fulfilled his commitment to Spielberg.

Within weeks of the original announcement, TriStar revealed that it was putting not one, but two, Peter Pan movies into production. Hollywood had already seen the duelling Robin Hood movies of the previous summer, but they at least were from separate studios. It was unheard of for the same studio to set up rival projects. The idea was hatched by TriStar's mercurial boss Peter Guber. Although they had green-lit *Hook*, TriStar had also been developing a new version of *Peter Pan* itself. The rights to the Barrie classic were owned by Dodi Fayed, who was a near neighbour of Guber's in Malibu. One morning Guber turned up at Fayed's house and announced that he had acquired 'the sequel to *Peter Pan*'. From there it was a short step to an article which appeared in *Variety* on 6 September to the effect that *Peter Pan* and *Hook* would film back to back, a technique which had brought success with the second and third instalments of the *Back to the Future* trilogy. While *Hook* would have Williams and Hoffman and be directed by Spielberg and written by Jim Hart, *Peter Pan* would star two unknowns as Peter and Wendy, with Joe Dante directing from a Lasse Halstrom script. Fayed would produce *Peter Pan* and executive produce *Hook*. Although the idea of filming back to back seemed attractive it was wildly impractical given the relative stages of pre-production on both pictures. While Fayed continued to prepare *Peter Pan*, Spielberg got ready to start shooting *Hook*.

Spielberg was delighted when Williams accepted the role of Peter Banning. He felt that the actor embodied all of the hidden, and not so hidden, child-like qualities which were necessary to be convincing. Williams was keen to do the film and to work with Spielberg, but he was less certain of being able to get a handle on the character.

> I really had to convince myself that I could play this [he remembers] ... It took a lot of hard work to get this really anal tone, to find one that is kind of lost but still believable as a man-boy – as a guy who suffers from a Peter Pan complex because he is, in reality, Peter Pan ... And finding that tone to make it boyish, lost, yet still a guy who makes a living basically screwing people as quickly as he can ... Steven has been amazing. At first you think here's a guy who basically deals in visuals. But no, he knows every movie that's ever been made. He's seen every movie twice. So he knows if someone did something before. And from that, he can give you an idea that goes beyond that.

Not long after filming started the pressure began to build. Playwright Tom Stoppard was brought on to do rewrites. Massive toy deals were done with Mattel, which increased pressure for the film to be in the cinemas for Christmas. More importantly, the film began to get more and more expensive. It was originally budgeted at $40 million, but as the real nature of the special effects needed to make Peter fly and the physical effects for the rest of the scenes became apparent, it was obvious that this figure would have to be taken with a liberal sprinkling of fairy dust. The budget quickly climbed to $50 million, then $60 million. Some sources put the final cost at $80 million, but the generally accepted figure seems to be closer to $60 million. Even so it was still one of the most expensive pictures ever made, despite the fact that Spielberg and his three principals – Julia Roberts had come on board as Tinkerbell – had deferred their salaries. They hadn't received a penny in wages for the film, choosing instead to take their fee in profit participation. But since this was 'first dollar' participation, it meant that TriStar could be committing up to 40 per cent of the film's gross receipts, making it harder still for the studio to turn a profit.

These problems may have confirmed some of the initial misgivings which Marsha Williams had about her husband taking part in *Hook*. Robin Williams and Marsha are very much a team, and although the final decision is his, the decision will not be taken without considerable input from her. In this case she had misgivings, both about the sheer scale and cost of the film, and the fact that they were essentially tampering with an icon. The fact that her husband stood to pick up the biggest pay-cheque of his life was neither here nor there.

'Money's never been the reason for me to recommend anything,' says Marsha Williams. 'Unless the entire country collapses we have as much as we'll ever need. I'm more interested in looking at what Robin hasn't done and seeing what's next. I'm prejudiced, but I've never seen anyone with his range.'

Hook ran into more production problems when Julia Roberts jilted her fiancé Kiefer Sutherland almost at the altar the week before she was due to start filming on *Hook*. At the same time she was beginning a relation-ship with the actor Jason Patric, and the two of them sought solace in Ireland as a respite from the packs of reporters and photographers who were following them. All of this put her participation in *Hook* in doubt, especially when she took off for Ireland. Although Spielberg now insists that there was never any real difficulty, there were growing suggestions at the time that he had threatened to replace her unless she turned up by an appointed date.

In the midst of all of this Williams and Hoffman were doing their best to keep things light on an increasingly difficult shoot. Having built a career on three films on which Hoffman had passed, Williams was delighted to finally be working with him. The two men enjoyed a fairly relaxed working relationship. Williams' prodigious mimetic skills meant he could do a spot-on impression of one of the parrots which was used to decorate Hook's galleon. Generally he would wait till things got slow and Hoffman was in the middle of a long speech before emitting a dead-on 'parrot' screech which brought proceedings to a halt. Hoffman would retaliate by teasing Williams about merely being a television actor. But together they conspired to keep the mood light. Williams, who had lost 20 pounds since *The Fisher King*, was often the target of his own humour as he pranced around in his green tights. And, just as he did in *The Fisher King*, he would entertain the cast and crew, especially the large numbers of child actors, with impromptu comedy spots between takes.

Still the film continued to run beyond its schedule. Studio bosses at TriStar were beginning to get nervous. The film was due to stop shooting at the end of July, but Spielberg told them he would need to shoot until at least the middle of August. This caused more pressure, because Hoffman was required to do re-shoots for Disney on his gangster movie *Billy Bathgate*. If filming on *Hook* went much past the end of August, then

The surreal poster image for *Toys* (1992) evoked the work of surrealist artist René Magritte, but in the end the film was too much of an indulgence on behalf of Barry Levinson for a talented cast including Williams, Joan Cusack and Michael Gambon to save.

A family moment. Robin and Marsha
with Zachary and Zelda in 1992.
After Zelda was born, Williams
promised if they had more children
there would be 'no more Zs'. Their
next child was Cody.

Robin Williams as the modern Hector,
one of five characters he played in Bill
Forsyth's rarely-seen *Being Human*
(released 1994). Forsyth's Scottish
accent gave Williams the inspiration
for the voice of his next screen
incarnation Iphagenia Doubtfire.

Robin Williams takes a breather
on the front stoop of the Hillard
household in *Mrs Doubtfire* (1993).
Williams frequently went out into
the street dressed in character just
to see how people would react.

The last of his lost boy roles – or so he claimed. Robin Williams as the grown up Allan Parrish in *Jumanji* (1995).

Robin Williams chose to play the straight role of Armand in the gay comedy *The Birdcage* (1996). He felt he had already done the drag stuff in *Mrs Doubtfire* and there were more possibilities with Armand. He was right.

Robin Williams and two drag queens at the post-première party for *The Birdcage* (1996). Although he has often been criticized for his camp caricatures Williams has been a strong and vocal advocate on behalf of gay rights.

No really, this is the last of the man-child roles. Williams allowed his friend Francis Ford Coppola to talk him into doing *Jack* (1996) but the lukewarm response suggested that Williams' instincts were right. It was time to move on.

Robin Williams with his best friend Billy Crystal. Having not worked together on film before, they ended up doing three movies together – *Hamlet, Father's Day* and *Deconstructing Harry* – inside a year (1997).

Robin Williams, man of the people. Williams is mobbed at the video launch of *Aladdin and the King of Thieves* (July, 1996). He agreed to voice the genie again after settling his differences with Disney.

Two masters of their craft. Williams took a small role in *Deconstructing Harry* just so he could watch Woody Allen work.

Williams and Matt Damon on Boston Common in *Good Will Hunting* (1997). This emotional speech is one of the key scenes in the movie and went a long way to landing the Best Supporting Actor Oscar for Williams.

One for all and all for a good cause. Billy Crystal, Whoopi Goldberg and Robin Williams at *Comic Relief 1998*.

A nervous Robin Williams brought his wife Marsha and his mother Laurie to the 1998 Academy Award ceremony for some moral support.

Williams and his fellow *Good Will Hunting* Oscar winners Matt Damon (left) and Ben Affleck celebrate backstage. Williams probably still wants to see some ID.

This one's for you Dad. Williams backstage at the Academy Awards when he dedicated his win for *Good Will Hunting* to his late father, Robert.

Williams with co-stars Cuba Gooding Jnr and Anabella Sciorra pose for the waiting photographers as they promote *What Dreams May Come* (1998) at Cannes.

Hoffman might not be available. The TriStar executives' anxiety was compounded by the fact that they still had not seen much evidence of what they were getting for their money. Spielberg had a clause in his contract which said they could not see daily rushes or assembled footage until he was ready. He did, however, reassure them that he was no stranger to this kind of pressure since he became used to tight deadlines on all three *Indiana Jones* pictures.

Williams' reaction to the pressure was similar to that of the rest of the cast. He chose to ignore it. 'I don't even ask,' he said in reply to a question about the rising cost of the film. 'I don't want to know. I just don't want that pressure. You can't go around worrying about the cost of the movie. No one took any money up front. We said, "Okay, we'll take it in the back end. We don't want to add any more to this".'

Williams clearly felt that he and Spielberg, Hoffman and Roberts had done their bit for the budget. Their only other responsibility was to make the best film they could. There are obvious parallels to be drawn between Williams' own childhood, in which he enjoyed a full and rich fantasy life, and Peter Pan himself. Peter Banning was the first of a number of man-child roles in which Williams would find himself locked over the next few years. But the notion of a lost childhood was reinforced not long before the film opened. On 25 November in San Francisco, Marsha Williams gave birth to their second child, a boy named Cody. As the film opened, it was inevitable that Williams' thoughts would turn to childhood and family.

> I believe childhood is a very precious time [he said], and I don't want to miss it with my children because I did miss it with my father. He was out working all the time and was always off round the country. So I didn't get a chance to see him very much and I miss that. I'm trying not to do the same thing with my children, and you have to balance it because it's a very precious thing. The line that sums it up in the movie is when Peter's wife says 'Don't miss it, because it's gone'. They only want to be with you up to a certain point, and they're basically looking at you going 'You're an asshole'. You have that time, maybe five or six years, when they want to know you and play with you and share with you. Then they start to grow away from you through biological necessity. I don't want to miss that with my children, but I did miss it as a child. My father loved me dearly, but I didn't spend time with him.

But Williams also conceded that, given what he does for a living, the magic of childhood may not last quite as long as in some other families.

My son [Zach] is eight now [he said at the time], and he saw *Hook*. The first
time I fly he turned to me and said, 'That's blue-screen. Right, Dad?' And I
said 'Yeah'. So his sense of wonder is tempered by this heavy knowledge of
all the technical stuff. But when my daughter saw it she just went 'Wow'.
You get to experience that again, you get to see the world again through her,
which is just wonderful.

TriStar chose an unconventional date to open *Hook*. It was released on
Wednesday, 11 December, with special previews the previous evening.
On the Tuesday night and the Wednesday the film took just over $2
million and the studios pronounced themselves thrilled. However, there
were others who decided to reserve judgement until the opening weekend
figures were in. By the following Monday, *Hook* had taken $14.2 million
from its opening weekend and $17.7 million in its first six days. Although
it was the clear box-office number one – taking almost twice as much as
Star Trek VI: The Undiscovered Country in second place – the figures were
still disappointing. There were some industry sources who called the film
'*Hudson Hook*', a reference to the financially disastrous Bruce Willis film
Hudson Hawk. That was overstating the case, but there is no doubt that
the figures were not as high as TriStar had been expecting. One factor
working against the film was its length – it ran for 144 minutes – which
reduced the number of screenings cinemas could have in a day. Nonetheless the film was by no means a flop; the figures were solid if unspectacular. Ultimately TriStar had the last laugh after all. *Hook* turned out to
have unexpected legs, and audiences defied the indifferent reviews to
come out and see it. By the end of its run in the United States it had taken
a respectable $119.7 million. It did even better in overseas markets, and
when foreign grosses were taken into account the film took almost $300
million world-wide. It then went on to be a huge hit on video, selling
millions of units and earning even more money.

By the time he had finished his chores on *Hook* both in terms of filming
and his round of publicity interviews, Robin Williams simply wanted to
go home to San Francisco. He had a new house and he wanted to spend
time with his new family.

This place is strange for me [he said of Los Angeles]. It's a fantasy life, just
very surreal . . . When you're in LA for more than a month, you bump into
your career too much. You start reading the trades, looking for your name.
You get paranoid about how you're doing. We're living in this rented house
in Bel Air . . . There's a gate, a little beeper, a guy that comes if you press the
beeper. What is that? Is that the way it's supposed to be? No. But it's the

reality of the place and that's why I don't live there. People do pretty horrible business things to each other and still try and hang socially there. I don't come down and hang out there. The house we just bought in San Francisco is at the mouth of the Bay, and you go from there through this beautiful park and up along the western beaches. It's incredible. It's nice to have distance between you and the world.

28

The Genius of the Lamp

When a man turns 40 it's time to take stock of his life. Robin Williams celebrated this particular landmark on 21 July 1991, while he was still filming *Hook*. As she had done with almost everything else in his life recently, Marsha took charge and arranged a surprise party for her husband at the ranch in Sonoma. She also organised a special birthday book. As early as March she had contacted all of the people who were important in Robin Williams' life and asked them to contribute to a book of memories. The book was duly presented to him at the party in front of a gathering which included major showbusiness names such as Steven Spielberg, Bette Midler, Billy Crystal, John Travolta, Bobcat Goldthwait, Kirstie Alley and Joan Baez, as well as people such as Adrian Cronauer, Dan Holzman and Barry Friedman who had also played their part in Williams' career.

As he looked back over his life at the age of 40, Williams must have been pleased with what he had accomplished. In personal terms the demons of drink and drugs had been defeated, he had a stable and happy relationship with a new wife, and, as he was heading into 1992, he had three children in whom he delighted. In career terms he was one of the top ten box-office draws in the country – his films had collectively grossed almost $600 million at the box-office – and he was able to command up to $8 million a picture; more importantly, he was able to move freely between serious roles and dramatic roles with relative ease and take his audience with him. He had also had two Best Actor nominations and was just about to pick up a third.

Of all the performances he had given since his renaissance in *Good Morning Vietnam*, the best was undoubtedly *The Fisher King*. Williams brought to Parry a touching pathos which made his madness all the more poignant and believable to the audience, without becoming maudlin. It is a performance which contains a large amount of sentiment without ever being sentimental. There was no real surprise when Williams was again nominated in the Best Actor category – his third in five years – when the Academy Award nominations were announced in February 1992. His fellow nominees were Warren Beatty for *Bugsy*, Robert De Niro for *Cape Fear*, Anthony Hopkins for *The Silence of the Lambs*, and Nick Nolte for *The Prince of Tides*.

This time round there was no clear favourite in what was generally regarded as one of the most even Oscar races for some years. The pre-Oscar tips were Nolte and Beatty. Nolte had surprised everyone with the sensitivity of his performance in *The Prince of Tides*, and he had also turned in an exceptionally strong performance in *Cape Fear*. Beatty on the other hand seemed to have gone out of his way to court the Academy. His film was the nominations kingpin with ten nominations, and he himself had gathered 13 nominations over the years as actor, director, producer and writer but had won only once, as Best Director for *Reds* in 1981. Beatty had even ended his status as Hollywood's most eligible bachelor by marrying his *Bugsy* co-star Annette Bening, and becoming a father. Surely, it was argued, such a track record could not easily be ignored. Williams and De Niro were both in with a shout, but the fact that neither *The Fisher King* nor *Cape Fear* had a Best Picture nomination might count against them. The only thing that was certain, according to Hollywood gossip, was that Anthony Hopkins had no chance. For one thing *The Silence of the Lambs* was perceived as a horror film – a category consistently ignored by the Academy – and for another it had been released in February of the previous year, six weeks before the last Oscars. In any event, after wins for Daniel Day-Lewis and Jeremy Irons in the two previous years it seemed unlikely that Oscar would leave the States three times in a row.

On the night, however, it was Hopkins, the rank outsider, who triumphed in what turned out to be a clean sweep for *The Silence of the Lambs*, which became the first film to take the five big awards – picture, director, actor, actress and screenplay – since *One Flew Over the Cuckoo's Nest* in 1975. Hopkins was as astonished as anyone. He was convinced that Nolte would win, but he admitted to having worn his lucky shoes just in case. For Robin Williams there was yet more disappointment. It was obviously easier for a camel to pass through the eye of a needle than for a former TV star and a comic to be recognised by the Academy.

By the time the Oscars had come around, Williams had almost completed another film. As he had said he would when he announced he was doing *Hook*, Williams had gone on from there to be reunited with his *Good Morning Vietnam* director Barry Levinson in *Toys*. Levinson had originally intended *Toys*, which he co-wrote with Jane Curtin, to be his début picture. It had been bought by Fox in 1978 on the understanding that he would direct it. But there was the inevitable change of studio regime and the new management didn't think the script was funny enough.

'Studio executives didn't know how to respond to it,' says Levinson, 'because they can't think of any other that it's like.'

Instead of making *Toys*, Levinson then went ahead and wrote and directed the seminal *Diner*, while *Toys* languished in Development Hell. It came close to being produced at Columbia, who wanted to make it with Levinson and Williams immediately after *Good Morning Vietnam*. But by the time the Vietnam comedy was finished, Columbia boss David Puttnam had left. The film would turn up from time to time in articles about Hollywood's best unproduced scripts, and that seemed to be where it would remain. Now, however, with the considerable combined clout of both Williams and Levinson the film was finally going into production. For Williams it was the chance to go back and do comedy after a lengthy absence.

> *The Fisher King* had some comedy, there was none in *Awakenings*, *Hook* has a few funny lines [he says]. It's nice to change the parameters and go against what people expect sometimes. It was nice to do *Dead Poets* because it suddenly allowed me much greater room to move. *Dead Poets Society* allowed me to do something like *Awakenings* because De Niro saw it and suggested I star with him. It gives me a much broader range, so that I can then go back and do the *Good Morning Vietnam* kind of thing, which is what I'm doing with *Toys*.

During pre-production for *Toys* Williams managed to squeeze in another memorable TV performance. Johnny Carson was retiring in May 1992 after 30 years as America's best-loved chat-show host on *The Tonight Show*. Carson, no mean comedian himself, was the king of late-night TV and Williams was one of his most favoured guests. In his final week on air Carson asked back some of his favourites. He had no studio guests for his farewell show, therefore the most important show of the week would be his second last. The show was broadcast on 21 May 1992 and Carson's guests were Robin Williams and Bette Midler. The programme aired not long after the Rodney King riots in Los Angeles, and Williams was on devastating form. He and Carson played off each other and each frequently reduced the other to tears of laughter. It was one of Carson's best interviews and it seemed appropriate that the best had been kept till last.

In *Toys*, Williams plays Lesley Zevo, son of a great toymaker – played by Donald O'Connor – who has to fight for the factory's future after his father dies. His uncle, a former military man played by Michael Gambon, takes over the company. All he wants to make are war toys until he then gets the idea of manufacturing war toys that shoot real bullets. Williams then has to enlist the aid of his sister, played by Joan Cusack, and some of the more peaceable toys to regain control of the family firm and his legacy.

Williams describes Gambon's character as 'F.A.O. Schwartzkopf', but behind the quick-witted pun on the world's most famous toy store, it's obvious that the strong anti-war message would have appealed to him. He was also delighted to be working with Hollywood legend Donald O'Connor, who plays his screen father before dying early in the film. Williams was so delighted to be working with O'Connor that he sent him a note when shooting was finished, thanking him for being 'such a great stiff'.

When Levinson originally conceived *Toys* almost 15 years previously, it had included ground-breaking ideas such as virtual reality and other concepts which were barely thought of at the time. Even if the finished film did not incorporate virtual reality itself, Levinson's wildly surreal vision was breathtaking to look at, but at the same time almost swallowed the actors whole. Williams was not alone in struggling to make an impact in a film which was a triumph of design over content. Bizarrely, given that it was Levinson who had finally provided an outlet for his comic potential in *Good Morning Vietnam*, Williams remains firmly shackled here by a very sentimental and cloying screenplay. Only once, in the scene where he delivers a pep talk to a series of nursery toys before the final battle for control of the company, is he allowed to cut loose. Williams' verbal gymnastics in that scene alone make you pine for what might have been had he been encouraged to do more.

Toys was aimed at the lucrative Christmas market. It was released in December 1992 to poor reviews and even worse box-office. The film ended up taking only $23.3 million at American cinemas, Williams' poorest return since he had originally teamed with Levinson for *Good Morning Vietnam*. But, bizarrely, even as *Toys* was flopping, Williams was already at the top of the box-office charts with another film.

Towards the end of shooting on *Hook,* Williams got a call from Jeffrey Katzenberg's office at Disney. Would he, wondered the Disney chairman, make some time to come over and have a look at some footage which they were putting together? Williams, a long-time animation fan, was intrigued and readily agreed. So, on a day off from *Hook,* he went across to Disney to meet animation directors Ron Clements and John Musker and animator Eric Goldberg. What they had to show him resulted in the most successful and popular role of Williams' career to date, as well as one which would plunge him into a bitter wrangle with the studio which had resurrected his career.

In April 1991, the Disney animation department was in the depths of despair. They had just screened an eight-minute black-and-white assembly of their new animated film. *Aladdin* was supposed to complete the 'fairy tale trilogy' of *The Little Mermaid* and *Beauty and the Beast.* But the consensus was that this version just didn't work. After a final viewing from Katzenberg the order came down to scrap it and start all over again.

Part of the problem was that the film simply didn't look right. The solution came from British animator Eric Goldberg, who was working on the genie. He had been searching every reference source he could find to come up with a look which would work on the genie. Almost by accident he came across the work of Al Hirschfeld, the brilliant caricaturist who can take an elongated curve and turn it into the most devastatingly accurate caricature. Goldberg started to work on the genie à la Hirschfeld and quickly realised that he had found the key. Using Hirschfeld as his starting-point, Goldberg came up with an elongated S shape which took the genie from being a puff of smoke coming out of the spout of Aladdin's lamp into a big-headed, lantern-jawed, sharp-witted comedy slave. This elongated S became the template for the rest of the design, and *Aladdin* was very quickly back in business.

As far as Clements and Musker, who had been responsible for *The Little Mermaid,* were concerned, there was only one person who could voice the genie. They had written the character with Robin Williams in mind, hoping that his quicksilver wit could be transformed into equally mercurial animation. Goldberg, who was in charge of animating the genie, agreed with Clements and Musker, but there were others who were less enthusiastic. Goldberg then went away and quietly assembled what amounted to a virtual screen test by taking samples of Williams' comedy and animating the genie to them. When Williams came over to Disney that late spring day in 1991, what he saw was the genie performing magic with his voice.

There was one bit [recalls Goldberg], where he said 'Tonight I'd like to talk to you about schizophrenia'. Then another voice would say 'No he doesn't. Shut up'. To illustrate that I had the genie grow a second head to argue with himself, so we could see how far we could take that approach to the character ... He [Williams] laughed his guts out. It was clear to him that we weren't going to take his comedy and make a mess of it.

Williams was convinced and, with the studio bosses, who had already seen the footage, equally certain, he became an enthusiastic conspirator in the comic mayhem of *Aladdin*. Williams already had some experience of animation. He had provided the voice for Batty Koda, a spaced-out, not too tightly wrapped bat in *FernGully ... The Last Rain Forest*. But that was nothing like this. This was Disney. At this stage the genie was still not much more than a minor supporting character, but the more Williams did, the more the character grew. In the end he recorded about 30 hours of material, which encouraged Disney to change the entire focus of the film and turn the genie into a major character. One of the improvisational techniques during their recording sessions echoed Williams' own days on the road. He would come into a studio and find a lot of props covered in sheets. Williams never knew what they were until the sheets were taken away and, just as he used to do with his box of toys on-stage, he would improvise at length once the sheets were taken away. Every utterance was transcribed and passed on to the animators, who would then use it to craft sequences such as Williams' show-stopping song *A Friend Like Me*. In that one song alone he becomes Arnold Schwarzenegger, Jack Nicholson, a kilted Scotsman, a Scottie dog, Ed Sullivan, a sheep, and – in a nod to the classic comedy show *Let's Make a Deal* – Groucho Marx and his prop duck.

'We weren't sure whether Robin was going to bring out his whole bag of tricks,' says Goldberg, 'but he did. So for the funny stuff I had to go as visually nuts as possible.'

Williams had become more excited about *Aladdin* than any project in recent memory. Part of the reason was that he was now the father of young children, and he saw in this movie the chance to leave a permanent legacy for them and for future generations. It was a way of giving something back to them for the joy they had brought him and he went more than the extra yard for Disney. For one thing there was no question of him charging anything like his normal seven-figure fee. He said he would do the job for the union rate – around $75,000 – the only proviso he made being that Disney should not exploit his name or his voice in their advertising. Disney were more than happy to agree. But the agreement

didn't seem to last very long and one day when Williams was watching
television he saw a TV commercial using his voice as the genie to sell
Disney merchandise. Williams had consistently turned down offers to
endorse products. The hamburger chain McDonald's were apparently
keen for him simply to name his price but he has always said no. His
father's experience with the car industry has left him very cagey about his
dealings with corporate America.

> It wasn't as if we hadn't set it out [recalls Williams of his deal with Disney].
> I don't want to sell stuff. It's the one thing I won't do. In *Mork and Mindy*
> they made Mork dolls – I didn't mind the dolls; the image is theirs. But the
> voice is me. I gave them [Disney] my self. When it happened I said to them
> 'You know I don't do that'. And they apologised; they said it was done by
> other people.

Williams was not satisfied with the explanation. He felt that a deal was a
deal and that Disney had broken their end of the agreement. The ill feeling
deepened when *Aladdin* was released in November 1992 – a month before
Toys – and went on to become the most successful film in Disney's history.
There was no doubt in the minds of many people that the film's success
was entirely down to Williams' extraordinary vocal performance. *Aladdin*
took $217.4 million in the United States alone. It then went on to sell 15
million copies in its first month in video release. Analysts estimate that
by the time revenues from international exhibition and ancillary sales are
added in, the film could have made around $750 million for Disney. Most
of this was clear profit for Disney, because once the production and
advertising costs have been taken into account the rest is a massive wind-
fall for the company, with no profit participation for the artists involved.

Williams was still smarting from the breach of the agreement not to
use his voice, which he felt was a betrayal, but his fellow actors were
aggrieved on his behalf at Disney's refusal to pay a bonus. There was, it
was pointed out, a clear precedent. After *Pretty Woman* had been a huge
success, Julia Roberts – who like Williams had no profit participation
agreement – was given an *ex gratia* bonus of $750,000. *Pretty Woman*
made $300 million for Disney, less than half what *Aladdin* was coining in
for them. Various industry sources put different figures on the amount
they felt was morally due to Williams. These ranged from $10 million to
$25 million, and none of them seemed excessive. But Williams' old friend
and *Awakenings* director Penny Marshall summed it up. 'I'd give him
whatever he wants,' she said, 'because he doesn't want that much.'

Marshall was quite correct. The money was not important to Williams who is not, by all accounts, materially obsessed. There was a principle at stake here and he had learned from his father that principles are more important than almost anything. It may have been that, whereas Disney had felt an obligation to Julia Roberts, they felt no such duty to Williams because in producing *Good Morning Vietnam* when no one else wanted it they had effectively given him his career. However, the longer the row went on the more damage was being done. When Williams was awarded a special Golden Globe award, for example, Disney, unbelievably in the light of the row, included it in a new wave of advertising for *Aladdin*.

'The mouse only has four fingers,' said Williams in one stinging rejoinder. 'It can't write a cheque.'

Disney eventually sent Williams a Picasso which is reportedly valued at more than $1 million as a peace offering. Williams accepted the painting – one in which Picasso imagines himself as Van Gogh – and it hangs in the living-room of his San Francisco home. But the damage had been done. He swore he would never make another film for Disney. He remained true to his word even when Joe Roth took over Disney's films division. Roth had come from Fox and was not involved in the *Aladdin* débâcle. Nonetheless, when he sent Williams a script, Williams returned it with a note saying that he knew that Roth was a very nice man but he still had a problem with the studio.

It was Roth who finally ended the feud almost four years after *Aladdin*. The movie had spawned a straight-to-video sequel, *The Return of Jafar*, in which Dan Castellaneta, the voice of Homer in *The Simpsons*, provided the voice of the genie. When Roth took over at Disney he was looking over the books and was astonished to find that, even without Robin Williams, *The Return of Jafar* had generated more profit for Disney than *Pretty Woman*. Almost immediately Roth called Williams to apologise in person for the way in which his original agreement had been breached. Disney then put out a press release to that effect. The *rapprochement* was sealed when Williams agreed to reprise his role as the genie in 1996 in another straight-to-video movie, *Aladdin and The King of Thieves*. Not surprisingly it was a huge international success.

'We made up,' said Williams succinctly some time afterwards. 'They apologised and that was all I wanted. They basically said, "We screwed him. Yes, we put out negative press and we're sorry." I said, "Thank you, you're a mensch, welcome back."

'That's all I wanted and they did it, and they did it publicly.'

29

There's No Face like Foam

Even though they had been married for more than three years, Robin and Marsha Williams were still the subjects of a whispering campaign. If he had ever doubted it before, Williams was very definitely being made aware of the fact that mud sticks. The mud which had been thrown by that *People* magazine cover story was sticking like glue. In almost every major interview, in almost every magazine profile, there was the mention of Marsha having been Zachary's nanny and – by implication, however veiled – the woman who wrecked Robin Williams' life. It would be fair to say that, in some quarters at least, Marsha Williams was still regarded with caution if not downright suspicion.

The whispering campaign intensified after an article in *The New Yorker* magazine in September 1993. The article was a profile piece on Marsha as she made her début as a producer. The tone, however, was unfortunate to say the least. Journalist Lillian Ross depicted Marsha as some kind of *über*-producer and supermom; a cross between Martha Stewart and D. W. Griffith. This was heady stuff for a woman without a single production credit to her name, and when it emerged that Ross's son Steven was a production secretary on the film the rumours flew thick and fast.

Marsha Williams had become used to defending herself in public and this was no exception.

First of all, it was something I really didn't solicit or want [she insisted]. I'm really pretty uncomfortable being interviewed and try to stay away from it ... Personally I was a bit offended for Lillian that one would reduce her writing to thinking that she would come out of retirement because her son answered phones on the production for a couple of weeks and that she could write a flattering piece as a result. I'm going to get a lot more trash and, frankly, I'm not thrilled about it. The first set of press that came out when Robin and I were together was horrible for my parents. It's like a feeding frenzy; they're looking for dirt.

The project which had put Marsha Williams back in the firing line was the film which would be the most successful of her husband's career, *Mrs Doubtfire*. Marsha Williams had read the original children's novel, *Alias Madame Doubtfire* by Anne Fine, some years previously and saw it as the perfect vehicle for Robin Williams. The book tells the story of a struggling actor who is divorced by his wife and loses custody of his children. He may be a lousy husband, but he is still a devoted father and will do anything to stay in touch with his children, even if it means impersonating an elderly woman so he can get a job baby-sitting his own kids. The book had been optioned by Fox but, with no producer attached, it was offered to Marsha to develop. The first thing she did was to form a production company, something they had both been talking about for some time. So, Blue Wolf was set up – Marsha Williams says the name is inspired by her husband, 'the blue-eyed wolf' – with *Mrs Doubtfire* as its first production.

It doesn't take much of a stretch of the imagination to see some parallels between the Williams's own life and the story in the film. Marsha Williams is adamant that it simply never occurred to her.

I never thought about it [she said at the time]. I can't think about what connections people are going to make. But there was a piece in a small movie magazine I saw recently. It talked about *Mrs Doubtfire* and then said, 'Are we the only movie magazine in America that noticed the parallel between Robin Williams' role and Marsha Garces Williams' role as nanny to the Williams clan?' But I was nanny to Zachary before we were involved, so what's the parallel? ... The thing for me that is sort of curious is that, had Robin picked me up in a bar, would that have made me a better choice? I have had 15 jobs in my life, and being a nanny was one.

Now being a producer was another, with both Robin and Marsha Williams receiving screen credits on *Mrs Doubtfire*. Although this was her first official job as a producer, Marsha Williams had been doing a similar job on a *de facto* basis for a long time.

'Actually, what I'm doing is to a great extent what I've been doing with Robin for several years,' she explained. 'I've been reading scripts for him, looking into possible projects, and giving him my opinions about all of it when he asks me. He doesn't always agree with me, and there have been movies he has embarked on without paying any attention to what I thought, but I've supported him in whatever decisions he's made.'

Marsha Williams had been around movie sets since *Good Morning Vietnam* and had been able to watch some highly effective producers at work. She had also worked closely with Robin on writing, rewriting and researching.

'She waded right into it,' says Williams of his wife's new job. 'She likes the challenge of producing. My name is on *Mrs Doubtfire* as producer, and we talk to each other about everything, but she does most of the work, and all that talking with other people. She has the patience to discuss a problem for hours and hours. I have to be busy preparing for my part. I tend to be more direct. I'll just say "That sucks".'

In making *Mrs Doubtfire*, Williams teamed up with another San Francisco resident, Chris Columbus. Columbus was a hugely successful director who had made his name with *Home Alone*, the most successful comedy in film history. He and Williams hit it off immediately when they met and they both had similar reasons for making the film. Columbus felt the film stressed the importance of family and he believes that they both made the film as a way of atoning for the amount of time they had each spent away from their children pursuing their careers. Both men agreed that the look of the character was vital to the success of the film. 'In the film,' says Columbus, 'if Robin's character doesn't fool the woman he'd been married to for 14 years, she won't hire him – and there's no movie.'

The key to Mrs Doubtfire herself came in the make-up and the costume. Williams had to draw once again on his experience at Juilliard, where he had taken a mask class in which they would put on masks and become a character.

It was like the costume of dreams [he joked about his Mrs Doubtfire make-up]. If you wear it she will come. Once I put the mask on – it wasn't really a mask, it was twelve separate pieces that took four hours to fit. Once that was on, plus the body suit, plus the orthopaedic socks and everything else, plus the frock and the sweaters, she started to emerge. The first thing was learning to relax your body a little bit in the walk, and to walk in those heels. To get the gravity of all that helped. The first make-up test we did was with a make-up which was very real, but she had so many liver spots she looked like a Jack Daniels poster child. We had to tone her down and give her that look you see in old Scottish ladies from Inverness who look like they're lit from within – especially after a couple of Glenfiddichs. We just tried to give her that softness, just as people see her, and they started to relate to her as an aunt or a relative.

Perhaps more than any of his other films, *Mrs Doubtfire* gave Williams the chance to combine comedy and drama very effectively. Mrs Doubtfire herself doesn't come into the film for more than half an hour, leaving Williams plenty of screen time to make an impression as the doting but feckless Daniel Hillard. Once she appears, however, it allows Williams to cut loose with both vocal and physical improvisation which makes the most of the man inside the woman. Finding the right voice for his *alter ego* had been somewhat problematic. Williams had experimented with a number of accents but nothing seemed quite right. Eventually the Scottish accent emerged as a result of Williams having spent months working with Glasgow film-maker Bill Forsyth on *Being Human*, a film which would be released after *Mrs Doubtfire*.

'The accent was in the back of my mind from working with Bill for four and a half months,' Williams recalls. 'Also, I had these teeth, kind of Julia Childs teeth, the kind that take you over. The first couple of tries sounded like Margaret Thatcher on steroids, then we pulled it back and softened it up a little bit.'

Although Mrs Doubtfire was supposed to be English rather than Scottish, Williams points out that most American audiences can't tell the difference. However, the choice of accent is appropriate since for years there had been a persistent rumour that Williams had been born in Edinburgh rather than Chicago.

'I think the story about me being from Edinburgh came about from an interview I did way before *Mork and Mindy*,' he explains. 'I was kidding with someone, a local paper reporter who was interviewing me, and I think he assumed because of the way I spoke I was from Edinburgh. I thought that was great. Sure, I performed once at the Festival, but he must have been on a lot of medication or something because he wrote that I was born there.'

The effect of transforming the chunky hirsute actor into a woman with whom you would cheerfully leave your children was quite remarkable. Chris Columbus compares the experience to a kind of multiple personality disorder: 'For me it was like working with two different actors. There were days when I worked with Robin and days when I worked with Mrs Doubtfire. It wasn't until the end of the shoot that I really started to treat her like Robin. Before that, whenever she came on to the set, everyone was a little more gentle with her, and I could almost feel myself wanting to help her across the street.'

Williams too noticed the change in the way people related to him and related to his character.

It's a weird thing [he says], the cast and crew treated her with a sort of genteelness, even though the big air-conditioner I had to blow cool air up my skirt was a bit of a give-away. But they would literally walk me in and make sure everything was all right for me. The reality came when I would wander off the set in full make-up and saw how other people treat older women in America. It's different. There are people who are very nice, but also there's a strange kind of neglect that you pick up once in a while. You'd be standing there and feel that no one would ever come and help you if you needed it. That only happened once in a while. We shot in a place called North Beach in San Francisco which was the closest thing they had to a red light district. I walked into a sex shop one day as Mrs Doubtfire and actually tried to buy a vibrator. The guy went with me for a few minutes until he made the connection with my eyes or something. It was great wandering off as her, the make-up was so good that it held up that way.

Mrs Doubtfire was released on 24 November 1993 to catch the Thanksgiving weekend which is the start of a highly lucrative six-week box-office window going through to the Christmas holidays. The film was a huge success with both public and critics and ended up grossing $219.2 million in the United States – a shade more than *Aladdin*, although the Disney movie grossed more in the long run once ancillary sales were taken into account. But not everyone was happy with the film. The then Vice-President Dan Quayle, who had previously taken Murphy Brown to task for becoming an unmarried mother, was unhappy with the film. The fact that Murphy Brown was a fictitious TV anchorwoman played by Candice Bergen seemed to have slipped past Quayle. However, he felt that *Mrs Doubtfire* was sending a negative message about family values.

Happy Dan has that Norman Rockwell painting view of American values [said a dismissive Williams]. The reality is that there are a lot of families that aren't necessarily first families, or families like Dan's ... the idea was that a family doesn't end with divorce. The reality in America – sad but true – is that it [divorce] is up to about 60 per cent, maybe higher, so second families move on from there. To have shown it as otherwise would have been a negative fantasy. It is a negative fantasy for a lot of therapists who work with children of divorced couples, because a child immediately thinks that the parents are going to get back together. Once they've established that they don't love each other but they love him, then it's something to work towards. That's the reality in America.

As a divorced father himself Williams knows whereof he speaks. Although his own split from Valerie Velardi was civilised, with no custody battles, there are moments when Daniel Hillard, the character he plays in the film, mirrors his own relationship with Zachary. And he admits that on occasion he did draw from life in his characterisation.

'What I wanted to do was just to try to put across something that my therapist was saying to me after my divorce,' he explains. 'Just focus on your child. Try and make things better for him. That's the only thing I bring to it.'

One of the things which so exercised Dan Quayle was the way the film ended. Daniel has forged a new relationship with his children as Mrs Doubtfire, and that relationship is strengthened when they discover his secret and realise how much he loves them. However, this is not the cue for a conventional happy ending. The film has an epilogue of sorts which shows that Daniel and his wife, played by Sally Field, do not get back together again. Instead their children have two parents who love them but simply choose to live apart. This epilogue was not in the original script from Randi Mayem Singer and Leslie Dixon. It was added in a director's rewrite by Chris Columbus with the full support of Robin Williams.

I think it's important that when kids see this picture they realise we aren't giving them a dishonest ending [says Columbus]. The parents don't get back together again, but we wanted kids to know that their family, if they come from a divorced family, was just as valid as the family next door with two parents. Also it was important that kids seeing this picture knew it wasn't their fault just because their parents got divorced ... In the original script Daniel and Miranda went off and got pizza together and reconciled. Robin, Marsha and I weren't interested in doing that kind of movie. We wanted a film which would be emotional where we could get a bit of a message across to kids.

30

Riddle Me This

From the moment he made his television début on *Mork and Mindy*, Robin Williams has been one of the entertainment industry's most endearing personalities. Audiences love him and this love is reflected in the roles he plays. Whether it's Adrian Cronauer, Peter Pan, Malcolm Sayer or Mrs Doubtfire, Williams does not play unsympathetic characters. For all that he talks about seeking variety in his work, it is only variety up to a point. He seems to want varied roles so long as they are varied likeable roles. Whether the audience would accept him as a villain is another matter entirely. Some actors, such as Morgan Freeman, have regrettably come to accept that their choice of roles is so inextricably linked with their screen persona that they simply cannot play a villain and take an audience with them. Robin Williams was perhaps reaching the same conclusion although, especially in the light of the success of *Mrs Doubtfire*, he did seem to be actively considering playing a villain.

> Anthony Hopkins said there is something very amazing when you play those characters [said Williams of villainous roles]. He said that even when he played Hitler there was an unexpected side that he found was very effeminate, and looking for those things was very interesting. That could be good for me, because I have been playing all these warm, giving characters. That's why in *Dead Again* it was nice to play this defrocked psychiatrist, who basically had his wires slightly crossed.

While no one seriously expected Williams to play Hitler, there was a hot

role in Hollywood which seemed to have his name written all over it –
and as an added bonus, it was a villain. The *Batman* franchise had become
a huge money-maker for Warner Brothers since Tim Burton brought the
character to the screen in 1989. *Batman*, in which Williams lost the role
of The Joker to Jack Nicholson, made $250 million in the United States
alone that summer. The sequel, *Batman Returns*, came along three years
later and took in $163 million. Warner, however, were unhappy with the
dark tone of the second film and wanted a lighter movie for the Caped
Crusader's third outing. Tim Burton was reluctant to go in that direction,
so he and Warner parted company over their creative differences and Joel
Schumacher was drafted in for the third film. With *Batman* star Michael
Keaton also leaving, the third film – *Batman Forever* – was the chance to
reboot the whole franchise. Val Kilmer took over as Batman, and this
time he would be battling evil in the form of The Riddler and Two-Face.
Tommy Lee Jones, fresh from his Oscar success on *The Fugitive*, was
pencilled in for Two-Face, and Robin Williams seemed tailor made for
the part of The Riddler. In terms of *Batman*'s rogues' gallery, The Riddler
was something of an oddity; he was not necessarily as dark as The Joker,
but his compulsion to leave clues in the form of riddles made him a much
quirkier character. Audiences knew him from Frank Gorshin's manic
characterisation on the *Batman* television series, and with that in mind
it seemed that this was the ideal role for Williams.

In public Williams was making all the right noises. 'I haven't read the
script but if it's one that I think I can play then I'd love to do it,' he said
when he was on the road promoting *Mrs Doubtfire*. 'I think I've played
enough nice characters so it's time to play a villain. The Riddler was
always a fascinating character in the comic books I've read. He's not as
menacing as some of the others, but he's more interesting. I'd love to play
it. If it was the right script, I'd do it in a second.'

While Williams was making positive noises, so too was Joel Schumacher, who conceded that in all probability Williams would play The
Riddler in *Batman Forever*. However, he insisted that nothing was definite
and even as he was saying so, Williams' management were denying that
anyone had been in touch about the role. Having been bitten once before,
Williams' agent was understandably reluctant to get drawn into any kind
of mating dance to allow his name to attract another actor to the movie.
Other actors had been mentioned – John Malkovich was considered for
a time – but it seemed that the role was Williams' if he wanted it.

While negotiations were going on – there was some dispute over Williams' $7 million fee, and the actor also wanted rewrites before he would
commit – another variable entered the equation in the shape of Jim

Carrey. Three smash-hit movies in a row with *Ace Ventura: Pet Detective,*
Dumb and Dumber and *The Mask* had turned the rubber-limbed Carrey
into Hollywood's hottest property. There wasn't a producer in town who
didn't want Carrey's name on a contract and Warner Brothers was no
different. On 2 June 1994 the shock announcement came that Robin
Williams was out of *Batman Forever* and Jim Carrey was in. Carrey would
be paid $5 million and apparently agreed to the role after only 30 minutes'
negotiation.

Williams made no direct comment at the time, but let it be known that
he had been unhappy with the script. He felt that the character in *Batman*
Forever was too intellectual and not as comedic as the character Gorshin
originated on television. He was also apparently concerned that The
Riddler would end up playing second banana to Tommy Lee Jones' Two-
Face. A few days later, however, Williams insisted that he had been ready
to play the part, only to discover that it was no longer on offer. Schumacher
for his part insisted that they simply became tired of waiting for Williams
to make up his mind and moved on accordingly.

Losing a role like this to Jim Carrey must have been a salutary experience for Williams. Carrey was the only actor in years who could rival
Williams for his verbal dexterity, and had the added bonus of incredible
physical comedy. Carrey was hotter than steam. His success put him on
the cover of *Newsweek* – the last comedian who had been there was
Williams himself almost ten years previously. Ironically, Carrey also lists
Williams as one of his biggest influences. But, even with the new kid in
town, Williams insisted there was more than enough room for both of
them.

> I think we do different things [he explained]. I think he does something
> quite unique and wonderful and I do something different. I'm still working,
> so as long as they don't say, 'I'm sorry, Robin, there's no more work for you.
> Jim has done everything and he's doing everything too. There are no more
> scripts for you, all comedy is Jim from now on. There'll be no more work
> for small hairy boys unless you want to do a musical of *Gorillas in the Mist*.'
> As long as they don't say that and I can do what I just did, then I'll be okay
> for a while. I appreciate what Jim does, it's great, and he does something so
> physical that it is wonderful. But I think there is room for different kinds of
> comedy.

While Robin Williams was losing the role of The Riddler to Jim Carrey,
audiences were seeing another side of him in American cinemas. Or
rather, a select few audiences were seeing another side of him. Williams

had spent a large part of the late summer of 1993 in Scotland filming *Being Human* with director Bill Forsyth. The film is a meditation on the nature of humanity and follows five men, all of whom are called Hector and all played by Robin Williams, through various periods of history. In the 6000-year span of the film Hector is variously a caveman, a Roman slave, a medieval Crusader, a sixteenth-century Portuguese nobleman, and finally a contemporary divorced New Yorker trying to be reconciled with his children.

Williams enjoyed the experience immensely. 'It's an unusual film,' he conceded. 'But it was a great thing to work on, especially with Bill. He makes wonderful strange movies. He just tries to get it exactly right.'

Marsha Williams was equally enthusiastic about the film. 'I see it as basically the realisation that after 6000 years we all still have the same needs,' she says. 'How have we evolved? The reality is we're still just human beings.'

Despite Robin Williams' enthusiasm, Warner Brothers, who had funded *Being Human,* were nowhere near as enthusiastic. The film that had been delivered by Forsyth was not what they had expected, although given Forsyth's track record of beautifully judged whimsical observation, how could they have expected anything different? They had spent $30 million on the film and despite extensive re-editing they were about to wash their hands of it. *Being Human* was eventually given a minimal release in the United States and Europe and not surprisingly sank without trace at the box-office. Those critics who did see it didn't think much of it, and audiences were simply not given the opportunity to make up their own minds.

The failure of *Being Human* did not matter a jot when it came to Robin Williams' pulling power in Hollywood. In box-office terms he was still anointed. He had starred in four films which had passed the magic $100 million mark – including two that broke the $200 million barrier – as well as starring in another which fell just short of the $100 million mark. Audiences loved him and, with a gap in his schedule after *Batman Forever* fell through, so did studios. Williams had been making noises about going back on-stage for a concert tour, especially after the gruelling business of filming *Mrs Doubtfire*. Live performance was becoming more and more appealing, especially after his recent hectic filming schedule. For Williams, performing on-stage was still the wellspring of his creativity.

Improvisation is total freedom [he says]. There's no dictating where or what you have to do. And it's a chance to use everything you know in one place. To do a Shakespearean play on George Bush – 'Neither a borrower nor a

Savings and Loan defaulter be' – you see, you have that freedom. No one
has to tell you. You can play with all that stuff. You can be anything you can
be.

But nothing was set in stone yet as far as a concert tour was concerned,
and if the right movie offer came along Williams could probably still be
tempted.

One likely offer which looked like succeeding was a film called *Crazy*,
which would have been produced by Ron Howard's Image company. The
film would also have reunited Williams with Mike Nichols, with whom
he had done *Waiting for Godot* at the Lincoln Center. Disney were also
making overtures, now that Jeffrey Katzenberg had left, to be replaced by
Joe Roth. Disney felt that Roth, who had given the go-ahead for *Mrs
Doubtfire*, might be the man to settle their increasingly embarrassing row
with Williams after *Aladdin*. Roth after all was the man who had been
responsible for Williams now being established in the $15 million a
picture bracket after the success of *Mrs Doubtfire*. Roth did indeed turn
out to be the peacemaker, but not just yet. In any event it's debatable
whether any amount of kissing and making up would have got Williams
interested in the project which Disney most wanted. They were keen for
a sequel to *Good Morning Vietnam* which would have put Adrian
Cronauer at the turbulent Democratic convention in Chicago in 1968.
The idea for the sequel came from Williams' manager Larry Brezner. Even
though he wasn't at the convention, Adrian Cronauer himself was keen
on doing another picture, which was tentatively titled *Good Morning
Chicago*.

The fly in the ointment was Williams himself, who was simply not keen
on the idea. 'They've written a couple of versions and they're getting
better,' he said, 'but why do a sequel unless you can do something quite
wonderful? You can't push it. The best sequels take the movie further. It's
also a hard call because the real man never went there, so now you're
fictionalising it.'

In the end Williams decided that his next film would be another family
comedy adventure. *Jumanji* is the story of Alan Parrish, a young boy who
is having a difficult relationship with his father. One evening he discovers
Jumanji, a strange board game with supernatural powers. The boy is
drawn into the game where he survives for more than 30 years until two
other children find the game and continue to play. Immediately the game
starts to manifest its bizarre powers and strange creatures begin to appear.
Amid all the weirdness the adult Alan Parrish, played by Williams, comes
back after being trapped inside the strange world of Jumanji for all that

time. Together the grown-up Alan and his new young friends have to play the game to its conclusion to save their town from being destroyed.

Jumanji is a special-effects romp directed by Joe Johnson, who had previously directed *Honey, I Shrunk the Kids*. For Williams there were once again parallels with his own life. How much of himself did he see in Alan Parrish, a little boy living alone in a big house with a stern and authoritarian father?

> I think maybe I was just possibly working out something from my own childhood [he admits]. Maybe I'm drawn to it because I sympathise with it. The character in *Jumanji* is an only child who gets picked on. I was that child who was picked on not only physically but intellectually too and it's like a whole other thing when you get both. But also there is a stage where you have to say 'Don't need to talk about that any more' and you can go on and play other characters.

Essentially *Jumanji* was a children's film. Williams abhors violence in real life, and as he grows older he admits to being drawn, just as he was with *Aladdin*, to films that he can take his own children to see. Unlike his earlier days Williams was now creating out of happiness rather than fear, and that was one of the overriding reasons for doing *Jumanji*.

> I love the fact that a film like *Mrs Doubtfire* can work for adults and children, [he says]. In *Aladdin* especially I used to get people coming up to me and going 'I was with my kid and I was laughing so much that my kid told me to shut up'. If the movie can be that funny, and there is stuff for children and there's stuff for you if you're there with your child, then that's great. It truly is a family film without being about talking down to children. You have to find something that works for both audiences, and that's why I do them. I do them because of my own children and for other people's children.

31

A Friend in Deed

In the life of actor Christopher Reeve, 15 September 1973 was an important date. At that stage Reeve was a prodigiously talented but still promising actor. International fame as Superman and with the Merchant-Ivory film-making partnership was still some years away. But on that autumn day when he turned up as an advanced student at the Juilliard school he met his fellow student – there were only two of them in the advanced group. Reeve remembers him as 'a short, stocky, long-haired fellow from Marin County, California, who wore tie-dyed shirts with track-suit bottoms and talked a mile a minute'. His classmate of course was Robin Williams. The two of them hit it off straight away and have remained close friends ever since. It was to Reeve that Williams would turn for advice for the lovelorn or just a kind word when he was feeling particularly miserable. It was also to Reeve that Williams turned when he thought he was about to make it big as Popeye, a role he hoped would do for him what Superman had done for his friend. There were no hidden agendas, no career points to be scored; Robin Williams and Christopher Reeve were simply as close as two friends could be.

More than 20 years after that first meeting, on 27 May 1995 the two friends had gone their separate ways in career terms. Williams was a household name with three Oscar nominations and a string of box-office hits to his name. Reeve was also a household name, but he had found the Superman tag a little difficult to shake off. The first three Superman films had been major successes, but the fourth one had done poorly at the box-office. Reeve was now carving out a new career on the stage and in character roles. On that day in May – Memorial Day weekend, the official start of summer in the United States – Reeve was indulging in another of his favourite pastimes. He had become passionate about horse-riding since he had had to learn it for a movie role some ten years earlier. Well and truly bitten by the bug, he had quickly become a passionate and accomplished equestrian. He was competing in a three-day event in Culpeper, Virginia on his favourite horse Eastern Express, which he had nicknamed Buck.

After the dressage round Reeve was handily placed and was looking forward to the cross-country event which was coming up next. Everything seemed to be going well and Buck took the first two fences with little difficulty. At the third fence, however, the horse simply stopped dead. Some reports said he had been startled by a rabbit, others that he had been spooked by some shadows. We will never be certain. What is certain is that the inevitability of Newtonian physics was demonstrated with sickening accuracy. Buck stopped and put his head down; Reeve, with nothing to stop him, went sailing over the horse's head. That would be bad enough, but normally a rider could try to do something to break his fall. Tragically and freakishly Reeve's hands were entangled in the bridle and he went crashing to the ground, taking the riding tack with him. Reeve landed on his head, breaking the first and second vertebrae in his neck. He was heard to say, 'I can't breathe.' Those were the last words he spoke until he woke up five days later in the University of Virginia hospital. Reeve had been flown there by helicopter when doctors at Culpeper realised that his injuries were so extensive they were well beyond the scope of their small hospital. He was paralysed, he could not breathe unaided, but all things considered he was lucky to be alive at all. The bones he had broken are the ones which are intended to be broken by a hangman's noose, causing almost instantaneous death.

The world was stunned by the news of Reeve's tragic accident. News bulletins the world over followed his progress during those first five days until he regained consciousness. His wife Dana never moved from his bedside, keeping vigil with his three children as he fought for his life. The news was also a devastating blow for Reeve's friends. Here was a man who was fit and vital and, at 43, in the prime of his life. This was a man who had made his name playing the most powerful man in the universe. But still he had been struck down suddenly and without warning. It was a powerful reminder if any were needed that celebrity does not automatically confer invulnerability.

When Robin Williams was told of his friend's accident he was shocked and stunned. When he finally discovered the extent of Reeve's injuries he was devastated almost beyond belief. The news was almost enough to tip him over into the sort of severe bout of depression he had not had for many years. 'When I heard about Chris that beat me up pretty bad,' he admits. 'Then I realised I couldn't be there for him like that. I had to be the friend that I had been before.'

Reeve, meanwhile, was still in hospital and still gravely ill. Doctors were waiting for him to recover his strength to the point where he would be strong enough to withstand a vital operation to reconnect his skull to his spine.

As he flitted in and out of consciousness he became aware of a new doctor in the room, one who appeared to be speaking with a strong Russian accent and a poor command of English. The new doctor was wearing a scrub hat and a surgical gown and he announced to the increasingly befuddled Reeve that he was his proctologist and that he had to conduct an immediate rectal examination.

'Five days after my accident I had a 50–50 chance to live,' Reeve would recall later. 'I was hanging upside down in a hospital bed and I looked and saw a blue scrub hat and a yellow gown and heard this Russian accent. There was Robin Williams being some insane Russian doctor.'

Robin Williams and Marsha had flown immediately from San Francisco to Virginia and quickly proved the old saw about laughter being the best medicine. 'I laughed,' Reeve recalls. 'And I knew for the first time I was going to be all right.'

There is no more passionate supporter of Reeve in his fight to regain the use of his legs than Robin Williams. If he was slightly in awe of Reeve's natural gifts when they were students together, he now yields to no one in his admiration of his friend's raw courage.

'How did he get through it?' Williams asks rhetorically. 'He has this amazing sense of purpose which drives him, and he gets through it with a sense of humour. His wife says he is the one who still uses phrases like "walk into the room". He's very focused on raising funds and raising consciousness.'

Nonetheless even the most optimistic scenario puts Reeve's recovery process at many years and at a cost of many millions of dollars. Williams' immediate aim was to get his friend off the respirator which had been helping him breathe. He was horrified to learn that a power cut near Reeve's home in Connecticut could have killed him had they not been able to hook up the respirator to a back-up generator. Williams has undoubtedly made some kind of direct financial contribution to Reeve's medical expenses as well as contributing his skills to the fund-raising efforts, but he is at pains to play down the extent of his involvement.

They [the media] put out this myth that we had made a blood oath in college to help one another [says Williams]. We didn't have that. I've done some things for him and I'll do others if he needs it. But the wonderful thing is that he is going to take care of himself. If he needs help I'll be there, but that's not to say that I have taken care of all of his medical expenses until the year 2010 or something. I haven't.

The story of the Reeve/Williams pact, which appears to have originated in the *Washington Post*, claimed that Williams had promised to pay his friend's medical expenses when his medical insurance ran out towards the end of 1995. It was the *Post* which pointed out that Reeve's annual medical bill was somewhere around the $400,000 mark, and claimed that 'if either made it in showbiz they would help the other in time of crisis'. Whether the story is true or not, and we must take Williams at his word, it nonetheless led to Robin Williams being praised in the US Senate.

Paul Simon, the senator for Williams' home state of Illinois, used his native son's example, however erroneously, as a stick to beat the Clinton administration's health policy. Taking the *Post* story at face value, Senator Simon praised Williams for his loyalty and generosity.

'I applaud what Robin Williams is doing,' he told the House. 'But something is wrong with our system when Robin Williams has to do that. And what about the millions of Americans who have no Robin Williams to help them? . . . Three cheers for Robin Williams! But three Bronx cheers [boos] for our short-sightedness in not protecting all of our citizens.'

Williams' reaction to Senator Simon's speech is not recorded, but it is likely to have been one of acute embarrassment. Williams was merely doing what he had been raised to do. He was helping a friend. He would do the same for Steven Spielberg when the director was shooting his Holocaust epic *Schindler's List*. At the end of a day spent recreating one of the most horrific and inglorious episodes in human history Spielberg would call Williams from the set in Poland and ask him to make him laugh. Williams would stay on the line no matter what the hour, telling jokes and doing 'schtick' until his friend had recovered his spirits sufficiently to tackle the next day's shooting.

Although Robin Williams and Christopher Reeve are not what you would call conventionally political animals, they are both driven by a strong sense of moral and social justice. It was this sense of decency and fairness which prompted Reeve to found The Creative Coalition in 1989. He set up TCC with two actor friends, Ron Silver and Susan Sarandon, as a lobby group to influence government policy on a number of issues including the environment, homelessness, funding of the arts and campaign funding reform. Every year TCC honours two people for their work in these fields. In January 1995, Reeve had told Williams that TCC wanted to honour him at its annual dinner in October for his work with Comic Relief, which was about to celebrate its tenth anniversary. Williams had agreed to accept the award, but it appeared that Reeve's accident a few months later had put paid to that plan. What only a handful of people, including Robin Williams, were privy to was that Christopher Reeve was planning on using that TCC annual dinner to re-enter public life.

Christopher Reeve was cheered to the echo as he was wheeled on-stage at the function room of the Hotel Pierre in Washington that October night. He was now in the process of coming off the ventilator and could speak haltingly through a 'sip-and-puff' process which involved taking in a small gulp of air and then speaking as he exhaled. Although he had forgotten to prepare anything, he managed to charm and entertain the audience of invited guests with a short but witty speech. He then introduced the main guest of the evening, Robin Williams.

In his inspiring and moving autobiography, *Still Me*, Reeve recalls that moment when Williams came on-stage and how effective his friend proved to be in normalising the situation.

> For the next twenty minutes he and I bounced off each other [recalls Reeve]. He took the curse off the wheelchair, going around behind it and pretending to adjust all the controls, referring to my breathing tube as a stylish new necktie and suggesting that I use the chair for a tractor pull. He told the audience that I had to be careful with the sip-and-puff control; if I blew too hard into the tube, I might pop a wheelie and blast off into the audience. The evening was transformed into a celebration of friendship and endurance.

His performance at that TCC gala may not have been the funniest in Robin Williams' career, but it was certainly one of the most meaningful. It re-established his friend as a man and not a cripple, and it was a typically warm and humane gesture by the comic. Williams remains uncompromising in his attitude towards Christopher Reeve. When people ask Williams how Reeve is doing, he will generally reply 'He's on a roll', just to watch the shock value. But Williams remains unstinting in his efforts. He and Reeve went to Puerto Rico together on a fund-raising trip for the American Paralysis Association in 1996, and in February 1998 Williams was one of the star guests at A Celebration of Hope, a gala evening in Los Angeles which raised more than a quarter of a million dollars for the Christopher Reeve Foundation.

'Tonight,' Williams told the glittering assemblage, 'we are here to help my friend and 250,000 other people get back on their feet again.'

It was a moving moment for a man who can frequently be moved to tears by the plight of others. When he spoke of Reeve in the early days after his accident it was not uncommon for Williams' eyes to fill with sadness. They are still prone to fill with tears, but these days they are prompted more by pride than anything else. To paraphrase the copy line from the first *Superman* film, he believes a man can walk.

Williams is an emotional man by nature, but especially where children are concerned. Steven Haft, who produced *Dead Poets Society*, recalls that his wife had a baby not long after Zelda Williams was born. As they were telling Robin and Marsha Williams the story of their own child's birth, Haft happened to mention that at one point in the delivery the nurse had to run out to deal with another mother whose baby was tragically stillborn.

'Robin and Marsha's first child had been born that year,' recalls Haft, 'and the story affected Robin so much he had to leave the room. A few minutes later I found him sitting by the crib, his hand on our son's back and tears streaming down his face.'

On the set of *Hook*, Williams was always available for child visitors. He was determined not to shatter the illusion of Peter Pan and would make time for the young tourists. He was also concerned that some of his co-stars, especially Julia Roberts who was going through a stressful period of her own, might not be able to give the youngsters the time he felt they deserved. Williams is also active in the StarBright Foundation, a charity which does its best to make wishes come true for terminally ill children.

Children respond to Williams' generosity of spirit. Their response is also very different and a good deal less hypocritical than the response he gets from some adults.

> They're very interesting and they're critical [says Williams]. They really let you know and it's wonderful when kids come up to you. I don't mind being Robert De Niro [from *Aladdin*] for a ten-year-old. It's really great that they respond. Before I went out to dinner with Chris one night I went to this thing at one of the hospitals for the StarBright Foundation. It's like a virtual world where these kids communicate with each other in different wards if they're in isolation. And all those kids came out about *Mrs Doubtfire* and the movies that affected them. One kid said he had seen *The Fisher King* when he was seven and it's wonderful when kids are affected like that. One child said he'd been in chemo for a while and he had watched *Aladdin* every day, twice a day and it had really helped him.
>
> They really want to hear the voice [he says of Mrs Doubtfire, who is

invariably the star of these private shows]. This little girl was at the hospital and they said 'He did *Jumanji*' and she went 'So'. And then they mentioned *Mrs Doubtfire* and I started to talk to her as Mrs D and she just started to laugh because the voice triggered something in her.

It's weird because sometimes kids will come up and do Jack Nicholson's voice from *Aladdin* and not even be aware of who they're doing.

32

The Lost Boy

Working in the film industry is a little like being in a different time zone on a semi-permanent basis. It can be particularly difficult for actors, who are the most conspicuous of the hired help in the film industry. A director can typically spend 18 months on a film from conception to final cut, and when he goes on the road to promote it, that is all he has to talk about. For some actors 18 months can encompass an entire career; Matt Damon, for example, went from being an unknown to a major player in less time. In the period that it takes a director to make one film an actor can make two or even three. Then, when the first of them is released and they have to do the publicity, they find themselves having to step back into a kind of time warp to try to remember what they were thinking about more than a year earlier in some cases.

That was exactly the situation in which Robin Williams found himself at the end of 1995 and beginning of 1996, when he was touring the world promoting *Jumanji*. Williams was well aware of the most frequently levelled criticism against him; namely that he was beginning to get stuck in a rut in his career choices. He had not been varying his roles of late, and after *Hook* and then *Jumanji*, and with the emotionally stunted Daniel Hillard in *Mrs Doubtfire* thrown in, he was becoming something of a poster boy for arrested development. *Jumanji* might possibly be the last time the audience would accept Williams as the man-child, no matter how well he did it.

'I think I have reached the limit,' he said. 'I think I have reached the end of the man-boy characters ... I think it was possibly just working something out from my childhood, but you reach a stage where you can play other characters.'

Quite why Williams wanted to work out these things from his childhood remains a mystery. He had been in therapy for a long time, since the break-up of his first marriage, and he must surely have addressed these issues many times in the privacy of the therapy sessions. Nonetheless he had been working it out and had realised that enough was enough. Williams claimed to be actively seeking other types of role. Indeed he was privately very pleased that he had just completed his first truly villainous performance. He had taken a small unbilled role – he was credited as 'George Spelvin' – in a film version of Joseph Conrad's novel *The Secret Agent.* Christopher Hampton was directing his own adaptation of the novel, and Williams had agreed to take a tiny role in a cast which included Bob Hoskins and Gérard Départieu. He was pleased with the end result and hoped it might help break the casting mould in which he was being set.

'I play the professor, the man who makes the bombs. It scared me quite deeply,' he said the morning after he had seen Conrad's political thriller for the first time. 'It was quite frightening and not warm in any way. I think it's time for me to play adults, no more cuddly folks.'

As it happened, no matter how convincing Williams is in *The Secret Agent* – and it is by no means a bad performance – it did him little good in career terms. The film, which was made by Twentieth Century Fox, was barely released in the United States and hardly anyone saw his first screen villain. Publicly Williams made no comment, but privately he must have been angry that a role which had been chosen with such care to enhance his dramatic range had been thrown into the cinematic dustbin. Ironically, however, when Williams was singing the praises of *The Secret Agent* while he was out promoting *Jumanji*, and when he was pledging to play more grown-up roles, he was just about to start work on his most obvious man-child role to date.

Francis Ford Coppola is one of the few genuine *auteurs* of American cinema. The first two parts of his *Godfather* trilogy are among the greatest American films ever made, and his Vietnam epic *Apocalypse Now* is an astonishingly surreal yet visceral look at the American involvement in Vietnam. But even icons have to eat. Coppola's films had not done especially well at the box-office recently and he had effectively become a director for hire. His version of *Dracula* was a success but it was scarcely his personal vision. Now he found himself working on a film which could only touch on his cinematic world view in the most tangential manner.

Coppola had signed on to direct *Jack*, a fantasy about a little boy with a rare but fictitious disease. This ailment means that he ages four years in biological terms for every calendar year. Hence by the time Jack is ten and in the fifth grade, he has the looks and physique of a 40-year-old man while still possessing the understanding and emotional maturity of a ten-year-old.

It's hardly surprising, given his recent track record, that Robin Williams was the first person the script went to. To his credit Williams did try to be true to his pledge about doing no more man-child roles. His initial response was a flat refusal. 'My first reaction was to say "No thanks, I've done this",' he recalls. 'But it was like they kept coming and then I kept saying "Please, I've done *Hook*, I've done *Jumanji*".'

Jack was being produced by Disney, but this had no effect on Williams' decision. As we have seen, Joe Roth's diplomatic courtship had paid off, and after Disney made a public apology Williams had willingly buried the hatchet. He bore no grudges and he wasn't deliberately holding out for more money or to make Disney squirm. He genuinely felt that there was nothing new that he could bring to the role. Disney, who were equally keen to have Williams back in their corporate fold, had one card left to play. They relied on Coppola's personal intercession. Williams and Coppola are neighbours in the Napa Valley, their properties backing on to each other. They are also partners in a San Francisco restaurant, The Rubicon, and they had been friends for 15 years. Williams had always wanted to work with Coppola and the feeling was mutual. The director went to work on his reluctant putative star and eventually wore him down.

> He started talking about it in a way that was very human [explains Williams]. I must say that I'm really glad that I went along for the ride. People might think that this movie is very bland, but it isn't. It talks about certain delicate things and there is a sadness to it. But it's what love is all about ... It's about reaching out and making connections, about relationships between adults and between kids ... It's a very human film and I'm very proud of it.

Filming *Jack* brought back memories of Williams' childhood both good and bad. In the early part of the film Jack is raised in virtual isolation from any other children, which must have recalled his own lonely early days in that big house. Inevitably too there were memories of the short, fat boy being bullied. But the film also rekindled memories of happier times from his childhood in Chicago. Times he had almost forgotten.

I remember once we moved to a new neighbourhood near Chicago and there were lots of kids on bikes [he recalls]. I remember moving from backyard to backyard, doing kid things and riding my bike everywhere. I remember we had a tree fort just like Jack and his friends do in the film. In the movie they get Jack to go and buy a copy of *Playboy,* and he can of course because he looks like an adult. Well, with us it wasn't *Playboy,* it was *National Geographic.*

Coppola had signed on Diane Lane and Brian Kerwin to play Jack's anxious parents, trying to make the most of what will inevitably be the short time they have with their son. But the bulk of the film deals with Jack's relationships with other kids. To get Williams into the right mood for the part, Coppola sent him on a camping trip with his half-dozen young co-stars.

I hung out with them at Francis's place for about three weeks [he says]. It was great because you assimilate behaviour without even knowing that you are picking it up. All of a sudden you have this weird combination shuffle and jump that a ten-year-old has and you don't bother about your shoes any more. It was really useful . . . The kids were like seven technical advisers and they would let you know when you went wrong. But you had to be in with them first, you had to know the dynamics of the group and how it worked. They form bonds and I had to be part of that.

As well as three weeks at Camp Coppola, as he came to call it, Williams also relied on his son Zach who was now 13. He remembered how difficult an age it can be for a boy and also how difficult it can be for a parent trying to deal with that. But for all of his efforts *Jack* was not a success. The film opened well enough on the strength of Williams' name, but reviews and word of mouth were against it. It seemed that Williams' instincts had been right; it had simply been a role too far. The public appeared to be tiring of watching Williams the man-child; they wanted the comedy of *Good Morning Vietnam* or *Mrs Doubtfire,* or the pathos of *The Fisher King* or *Dead Poets Society.* In the end *Jack* took $58.6 million at the American box-office, which was respectable but not what Williams was becoming used to.

By the time *Jack* was released in the autumn of 1996, Williams had had four films in a row which had broken $100 million at the American box-office. Ironically the most recent of these was *The Birdcage,* a film which he had completed before *Jack* and which gave him another shot at breaking out of those man-child shoes. *The Birdcage* was an Americanised version of the classic French comedy *La Cage aux Folles*, which had already been a huge international hit in its own right as well as spawning a successful stage musical. In the original two gay Frenchmen are thrown into a panic when the straight son of one of them announces that he is about to be married. The meeting of the prospective and very strait-laced in-laws is a potential nightmare. If they discover his father is gay and living with another man, then the whole thing will be off. In desperation his father's partner pretends to be the boy's mother and the whole things descends into hilarious farce.

The Birdcage, which was written by Elaine May and directed by Mike Nichols, the combination which effectively defined American satire in the Sixties, relocates the action from France to Miami's gay enclave on South Beach. Williams plays Armand, who has lived for 20 years with his flamboyant lover Albert, a career-making performance from Nathan Lane. Then Armand's straight son, played by Dan Futterman, turns up unannounced to reveal that he is to be married to his college sweetheart, played by Calista Flockhart. She is the daughter of Gene Hackman's right-wing senator, whose family values platform is being seriously undermined by a sex scandal. He decides that the wedding might be just the thing to take the political heat off, so he and his wife, Dianne Wiest, head for Miami to meet the new in-laws. The last thing they expect is a gay couple, so Lane drags up with hilarious consequences.

Williams' initial reaction when he was offered the movie was to turn it down. He felt it was a mistake to remake a classic, but once he read the few pages of the script that he had been sent he was laughing so loud that he knew it could work on its own terms. Williams had only one further reservation. He had been offered the part of Albert the drag queen, but he wanted the role of Armand.

'First of all I've done that,' he said to explain his choice. 'I wanted to try something different. I wanted to play off of him. I still get to go nuts many times, but it was like learning a whole different job.'

Subconsciously Williams' choice of Armand over Albert may also have been a reaction to another criticism. Over the years Williams had been criticised by gay groups for the extravagant way in which he had portrayed them in his stand-up performances. It was an issue that he had addressed at some length in his 1992 *Playboy* interview.

I understand what they're talking about and I have tried to cut back a little [he conceded]. I can see their point because they have always been portrayed as being that way. But don't tell me, if you walk down a street in San Francisco, you won't see a lot of people like that . . . How do you not offend anyone? Finally you just say, 'Fuck it. I have to do what I do. If it pisses you off, I still do other things that piss other people off.' I've got the born-again Christians after my ass because I defend gays, and gays are mad at me because I do effeminate characters. You can't keep modifying or you're like a chameleon in front of a mirror.

Once he had got the choice of role squared away, the other major attraction for Williams was the chance to work on film with Mike Nichols, who had directed him on the stage in *Waiting for Godot*. Throughout his career Williams has made impeccable choices of the directors he works with. From Robert Altman through George Roy Hill through Peter Weir through Francis Ford Coppola he has worked with the best. He has also consciously chosen directors who will challenge him and stretch him and bring out the best in him.

> Working with Mike Nichols was amazing [he says]. In terms of comedy he is the best. He was amazing to work with. That's why in *The Birdcage* I took the more masculine of the two. I didn't want to do the drag part, not only because I had already done the drag thing in *Mrs Doubtfire*, but also because I had faith that if I worked with Mike I could find a different level of comedy, and I did. It was great. He really helped me find that other level. We would try wonderful outrageous things, but I knew he would pick the best. I wasn't afraid.

The lack of fear had come to typify Williams' whole life in the Marsha era. It had taken hold first of all in his private life, and now it was spilling over into his professional life as he began to create things out of happiness rather than stark terror. Williams' performance as Armand is a little gem. It is remarkably restrained for a man who was once described as 'the Tasmanian devil of comedy'. There is a touching and loving core about Armand which Williams manages to bring out while still being able to throw hissy fits with the best of them when the script demands.

The Birdcage, like *Mrs Doubtfire*, also allowed Williams to sermonise, however discreetly, about the importance of real family values as opposed to the false values of Gene Hackman's character.

> Lots of Americans look at San Francisco and say 'That place is crazy' [he explains]. But I used to live at 19th and Castro, and it's a neighbourhood. Yeah, there are a lot of gay men and gay women, but it has the same values as your neighbourhood. They want peace and quiet. They want to live their lives, and they do have children from previous marriages, artificial

insemination, a hundred different ways. It's family oriented. People don't acknowledge it, but that's the reality.

Whether audiences took Williams' subliminal message on board or not, they flocked to *The Birdcage* in droves. The film grossed $124.1 million in the States and in the process helped to kick-start the ailing MGM studio which was slowly getting back on its feet after years of financial limbo. It was strong and compelling evidence to back up what Williams already knew – that there would be no more man-child parts.

By the time *The Birdcage* came out he was already committed to *Jack* and indeed had begun filming. But he was adamant that *Jack* would mark the end of this particular phase of his career. The epiphany apparently came one day during shooting as he was sitting on a playground swing. 'This is the last one,' he said to himself. 'This is the ultimate one. This is the metaphor gone beyond hyperbole and into simile. I can't do it any more after this. I'm 45. This is way beyond the Peter Pan syndrome.'

So far, he has remained true to his word.

33

Free at Last

Robin Williams never set out to be a comedian. He wanted to be an actor; the comedy was a defence mechanism he happened to be good at. It was something he had started because he couldn't get work in legit theatre, and after a while it became too difficult for him to give up. Now in his mid-forties he was starting to have some second thoughts. There was only so long that he could continue doing comedy without become passé. Very few comedians have long shelf lives and Williams' had been longer than most. Perhaps it was time to stretch the acting muscles more rigorously than he had been doing of late.

Williams began to seek out projects which would challenge him as an actor. One was a film about the assassination of San Francisco's gay leader Harvey Milk. *The Mayor of Castro Street*, as the project was known, had been in development with Williams' good friend and fellow San Franciscan Gus Van Sant. The two men had wanted to work together for some time and the script was gelling slowly but surely, even if it wasn't quite there yet. Another project he was keen on was *Damien of Molokai*, the inspiring story of a priest who founded a leper colony on the island of Molokai. Father Damien eventually contracted the disease and died himself, but was later canonised by the Catholic Church. There was also the possibility of doing a new version of *Don Quixote*, with John Cleese as Cervantes' deluded hero and Williams as his faithful Sancho Panza. This looked like being his next project until the financing fell through inexplicably at the last minute.

Then, with his wife Marsha under the auspices of their Blue Wolf company, Williams was also developing the story of cartoonist and humorist John Callahan. Callahan is a quadriplegic and a recovering alcoholic, and Williams had been talking about doing this one since the time of *Mrs Doubtfire*.

> He's really been through it [says Williams], but he also has a great, totally uncompromising way of looking at his life. Here's someone who is very unsentimental about everything he does. His cartoons are deadly. One shows two people, a blind guy and a blind woman sitting in the daylight, with the sun just streaming in, and the blind man is courting her, saying 'The night is made for lovers'. He's not afraid to talk about it.

Most of these projects would remain in the pipeline for several years. In the meantime Williams was trying to concentrate on some character work and staying out of the limelight. As well as the sinister professor in *The Secret Agent*, he had also played Osric in Kenneth Branagh's version of *Hamlet*, and before that he had played a crazed Russian doctor – a rehearsal for his performance with Christopher Reeve – in *Nine Months* for Chris Columbus. He had also been obliging his friends. He did a brief cameo as a mime teacher for Bobcat Goldthwait in his directing début *Shakes the Clown*. Then he obliged Steven Spielberg with a single-scene cameo as a night-club owner in the drag comedy *To Wong Foo, Thanks for Everything, Julie Newmar*, which Spielberg was producing.

'I just want to work with characters, with great ensembles of people,' he insists. 'You kind of have to say [to the fans], "If you're disappointed I'm sorry, but I have to keep trying new things for the sake of my own sanity".'

Williams also did another film with Disney. He had agreed to reprise his role as the genie in a third *Aladdin* movie, *Aladdin and the King of Thieves*. The straight-to-video movie had actually started shooting, with Dan Castellaneta once again providing the voice of the genie. Then, with about a third of the film already animated, Joe Roth reached his *rapprochement* with Williams. When Williams signed on, Castellaneta was out and Williams was in.

'I went into a room and started improvising and these guys kept throwing things at me,' says Williams, describing an experience similar to that first turn on *Aladdin*. 'It just got wild. They let me play. That's why I loved it – it was like *carte blanche* to go nuts.'

Williams' fee for this one was more than the union scale of $75,000 that he got for *Aladdin*, but there was still no profit participation on a video which was expected to sell around 10 million units. Disney for their part were still forbidden to use his name or his voice to sell anything connected with the film.

'When your name's above the title, there's a lot of pressure on you,' says Williams, explaining his recent choices. 'When you're a supporting actor, you're just free to do the character.'

That's all very well, but nobody earns more than $20 million a year – Williams earned a reported $23 million in 1996 and $27 million in 1997 – by doing character roles. He still had to be on the look-out for those big starry vehicles which would enable him to pull down the $15 million pay-cheques. One such vehicle seemed to be *Father's Day*, like *The Birdcage* – and *Nine Months* for that matter – a Hollywood version of a successful French film. The French version was called *Les Compères* and starred Michel Richard and Gérard Départieu. The plot concerns a woman looking for her missing son. Unable to find him, she calls two old flames and enlists their aid by telling each of them that he is the father of the missing boy. Neither of them is aware of the other and in the course of the film they team up, discover their mutual secret, and at the same time find out by proxy about the joys of parenthood.

Although Robin Williams and Billy Crystal had been close friends since their early days on the comedy circuit, they had never made a film together. Their screen appearances had been limited to their Comic Relief specials with Whoopi Goldberg. Bizarrely, by the time they started shooting together in *Father's Day*, it was their third screen team-up in a year. Billy Crystal had also appeared in *Hamlet*, and Williams had taken a small but telling role in Woody Allen's *Deconstructing Harry*, in which Crystal was second lead. Williams' cameo about a man whose life is so unfocused he is literally out of focus in the film is one of the best jokes in Allen's movie. Williams has barely a handful of scenes, but he took the part just to be on a Woody Allen set and watch him work.

In *Father's Day*, Crystal is the sharper, more successful of the pair. Williams plays a struggling poet who is prone to lachrymose anxiety attacks at the drop of a hat. Appearing with such a close friend in such high-pressure circumstances could have been stressful, but Williams insists the experience was nothing but positive.

For me it was great getting to know him as a friend over the years [he explains], and someone might think that doing a movie together would tax the marriage, but we still love each other. Actually I got to know him better because you spend so much time together doing a movie. I got to really know him and talk about things and in the process I learned a lot about his past. He was telling me about his father and that was great. These talks were actually in the movie at one point. He has a wonderful thing where he talked about a real dream he had about his father and I said, 'You have to use that. It's such an amazingly powerful thing.' It's something that may seem very specific, but I think anybody who has lost their father would relate to what it was. Then the movie ended up going more with the comedy stuff, but that is one of the things that was very powerful.

Father's Day was the sort of movie which everyone thought would be a huge hit in the summer of 1997. It had two popular stars, a proven formula, and the expectations were very high. They had even arranged a rare television appearance for Crystal and Williams on *Friends* in the week of the film's release. It was also opening in mid-May, just before the all-important Memorial Day weekend. The idea was that it would hit the box-office with a bang and then clean up before the perceived summer heavyweights, *The Lost World: Jurassic Park*, *Men in Black* and *Batman and Robin*, came along. It all went horribly wrong, however, and *Father's Day* finished a poor second on its opening weekend to the sci-fi epic *The Fifth Element*. It was a poor summer all round for Warner Brothers, who were hitting a box-office slump not only with *Father's Day* and the *Batman* movie but also their other summer entry *The Conspiracy Theory*. This one also underperformed despite the presence of Mel Gibson and Julia Roberts.

The fact that Warners were in such a slump meant that very little of the blame for the failure of *Father's Day* attached itself to any of the stars. Industry pundits blamed Warner's slightly old-fashioned way of packaging high-priced star vehicles when the rest of the industry had moved on from that. This set the bar so high in terms of movie costs that it would be difficult to make money in what Williams referred to as a 'Darwinian summer' at the box-office. Natural selection did come into play and *Father's Day* was a major loser.

Williams, however, was a prodigious and apparently tireless worker and he was able to turn this work ethic to his advantage. If he had missed out on the summer box-office there was always the Christmas holidays. Williams was already hard at work on a new film for Disney which was tipped to be one of the big holiday hits of 1997.

Disney was remaking *The Absent-Minded Professor*. The original starred Fred MacMurray as a scientist who invented a remarkable elastic compound which he called 'flying rubber' – or Flubber – which allowed anything it came into contact with to effectively defy gravity. *The Absent-Minded Professor* had been the highest-grossing film of 1961 and had spawned a sequel, *Son of Flubber*. Now Williams was taking on the

MacMurray role in a remake called simply *Flubber*. He was playing Professor Philip Brainard, a man so preoccupied with his work that he forgets everything else – even his wedding day. When he invents the miraculous Flubber it seems all his troubles are over, but before that can happen he has to prevent some unscrupulous rivals from getting their hands on it.

Williams claims to be not very astute when it comes to judging a script. He points out that he wanted to turn down *The Birdcage*, for example. On the other hand his instincts also told him not to go with *Jack* or *Father's Day* in their initial form, so his judgement may not be that bad. For *Flubber*, however, he did some market research. He held a private screening of *The Absent-Minded Professor* for five-year-old Cody and asked if he thought he should do his own version. When Cody said he should, Williams signed on.

'This film was made for kids, make no mistake about that,' says Williams. 'You can't say, "I was trying to achieve scientific reality." That's bullshit. It's a children's movie, and when I took mine to the première of *Flubber* they were laughing like crazy, which is a good sign. And the audience was full of kids and they were laughing too.

'My kids don't analyse what I do,' he continues. 'They don't say, "Hey Dad, your acting has less depth than Fred MacMurray." They just have a natural reaction to a film and they laugh if they think it's funny. And that's the way it should be.'

In *Flubber*, as in *Hook* and *Jumanji*, Williams was extensively involved in optical effects. He has a number of scenes in which his car flies, courtesy of a tank full of Flubber, and others where he bounces ceiling-high because of the effects of the stuff. And when he's not flying around himself, he has to share almost every scene either with Flubber, a green computer-generated goo with a personality of its own, or Professor Brainard's flying robot Weebo.

> There are other people in the room so I still had someone to talk to [he says of the lonely experience of acting to nothing for computer-generated imaging]. I was a mime so I had a running start on that stuff, so you start from there and you just play and improvise. The animators pick what they like, so it wasn't as hard as it seems ... Once they have explosions and things breaking, then it becomes a little more precise. But in the scenes when you first see it [Flubber] when I discover it, they let me try a lot of different things.

Flubber also meant Robin Williams had to log more flight time in his flying harness for the aerial scenes.

I've got more flying time than Mary Martin [he jokes]. They put you in the same kind of pants and they have this thing called a nitrogen ram which pulls you up in the air. They can go 50 or 60 feet up if you want to go that high, and they can bring you down to within an inch of the floor – or through the floor if you choose – and then back up again 15 or 20 times.

It's a ride [he says enthusiastically]. They would go 'We've got it' and I would want to try again and again. It's fun. It's not a stunt in the sense that there is no real danger, or if there was they didn't tell me. On *Hook* they used to have eight guys on a pulley, but with this it's like a system of nitrogen ratchets. It's very precise and they test it with sandbags. It's a bit like watching a hanging.

Flubber was Disney's major family movie release for the Thanksgiving season in November 1997. It was opening on Thanksgiving weekend against what was perceived to be stiff competition in the shape of the keenly anticipated but twice-delayed *Alien Resurrection*. Not only that, but *Flubber* was also following on from Fox's high-priced animated version of *Anastasia* which had opened strongly over the previous weekend. The reviews for *Flubber* had not been overly enthusiastic. Director Les Mayfield seemed to be at a loss to know what to do with Williams' character. There are so many effects and so much mayhem in some scenes that Williams has nothing to do, and for much of the film he plays second fiddle to a lump of computer-generated green jelly. But, as Williams pointed out, *Flubber* was made for kids not critics. It finished the five-day Thanksgiving weekend in top spot at the box-office with a shade under $36 million. *Alien Resurrection* trailed well behind in second place with just under $26 million.

Although it started with a bang, *Flubber* didn't demonstrate the staying power for which Disney might have hoped. One of the box-office trends of the Nineties was that films tended to have shorter shelf lives – the total box-office take is now roughly three times the opening weekend, compared with five times around ten years ago. *Flubber* was a shining example of this theory, finishing up with just over $96 million at the American box-office.

Flubber had just fallen short of the $100 million mark, which was becoming a trademark of Robin Williams films in the Nineties. If Williams was concerned about his appeal slipping, however, he need not have been. The best was only a matter of weeks away.

34

Let's See Some I.D.

By the end of its second weekend *Flubber* was already running out of steam. The box-office charts showed that it had dropped off 58 per cent from its opening. That still meant a healthy $60 million in the first twelve days, but that would also turn out to be around two-thirds of its entire box-office take. Further down the charts on *Flubber*'s second weekend came an entry which made interesting reading. *Good Will Hunting* had entered the charts in 19th position. It was only playing on seven screens but it had taken more than quarter of a million dollars. Significantly its per screen average – often a better indicator of how a film is performing than the box-office total – was the highest in the chart at a thumping $38,897. This effectively meant that the film was playing to sell-out crowds. Robin Williams was also in *Good Will Hunting*, and this box-office chart provided a snapshot of the two sides of his career. *Flubber* was a popcorn movie he had made for his kids; *Good Will Hunting* was the movie he had made for himself. It was a serious movie which gave him his best role since *The Fisher King*.

Good Will Hunting stars Matt Damon, in the title role of Will Hunting, and Ben Affleck. They are lifelong friends from the South Side, the toughest part of Boston. Affleck is a demolition worker and Damon is a janitor at MIT (Massachusetts Institute of Technology). Damon is also a mathematical genius who has serious personality disorders as a consequence of his abusive childhood. When MIT professor Stellan Skarsgaard discovers him solving one of the complicated problems he has left on the blackboard for his students, he becomes intrigued by Damon. By this time Damon's temper has landed him in trouble with the law, again. Skarsgaard persuades the judge not to jail him on two conditions; the first that he is released into his custody, the second that he undergoes therapy. After trying a series of doctors without success, Skarsgaard finally turns in desperation to his old friend Robin Williams. At one time Williams was a brilliant psychiatrist doing ground-breaking work with traumatised Vietnam veterans, but the death of his wife has left him alone, bitter and brooding. He eventually agrees to see Damon, and after an inauspicious start they begin to build a relationship. Williams, like Damon, comes from the South Side and, like Damon, he too was abused as a child. In the course of their sessions together both find a way to deal with their own problems and get on with their lives.

Before *Good Will Hunting* was released, its co-writers Damon and Affleck, who are 28 and 26 respectively, were regarded as two of Hollywood's most promising young actors. Affleck was tipped for great things after his performance in Kevin Smith's *Chasing Amy.* Damon, however, was thought to be the brighter prospect after starring in *The Rainmaker,* which had just opened, and being cast by Steven Spielberg in the title role in his war epic *Saving Private Ryan.* Like the characters they play in *Good Will Hunting,* Damon and Affleck have been friends since they were ten years old. *Good Will Hunting* has its origins in a one-act play Damon wrote at Harvard before he dropped out. Over the years the two friends expanded it, honed it, and in the end transformed it into a movie script for which they both took equal credit. Although Damon has the lead role in this one, they have an understanding that Affleck will take the lead in their next script. Eventually they managed to interest Castle Rock Pictures in making the film, which was gathering a lot of interest in young Hollywood. Castle Rock however wanted to cast two actors who were the same age as Affleck and Damon, but better known. This proved to be a deal-breaker. Castle Rock gave them two months to come up with a buyer who would reimburse them for the money they had spent developing the script, otherwise it would stay with them and they would go with the big names. Happily Miramax was willing to step in, and also willing for Damon and Affleck to take the roles they had written for themselves. Gus Van Sant was then attached as director, and by one of those fortunate coincidences he and Robin Williams finally got the chance to work together. Damon and Affleck had written the role of Sean Maguire with Williams, or something they described as a Robin Williams type, in mind. When he saw the script he had no doubt in his mind that he was going to do this film.

'When I met the boys [Ben and Matt] for the first time I said "Let's see some I.D.", ' says Williams, who could not believe that a script which dealt in such a mature way with so many life experiences could have been written by such young men. He also recognised that this was a long way from the man-child rut in which he had recently become mired.

When I do a movie like *Good Will Hunting* I do it because the story works [he explains]. I read it and thought I would be insane to pass this up. A movie like *Awakenings* is a serious movie, a movie like *Deconstructing Harry* which is really dark comedy I did because I really just wanted to be in the same room with Woody Allen and see what it's like to work with him. It's not a duel (with lighter roles), it's a conscious choice. I do a children's movie because I have children and I want something for them to see, and then I do these serious movies and I like to have access to both. To do all these different movies is important to me, and to do a stand-up comedy routine like I still do in clubs is just as valuable.

The writing is better for the serious roles [he continues]. So far in the serious films the scripts ... have a certain quality of writing about them. You've seen the quality of the writing that these two guys wrote, and then I met them and went 'Now who wrote this really?' Because you see the depth of perception in the things that they talk about and you go 'This is something that I want to be part of'. It's a supporting part, but it's a great ensemble. It's just like being in *The Birdcage*, it's a great ensemble, I like being in a supporting part more than I like being a star ... For me it's just as meaningful and in some ways more relaxing to do that and to work with someone like Gus Van Sant, who's very relaxed. I enjoy doing the effects movies. I love computers, I love being on-line and I love playing computer games, so for me an effects movie like *Flubber* or *Jumanji* is just another live-action computer game with myself as part of the game. To do a serious movie is really good exploration and it pushes the envelope of people's perceptions of what I can do. I was training to be an actor. John Houseman said, 'Mr Williams, you are damaged but interesting.' It's part of what I hope to do eventually is to be acting once again.

Although he still loves comedy, especially stand-up, and he still sneaks into comedy clubs late at night to do impromptu sets to keep his creative juices flowing, Williams appears to be coming round more and more to the fact that he really wants to be an actor. By this time he had reached the stage where the combination of commercial success and creative security meant that he was really enjoying film-making for the first time in his career.

Two of the most difficult scenes of Williams' career come in *Good Will*

Hunting. The first is after Sean and Will have had their first disastrous session together. The next time they meet Sean takes him out on to Boston Common and tells him about life, and how little Will really knows about life. It is a remarkable scene. Damon and Williams are sitting side by side on a bench, not looking at each other but staring straight ahead. Williams then pours out his soul to Damon and by extension to the audience. We hear of his Vietnam experiences, the death of his wife, his complete loss of faith, in a remarkable four-minute speech. The camera is on Williams almost continually; the only cut comes when Van Sant moves from right profile to left profile about half-way through. It is a searing and deeply affecting scene without a trace of mawkishness or sentiment. Similarly, towards the end of the film when Sean finally gets through to Will in his consulting room, Williams is faced with another tough challenge. Will has finally opened up and revealed his abusive childhood, and Sean has revealed that he had a similar experience with his own father. Sean then tells Will that it's not his fault, none of it is his fault. This is perhaps the first time in Will Hunting's life that anyone has understood the burden of guilt he has been carrying and attempted to lift part of it from his shoulders. The line is repeated nine times until Will finally breaks down and sobs in Sean's arms. As the camera pulls back, they are both weeping – as the script says, 'two lonely souls being father and son together'.

Each of these scenes is technically extremely difficult. In the Boston Common scene Williams has to be completely submerged in the character, there can't be so much as a gesture or a facial tic to distract the audience. Similarly, as he tells Will nine times that it's not his fault, there cannot be a variation of tone or inflection. Both scenes require Williams to totally serve the script, something he has not always been able to do in the past. There cannot be a trace of the sentiment which he allowed to creep in to *Dead Poets Society* to colour the audience's perception of the scenes. Williams nails both scenes so well that it's hard to imagine anyone else playing them. The combination of commercial success and creative security had given Williams a new confidence in his performance. According to Gus Van Sant, he now knew exactly what was required of him and how he was going to go about it.

I didn't have to do a lot of directing [says Van Sant]. I was possibly doing things intuitively. When we discovered the role, he [Williams] said he was going to do something that he hadn't done before. I pretty much tried to stay out of his way and didn't give him specific pointers during the shoot. Generally, whatever I did say, he would disagree with. A number of times I would say 'You could do it this way' and he'd say 'No, no, no' and then do it a completely different way, the way he wanted to. So my direction was more as an observer, making sure everything was going right and staying out of the way. I once saw this Jack Lemmon interview on TV and the only criticism of directors he had was that if things are going really well, they didn't need to get involved because it only confused matters. If the actor was on a run it was better if the director stood back. That's what I did.

Williams continued in serious vein after *Good Will Hunting* by going into *What Dreams May Come*. This is a fantasy directed by New Zealand film-maker Vincent Ward about a man's journey through the Afterlife. This modern-day Orpheus tale combines both effects and drama, since the Afterlife is being created on a virtual set, with Williams and co-stars Cuba Gooding Jnr and Annabella Sciorra completing some location shooting in Montana.

It's Vincent's sense of the visual that made me agree to this [explains Williams]. Have you ever seen his film *The Navigator*? If it had been anyone else I don't know if I would have done it. The guy I play is married to an artist who does all these landscapes, and when I die it's like I'm in one of her paintings. It's basically Orpheus and Eurydice. There's something quite wonderful and at the same time quite scary about this film.

After *What Dreams May Come*, which was due for release in the autumn of 1998, Williams went straight on to location filming in Poland and Hungary for another challenging role in *Jakob the Liar*.

It's based on a novel by a survivor of the Lodz ghetto [he says]. It's a fictional account of a Polish Jew in 1944 who hears a radio in a German commandant's office and he figures out that it's about a battle being fought on the Polish border. From that he realises that the Russians aren't that far away. He's in the ghetto and they have no other news or access to other news, and it's about what he does when he tells people this news, the effect it has on them, the hope it brings them, and how it changes people's lives. He only hears one broadcast so he has to keep making things up – hence the title Jakob the Liar – so he keeps bringing more news and tries to keep people going with it, and it's that effect. It's basically a character-driven story. It has Armin Mueller Stahl, Alan Alda, Bob Balaban and I think it's quite unique. I made the film because the story is so powerful and so interesting, and that's what I want to do from now on.

His next interesting story is *Patch Adams*, in which he plays the real-life doctor who founded The Gesundheit Institute, a holistic health-care system which is based on the healing power of laughter. After *Patch Adams*, he moves on to *First Person Plural*, the true story of a man with multiple personality disorder, which Disney acquired for Blue Wolf for more than $1 million.

It's safe to say that Robin Williams is a much-changed man, not only personally but also as a performer. It is inconceivable to think of the man who struggled beneath the latex in *Popeye* being the same man who could star in *Good Will Hunting*. Williams has learned not to fear the silences any more. He has learned to cherish the down time and be grateful for his second chance. There was a time when he was defined by what he did on-stage; now he is defined by what he does off-stage, in his own home. His family has become the most important thing in his life. He no longer has fits of depression, instead he has constructively turned them to moments of quiet contemplation.

'People expect a certain level from you,' he says. 'I have learned to be quiet now, but if I am quiet, or just out walking along or watching something, they think something's wrong. It's that thing of people always wanting you to be on, but there are times when I am just very quiet.'

These quiet moments come most frequently at home with his family, where he retreats to find some sanity and decency in the world. He has acknowledged that it was his family who helped him combat and defeat his depression.

'I have great friends, and my wife and family are extraordinary,' he says. 'It's people who get me through all of that, but especially my children, who are stunning. We were sitting at breakfast one morning and my little girl said "Isn't it wonderful, Cody's not talking". My wife said "That's because he's eating". And Zelda said "I can dream can't I?" Stuff like that keeps me going, that simple human contact.'

His family have also helped him adjust to his fame. He is no longer driven by it and no longer a hostage to it. His celebrity has become a tool to help make his life easier, not a rod for his own back.

You can't take it seriously [he says simply]. You can't worry if you make movies that don't make $100 million. It's a roulette wheel. You can only look at a script and say, 'Does the story appeal to me? Is it something that I should be doing? Is it something that only I can do?' The truth is with *Flubber* there are about 25 guys who could have played this part, honestly. It's an effects movie that I can bring a certain kind of fun to. A movie like *Good Will Hunting* on the other hand, while there are others who can play that part, I think I can bring something quite unique to it. When I get a script now I try to find those things that you can do, that you can really kick the shit out of and yet explore and have a good time doing and push the envelope a little.

Will it make hundreds of millions? I don't know and I don't care [he continues]. If *Good Will Hunting* makes hundreds of millions of dollars that would be wonderful for the people who invested in it, but for me I got a chance to be in a good movie, to be in a story that has some depth, and that's worth it. I did *Flubber* for children and that's worth it too. I don't want to demean children's movies, they have a right to be entertained, just like adults have a right – if they want to go and see *Air Force One* with things blowing up and a guy hanging on the wing of a plane, they have a right to, that's entertainment. But in the process of doing that, if you can find other things good, that's the drill.

Fame for me has come and gone about 15 times [he says philosophically, considering the 'power lists' of *Premiere* magazine and *Entertainment Weekly*]. Been there, number 1, number 5, number 8, number 12, number 30. It's a very surreal thing. That's why I live in San Francisco – when you pass a nun dressed in leather that gives you a different perspective. I live there because you really don't want to have to worry about your career constantly. I mean parking lot attendants give you scripts in Los Angeles. In San Francisco people accept me as me, they know I've done movies, but that's just part of it. I can go to a bike shop and buy some weird bike and hang out and talk to bike messengers and then I can get on my bike and ride 40 miles across the Golden Gate to some other place, to woods, and be totally alone, and that's wonderful.

The other thing is surreal, it's like a Mardi Gras float. I'm not having to say it isn't fun and there aren't perks with being famous, but the other part is having a life and having a life as an adult. I'm a father, I'm 46 years old, I have three kids and I love them madly, and I have to be an adult.

And the Winner Is . . .

Despite what they say in public about acting not being a competitive sport, and awards not really meaning anything, all actors have entertained the notion at least once in their lives of standing on the stage on Oscar night thanking their parents, their agent, their guru, and everyone else they can think of. But for all that, an Academy Award remains a quixotic honour. Great actors such as Richard Burton and Peter O'Toole have never won. Martin Scorsese, possibly the most influential director of his generation, has also continually been overlooked by the Academy. At the same time less notable talents have picked up almost inexplicable Oscars.

Some bear the snub better than others. Martin Scorsese has now become philosophical about the fact that he may never win. However, he has made no secret of the fact that he genuinely wanted to win an Oscar. So too did Robin Williams. He had been nominated three times as Best Actor – for *Good Morning Vietnam*, *Dead Poets Society* and *The Fisher King* – and each time he came away with his acceptance speech unheard.

It's so much fun to go along and go, 'Grrrr. Oh somebody else won? Oh good for you. La de da' [he says with some candour]. I'd like to win one so that I could pick it up and say, 'Look, Oscar hasn't got any balls.' I've had friends win and some day it would be nice. I don't want to win one of those awards for being 100.

For a while I was trying to look for movies. It was like 'This is your Academy Award-winning movie'. But if you do that, it's like trying to kiss your own ass – you can't do it. I'm not that flexible. Now I just try and find movies that I just enjoy making, because if you are going to spend four, five, or six months of your life doing something, it had better be something that you enjoy doing. You have to be willing to put your heart and soul into it rather than trying to achieve some award that may not happen.

Good Will Hunting was a project that Williams had put his heart and soul into and had given him huge creative satisfaction. He also gained a great deal of financial satisfaction, since he waived his fee in return for a 15 per cent profit participation in a film which stayed in the US box-office charts for six months and earned almost $140 million. But his performance attracted a lot of attention during the annual end-of-year round of award ceremonies. Although his name was above the credits, Williams was playing a supporting role and it could be argued that going for Best Supporting Actor might give him a better shot at winning. However, the films competing for the 1997 Academy Award featured some of the best supporting performances of recent years. The candidates included Robert Forster and Robert De Niro from *Jackie Brown*, De Niro again from *Wag the Dog*, Anthony Hopkins and Morgan Freeman from *Amistad*, Guy Pearce, Russell Crowe, Kevin Spacey and James Cromwell from *L.A. Confidential*, Burt Reynolds from *Boogie Nights*, Billy Zane from *Titanic*, Greg Kinnear from *As Good As It Gets*, Billy Connolly from *Mrs Brown*, Al Pacino from *Donnie Brasco*, Tom Wilkinson and Mark Haddy from *The Full Monty*, and Williams and Ben Affleck from *Good Will Hunting*. This was bound to be one of the most competitive Best Supporting Actor categories in years, especially since most of the other Oscar categories seemed cut and dried.

In the end there were some shocks and some glaring omissions when the Academy Award nominees were announced in February 1998. The Academy voters had indeed nominated Williams, and his fellow nominees were Burt Reynolds, Greg Kinnear, Anthony Hopkins and Robert Forster. Pundits quickly decided it was a two-horse race. Hopkins could be eliminated for being a previous winner and for starring in a film which the Academy seemed to have overlooked; likewise Forster had appeared in a film which also seemed to have found little favour with the Academy, while Kinnear suffered from something which Williams knew all about in that he was a TV star and perceived as a comedian.

Two other award ceremonies have been deemed to be significant in deciding the final fate of the Academy Award. The first is the Golden Globe awards, which are voted on by Hollywood's Foreign Press Association. Some of their choices have been odd to say the least, but with national television coverage and support from the major studios, these awards have gained bell-wether status. Perhaps a more reliable indicator might be the relatively new Screen Actors Guild awards. These are seen as a better guide because the same people vote for them, i.e. SAG members, as vote for the Academy Awards.

Burt Reynolds drew first blood by winning the Golden Globe for his role as a porn-movie mogul in *Boogie Nights*. Reynolds' sly and ironic performance was seen by some as a self-deprecating nod to his old screen image, as well as capping a comeback which had been simmering for some years. However, by March the momentum seemed to be running away from Reynolds, especially when stories began to circulate that he hadn't been too enamoured of *Boogie Nights* in the first place.

Williams evened the score by taking Best Supporting Actor at the SAG awards. 'I was sitting over there sweating like Marlon Brando after Thai food,' he joked on accepting his award. 'I'm stunned.'

With the Oscars only three weeks after the SAG awards, Williams was deemed to have the edge in what was still being seen as a close race. On the night Williams went along with his wife and his mother. He and Marsha sat in the orchestra section of the Dorothy Chandler Pavilion, where the major names are seated, with the rest of the *Good Will Hunting* contingent. The film had nine nominations overall, including one for Affleck and Damon who would win for Best Original Screenplay.

In the end, when the envelope was opened and the winner's name was finally announced, it was Robin Williams. Burt Reynolds had to be as good as his pre-show quote when he had suggested that if he lost we would see the best piece of acting he had ever done. As a plainly stunned Williams hugged his wife before bounding up the steps to a standing ovation from the orchestra section, a tight-lipped Reynolds applauded but did not get to his feet. Williams embraced his best friend Billy Crystal, who was the Oscar night master of ceremonies, before admitting to a new phenomenon.

'Ah man!' he said. 'This might be the one time I'm speechless.'

A speechless Robin Williams is as likely as a politician declining a sound-bite. He did make a speech, in which he thanked Marsha eloquently, and then pointed to his *Good Will Hunting* co-star and said, 'Matt, I still want to see some I.D.'

In the midst of his greatest triumph he still found time to think of his parents. He thanked his mother, but especially his father. 'I want to thank my father up there,' he said, gesturing to the ceiling of the auditorium, and praised his father for not standing in his way when he made the decision to be an actor. Then the old performance junkie kicked in again as Williams recovered his composure sufficiently to impersonate Groucho Marx and duck-walk off the stage carrying his Oscar.

Afterwards Williams admitted to being genuinely stunned. He said he had not expected to win on any of his previous nominations and this was no exception. 'I didn't think I had a chance, and when they said it, I was shocked,' he said. 'This is a wild night. It's just insane. I'm very proud. This is an extraordinary piece and the first time I read it I wanted to do it.'

But Williams also said he hoped that his win might end the stigma against comedians. 'I was trained as an actor,' he pointed out. 'it's not like they had to medicate me. People think a comedian is a slightly damaged person. It's like "You're a comedian, go over there. Stay. Good".'

The irony of the evening would not have been lost on Robin Williams. He, as an alleged comic actor, had finally won an Oscar playing a straight role, while Jack Nicholson as a straight actor had won Best Actor for a comic role in *As Good As It Gets*.

Irony aside, it mattered not a jot. The camel had finally passed through the eye of the needle.

FILMOGRAPHY

Can I Do It ... Till I Need Glasses? (1977)

Director I. Robert Levy; script supervisor Sandy King. Running time 72 mins.

Cast: Victor Dunlap, Moose Carlson, Walter Olkewicz, Joey Camen, Amy Kellog, **Robin Williams**

Williams filmed some sequences for this insipid sex revue after his success in *Mork and Mindy*. The film premièred without his contribution, which was added later.

Popeye (1980)

Director Robert Altman; producer Robert Evans; screenwriter Jules Pfeiffer. Running time 114 mins.

Cast: **Robin Williams (Popeye)**, Shelley Duvall, Ray Walston, Paul Dooley, Paul Smith, Linda Hunt

Robin Williams plays a latex-enhanced version of L. C. Segar's famous comic-strip sailor.

The World According to Garp (1982)

Director George Roy Hill; producers George Roy Hill, Robert L. Crawford; screenwriter Steve Tesich. Running time 136 mins.

Cast: **Robin Williams (T. S. Garp)**, Mary Beth Hurt, Glenn Close, John Lithgow, Hume Cronym, Jessica Tandy

Williams is the eponymous hero in John Irving's account of an unconventional young man and his remarkable mother.

The Survivors (1983)

Director Michael Ritchie; producer William Sackheim; screenwriter Michael Leeson. Running time 102 mins.

Cast: Walter Matthau, **Robin Williams (Donald Quinelle)**, Jerry Reed, James Wainwright, Kristen Vigard, John Goodman

Williams plays an insecure man who takes survivalist training to absurd levels after identifying a criminal.

Moscow on the Hudson (1984)

Director Paul Mazursky; producer Paul Mazursky; screenwriters Paul Mazursky, Leon Capetanos. Running time 115 mins.

Cast: **Robin Williams (Vladimir Ivanoff)**, Maria Conchita Alonso, Cleavant Derricks, Alejandro Rey, Savely Kramarov, Elya Baskin

Williams is a Russian musician who has to try to adapt to life in the United States after defecting in Bloomingdales.

The Best of Times (1986)

Director Roger Spottiswoode; producer Gordon Carroll; screenwriter Ron Shelton. Running time 104 mins.

Cast: **Robin Williams (Jack Dundee),** Kurt Russell, Pamela Reed, Holly Palance, Donald Moffat, Margaret Whitton, M. Emmet Walsh.

Williams is a mild-mannered bank manager whose life is frustrated by the memory of missing a big play in a football game 20 years previously.

Club Paradise (1986)

Director Harold Ramis; producer Michael Shamberg; screenplay by Brian Doyle-Murray, based on a story by Tom Leopold, Chris Miller III, Harold Ramis and Ed Roboto. Running time 104 mins.

Cast: **Robin Williams**, Peter O'Toole, Rick Moranis, Jimmy Cliff, Twiggy

Williams is a Chicago fireman who is persuaded to sink half his severance pay into a run-down Caribbean resort.

Seize the Day (1986)

Director Fielder Cook; producer Robert Geller; screenplay by Saul Bellow and Ronald Ribman, based on a story by Saul Bellow. Running time 93 mins.

Cast: **Robin Williams (Tommy Wilhelm)**, Joseph Wiseman, Jerry Stiller, Glenne Headley, Richard B. Shull, Tony Roberts

Williams' first genuinely dramatic performance as a salesman who seeks nothing more than the approval of his flint-hearted father.

Dear America: Letters Home from Vietnam (1987)

Director Bill Couturie; producers Bill Couturie, Thomas Bird; screenplay by Richard Dewhurst and Bill Couturie, based on the book *Dear America, Letters Home from Vietnam*. Running time 87 mins.

Voice cast includes narration from **Robin Williams**, Robert De Niro, Ellen Burstyn, Kathleen Turner, Michael J. Fox, Willem Dafoe and many others

Williams is one of many star names who contributed their voices to this intensely moving collection of letters from American soldiers in Vietnam to their loved ones at home.

Good Morning Vietnam (1987)

Director Barry Levinson; producers Mark Johnson, Larry Brezner, Ben Moses, Harry Benn; screenwriter Mitch Markowitz. Running time 120 mins.

Cast: **Robin Williams (Adrian Cronauer)**, Forest Whitaker, Tung Thanh Tran, Chintara Sukapatana, Bruno Kirby, Robert Wuhl, J. T. Walsh

Williams' breakthrough role as an Army radio disc jockey whose irreverent rantings make him a folk hero among the troops and a thorn in the side of his superiors.

The Adventures of Baron Munchausen (1989)

Director Terry Gilliam; producers Thomas Schuhly, Ray Cooper; screenplay by Charles McKeown and Terry Gilliam, based on the stories of Rudolph Erich Raspe. Running time 126 mins.

Cast: John Neville, Eric Idle, Oliver Reed, Charles McKeown, Bill Paterson, Uma Thurman, **Robin Williams (King of the Moon)**

Williams contributes a very funny but unbilled cameo in Gilliam's lavish interpretations of Raspe's flights of fantasy.

Dead Poets Society (1989)

Director Peter Weir; producers Steven M. Haft, Paul Junger Witt, Tony Thomas; screenwriter Tom Schulman. Running time 128 mins.

Cast: **Robin Williams (John Keating)**, Robert Sean Leonard, Ethan Hawke, Josh Charles, Kurtwood Smith

Williams plays an inspirational English teacher who encourages his impressionable young charges to 'carpe diem' – seize the day.

Awakenings (1990)

Director Penny Marshall; producers Walter Parkes, Larry Lasker; screenplay by Steve Zaillian, based on the novel by Oliver Sacks. Running time 121 mins.

Cast: **Robin Williams (Dr Malcolm Sayer)**, Robert De Niro, Julie Kavner, John Heard, Ruth Nelson, Penelope Ann Miller

Williams is a brilliant neurologist whose work with patients in a post-vegetative state enables them to have some semblance of a life.

Cadillac Man (1990)

Director Roger Donaldson; producers Charles Roven, Roger Donaldson; screenwriter Ken Friedman. Running time 97 mins.

Cast: **Robin Williams (Joey O'Brien)**, Tim Robbins, Pamela Reed, Fran Drescher, Zack Norman, Annabella Sciorra

Williams is a hustling car salesman who ends up negotiating for his life when a crazed gunman bursts into his showroom.

Dead Again (1991)

Director Kenneth Branagh; producers Lindsay Doran, Charles H. Maguire; screenwriter Scott Frank. Running time 107 mins.

Cast: Kenneth Branagh, Emma Thompson, Andy Garcia, **Robin Williams (Doctor Cozy Carlisle)**, Campbell Scott, Wayne Knight

Williams plays a cameo as a disbarred psychologist in Branagh's Hitchcockian mystery.

The Fisher King (1991)

Director Terry Gilliam; producers Debra Hill, Lynda Obst; screenwriter Richard La Gravenese. Running time 137 mins.

Cast: **Robin Williams (Parry)**, Jeff Bridges, Mercedes Ruehl, Amanda Plummer

Williams is a man driven to madness by the senseless killing of his wife.

Hook (1991)

Director Steven Spielberg; producers Kathleen Kennedy, Frank Marshall, Gerald R. Molen; screenplay by Jim V. Hart and Malia Scotch Marmo, based on the story by Hart and Nick Castle, adapted from the original stage play and books by Sir James M. Barrie. Running time 144 mins.

Cast: Dustin Hoffman, **Robin Williams (Peter Banning/Peter Pan)**, Julia Roberts, Bob Hoskins, Maggie Smith, Caroline Goodall

Williams is Peter Pan as a grown man who has lost his identity.

Shakes the Clown (1991)

Director Bobcat Goldthwait; producers Paul Colichman, Ann Luly-Goldthwait; screenwriter Bobcat Goldthwait. Running time 83 mins.

Cast: Bobcat Goldthwait, Julie Brown, Bruce Baum, Steve Bean, **Robin Williams (Mime Jerry)**

Williams makes an unbilled cameo as a mime teacher.

Aladdin (1992)

Directors John Musker, Ron Clements; producers John Musker, Ron Clements; screenwriters Ron Clements, John Musker, Ted Elliott, Terry Rossio. Running time 90 mins.

Cast (voices): Scott Weinger, **Robin Williams (Genie)**, Linda Larkin, Jonathan Freeman, Gilbert Gottfried

Williams is the voice of the genie in this animated adventure.

FernGully . . . The Last Rain Forest (1992)

Director Bill Kroyer; producers Wayne Young, Peter Faiman; screenplay by Jim Cox, based on the FernGully stories by Diana Young. Running time 76 mins.

Cast (voices): Tim Curry, Samantha Mathis, Christian Slater, Jonathan Ward, **Robin Williams (Batty Koda)**, Grace Zabriskie

Williams provides comic relief as a spaced-out bat in this ecological animated feature.

Toys (1992)

Director Barry Levinson; producers Barry Levinson, Mark Johnson; screenwriters Barry Levinson, Jane Curtin. Running time 121 mins.

Cast: **Robin Williams (Lesley Zevo)**, Michael Gambon, Joan Cusack, Robin Wright, LL Cool J, Donald O'Connor

Peaceable Williams tries to regain control of the family toy firm from his militaristic uncle.

Mrs Doubtfire (1993)

Director Chris Columbus; producers Marsha Garces Williams, Robin Williams, Mark Radcliffe; screenplay by Randi Mayem Singer and Lesley Dixon, based on the novel *Alias Madame Doubtfire* by Anne Fine. Running time 125 mins.

Cast: **Robin Williams (Daniel Hillard/Mrs Iphigenia Doubtfire)**, Sally Field, Pierce Brosnan, Harvey Fierstein, Polly Holliday

Williams is a struggling divorced actor who impersonates an elderly babysitter to see his kids.

Being Human (1993)

Director Bill Forsyth; producers David Puttnam, Robert F. Colesberry; screenwriter Bill Forsyth. Running time 122 mins.

Cast: **Robin Williams (Hector)**, Kelly Hunter, John Turturro, Anna Galiena, Vincent D'Onofrio

Williams plays five men named Hector in a story spanning 6000 years.

Jumanji (1995)

Director Joe Johnston; producers William Tietler, Scott Kroopf; screenwriters Jim Strain, Greg Taylor, Jonathan Hensleigh. Running time 104 mins.

Cast: **Robin Williams (Alan Parrish)**, Jonathan Hyde, Kirsten Dunst, Bradley Pierce, Bonnie Hunt

Williams is a small boy trapped in a board game who emerges as an adult 26 years later.

Nine Months (1995)

Director Chris Columbus; producers Ann Francois, Michael Barnathan, Mark Radcliffe; screenwriter Chris Columbus. Running time 103 mins.

Cast: Hugh Grant, Julianne Moore, Tom Arnold, Joan Cusack, Jeff Goldblum, **Robin Williams (Dr Kosevich)**

Williams contributes a short cameo as a Russian gynaecologist.

To Wong Foo, Thanks for Everything, Julie Newmar (1995)

Director Beeban Kidron; producer G. Mac Brown; screenwriter Douglas Carter Beane. Running time 109 mins.

Cast: Wesley Snipes, Patrick Swayze, John Leguizamo, Stockard Channing

Williams has a one-scene cameo as the owner of a gay night-club.

The Birdcage (1996)

Director Mike Nichols; producer Mike Nichols; screenwriter Elaine May. Running time 119 mins.

Cast: **Robin Williams (Armand Goldman)**, Gene Hackman, Nathan Lane, Dianne Wiest, Dan Futterman, Calista Flockhart, Hank Azaria

Williams is a gay but subdued night-club owner whose straight son is bringing his reactionary prospective in-laws to dinner.

Hamlet (1996)

Director Kenneth Branagh; producer David Barron; adapted screenplay by Kenneth Branagh, based on the play by William Shakespeare. Running time 238 mins.

Cast: Kenneth Branagh, Julie Christie, Derek Jacobi, Kate Winslet, Billy Crystal, **Robin Williams (Osric)**

Williams plays a courtier in this full-length adaptation of Shakespeare.

Jack (1996)

Director Francis Ford Coppola; producers Ricardo Mestres, Fred Fuchs, Francis Ford Coppola; screenwriters James De Monaco, Gary Nadeau. Running time 113 mins.

Cast: **Robin Williams (Jack Powell)**, Diane Lane, Brian Kerwin, Jennifer Lopez, Bill Cosby, Fran Drescher

Williams plays a boy who ages four times as fast as normal children.

Joseph Conrad's The Secret Agent (1996)

Director Christopher Hampton; producer Norma Heyman; screenplay by Christopher Hampton, based on Joseph Conrad's novel. Running time 95 mins.

Cast: Bob Hoskins, Patricia Arquette, Gérard Départieu, **Robin Williams (The Professor)**

Williams is billed as George Spelvin in his role as a sinister bomb-maker.

Father's Day (1997)

Director Ivan Reitman; producers Joel Silver, Ivan Reitman; screenplay by Lowell Ganz and Babaloo Mandel, based on the film *Les Compères* by Francis Veber. Running time 102 mins.

Cast: **Robin Williams (Dale Putney)**, Billy Crystal, Julia-Louis Dreyfuss, Nastassja Kinski, Bruce Greenwood

Williams plays one of two men searching for a missing boy each believes is his son.

Flubber (1997)

Director Les Mayfield; producers John Hughes, Ricardo Mestres; screenwriters John Hughes, Bill Hall. Running time 95 mins.

Cast: **Robin Williams (Professor Philip Brainard)**, Marcia Gay Harden, Christopher McDonald, Raymond J. Barry, Clancy Brown, Ted Levine, Wil Wheaton

Williams is an absent-minded scientist who invents a substance which defies gravity.

Good Will Hunting (1997)

Director Gus Van Sant; producer Lawrence Bender; screenwriters Matt Damon, Ben Affleck. Running time 126 mins.

Cast: **Robin Williams (Sean Maguire)**, Matt Damon, Ben Affleck, Stellan Skarsgaard, Minnie Driver, Casey Affleck

Williams is a therapist trying to help a troubled mathematical genius.

BOX OFFICE

Robin Williams' films have grossed more than $1 billion at the American box-office. These are his top ten earners in the domestic market.

1.	*Mrs Doubtfire*	1993	$219.2 million
2.	*Aladdin*	1992	$217.4 million
3.	*Good Will Hunting*	1997	$138.3 million*
4.	*The Birdcage*	1996	$124.1 million
5.	*Good Morning Vietnam*	1987	$123.9 million
6.	*Hook*	1991	$119.7 million
7.	*Jumanji*	1995	$100.4 million
8.	*Dead Poets Society*	1989	$95.9 million
9.	*Flubber*	1997	$92.9 million
10.	*Nine Months*	1995	$69.7 million

Good Will Hunting was still on domestic release in the United States as at 1 August 1998.

AWARDS

Robin Williams has won awards in almost every sphere of entertainment. The only one to elude him so far is a Tony for a Broadway performance. Here are his other major honours.

1979
Golden Globe: Best Actor in a Comedy Series, *Mork and Mindy*
Grammy: Best Comedy Recording, *Reality . . . What a Concept*

1987
Emmy: Best Individual Performance in a Variety or Music Programme, *A Carol Burnett Special*
Golden Globe: Best Actor in a Comedy, *Good Morning Vietnam*
Grammy: Best Comedy Recording, *A Night at the Met*

1988
Emmy: Best Individual Performance in a Variety or Music Programme, *ABC Presents A Royal Gala*
Grammy: Best Comedy Recording, *Good Morning Vietnam*
Grammy: Best Recording for Children, *Pecos Bill*

1991
Golden Globe: Best Actor in a Comedy, *The Fisher King*

1992
Golden Globe: Special Achievement, *Aladdin*

1993
Golden Globe: Best Actor in a Comedy, *Mrs Doubtfire*

1998
Academy Award: Best Supporting Actor, *Good Will Hunting*
Screen Actors Guild: Best Supporting Actor, *Good Will Hunting*

SOURCES

I Love You in Blue
Playboy October 1982; *San Francisco Chronicle* 19 October 1987; *Esquire* June 1989; *New York Times* 11 November 1990; *Playboy* January 1992; *New York* 22 November 1993
David Halberstam: *The Fifties* Fawcett Columbine 1998

School Daze
Author's interviews with Robin Williams, January 1988 and February 1996; US press junket for *Jack* 1996
Playboy October 1982; *San Francisco Chronicle* 19 October 1987; *New York* 22 November 1993

In Old Tiburon
Author's interview with Robin Williams, January 1988
Playboy October 1982; *New York Times* 11 November 1990; *Playboy* January 1992; *New York* 11 November 1993

It's a Helluva Town
Author's interview with Robin Williams, January 1988
Harpers magazine February 1979; *Playboy* October 1982; *Premiere* January 1988; *New York Times* 11 November 1990; *Playboy* January 1992

Damaged but Interesting
Siobhan Synnot interview with Robin Williams, February 1998
Playboy October 1982; *Premiere* January 1988; *New York Times* 11 November 1990; *Los Angeles Times* 8 December 1991
Christopher Reeve: *Still Me* Random House 1998

Fly Like an Eagle
Author's interview with Robin Williams, January 1998
Rolling Stone August 1979; *Playboy* October 1982; *Premiere* January 1988; *New York Times* 11 November 1990; *New York Newsday* 24 September 1991; *Playboy* January 1992; *Esquire* November 1993
Mary Ellen Moore: *The Robin Williams Scrapbook* Tempo 1979

Sock it to Me
Rolling Stone August 1979; *Playboy* October 1982; *New York* 11 November 1993
People Entertainment Almanac 1988
Alex McNeil: *Total Television* Penguin 1996

My Favourite Orkan
Author's interview with Robin Williams, January 1988
Playboy October 1982; *Premiere* January 1988; *New York* 22 November 1993
Mary Ellen Moore: *The Robin Williams Scrapbook* Tempo 1979
People Entertainment Almanac 1988
Alex McNeil: *Total Television* Penguin 1996

Nanoo, Nanoo
Author's interview with Robin Williams, January 1988
Playboy October 1982
Mary Ellen Moore: *The Robin Williams Scrapbook* Tempo 1979
Alex McNeil: *Total Television* Penguin 1996
Mork and Mindy pilot episode viewed at the Museum of Television and Radio, New York

'Mork, Robin . . . Robin, Mork'
Author's interview with Robin Williams, January 1988
Playgirl March 1979; *Rolling Stone* September 1982; *Playboy* October 1982; *New York* 22 November 1993
People Entertainment Almanac 1988
'Mork Meets Robin Williams': *Mork and Mindy, Vol. 4* Paramount Video

I Yam What I Yam
Author's interview with Robin Williams, January 1988; Siobhan Synnot interview with Robin Williams, February 1998
Rolling Stone August 1979; *Rolling Stone* September 1982; *Playboy* October 1982; *Rolling Stone* February 1988; *New York Times* 11 November 1990
Peter Biskind: *Easy Riders, Raging Bulls* Simon & Schuster 1998

The Midas Curse
Author's interview with Robin Williams, January 1988
Playgirl March 1979; *Rolling Stone* September 1982; *Playboy* October 1982; *Rolling Stone* February 1988; *Los Angeles Times* 8 December 1991; *New York* 22 November 1993

Consequences
Author's interview with Addison Arce, July 1995
Rolling Stone September 1982; *Playboy* October 1982; *Rolling Stone* February 1988; *New York* 22 November 1993

Beautiful Boy
Playboy October 1982; *Rolling Stone* February 1988; *New York Times* 11 November 1990; *Playboy* January 1992; *New Yorker* September 1993; *New York* 22 November 1993

Enter Marsha
Rolling Stone February 1988; *People* 22 February 1988; *Redbook* January 1991; *Rolling Stone* February 1991; *Playboy* January 1992; *New Yorker* September 1993; *New York* 22 November 1993; *Cosmopolitan* April 1994

Growing Up
Author's interview with Robin Williams, January 1988
Rolling Stone February 1988; *People* 22 February 1988; *Esquire* June 1989; *Redbook* January 1991; *Rolling Stone* February 1991; *Playboy* January 1992; *New Yorker* September 1993; *New York* 22 November 1993

'Goood Mooorning Heraklion!'
Author's interview with Adrian Cronauer, February 1998
Premiere January 1988

From the Delta to the DMZ
Author's interview with Robin Williams, January 1988; author's interview with Adrian Cronauer, February 1998
Premiere January 1988; *People* 22 February 1988; *New York* 22 November 1993
Levinson on Levinson Faber & Faber 1992

A Death in the Family
San Francisco Chronicle 19 October 1987; *Rolling Stone* February 1988; *Playboy* January 1992

Waitin'
Author's interview with Robin Williams, January 1988; Siobhan Synnot interview with Robin Williams, February 1998
New York Post 12 December 1988; *New York Newsday* 24 September 1991; *Playboy* January 1992
Anthony Holden: *The Oscars* Little, Brown 1993
John Harkness: *The Academy Awards Handbook* Pinnacle 1997

Waiting for Godot, viewed at the Museum for the Performing Arts, New York

Dances with Lepers
Rolling Stone February 1988; *People* 22 February 1988; *Esquire* June 1989; *Playboy* January 1992

Oh Captain, My Captain
San Francisco Chronicle 27 April, 8 June, 10 October (all 1988); *Rolling Stone* February 1988; *New York Times* 11 November 1990; *Playboy* January 1992
Nancy Griffin and Kim Masters: *Hit and Run* Touchstone 1986

A Little Spark of Madness
Author's interview with Dan Holzman, March 1998; author's interview with Barry Friedman, March 1998
Esquire June 1989; *Playboy* January 1992; *Premiere* January 1990
Robin Williams: Off the Wall, viewed on Comedy Central 24 March 1998
An Evening with Robin Williams CIC Video
An Evening at the Met Vestron Video

Do You Take This Woman
Life 10 April 1989; *Esquire* June 1989; *People* 12 August 1991; *New York Newsday* 24 September 1991; *Redbook* January 1991; *Los Angeles Times* 8 December 1991; *New Yorker* September 1993
Anthony Holden: *The Oscars* Little, Brown 1993
John Harkness: *The Academy Awards Handbook* Pinnacle 1997

The Thief of Bad Gags?
Author's interview with Oliver Sacks, February 1991; Siobhan Synnot interview with Robin Williams, February 1998
Premiere January 1988; *Time* 21 May 1990; *New York Times* 11 November 1990; *Premiere* January 1991; *Rolling Stone* February 1991; *Playboy* January 1992

A Chink in the Armour
Author's interview with Robin Williams, February 1996
New York Times 11 November 1990; *New York Newsday* 24 September 1991; *San Francisco Chronicle* 10 September 1991; *San Francisco Chronicle* 8 November 1991; *Playboy* January 1992; *San Francisco Chronicle* 22 February 1992; *San Francisco Chronicle* 30 July 1992; *New York Daily News* 31 July 1992

Think Happy Thoughts
Author's interview with Robin Williams, February 1992; author's interview with Dustin Hoffman, February 1992
Daily Variety 7 August 1990; *Variety* 15 August 1990; *Daily Variety* 2 February 1991; *Variety* 18 February 1991; *Daily Variety* 9 June 1991; *Daily Variety* 16 June 1991; *Variety* 29 July 1991; *Daily Variety* 13 December 1991; *Daily Variety* 16 December 1991; *Variety* 23 December 1991; *Los Angeles Times* 8 December 1991; *People* 23 December 1991; *Playboy* January 1992; *Daily Variety* 1 December 1992; *New York* 22 November 1993

The Genius of the Lamp
Author's interview with Robin Williams, February 1992; author's interview with Robin Williams, February 1996; Siobhan Synnot interview with Robin Williams, February 1998
Premiere December 1988; *Premiere* December 1992; *New York* 22 November 1993; *Variety* 12 September 1994; *TV Guide* 16 December 1996; *Screen International* 12 December 1997
Anthony Holden: *The Oscars* Little, Brown 1993
John Harkness: *The Academy Awards Handbook* Pinnacle 1997
Levinson on Levinson Faber & Faber 1992

There's No Face like Foam
Author's interview with Robin Williams, January 1994; author's interview with Chris Columbus, January 1994; Siobhan Synnot interview with Chris Columbus, January 1994
New Yorker September 1993; *New York Newsday* 21 November 1993; *Los Angeles Times* 22 November 1993; *New York* 22 November 1993; *St Louis Post-Dispatch* 8 December 1993; *Screen International* 12 December 1997

Riddle Me This
Author's interview with Robin Williams, January 1994 and February 1996
Entertainment Weekly 1 October 1993; *Los Angeles Times* 21 November 1993; *Entertainment Weekly* 3 June 1994; *People* 23 May 1994; *USA Today* 8 June 1994
David Frost Interview (May 1991), viewed at the Museum of Television and Radio, New York

A Friend in Deed
Author's interview with Robin Williams, February 1996 and May 1997
New York 22 November 1993; *People* 30 October 1995; *USA Today* 3 February 1998
Christopher Reeve: *Still Me* Random House 1998

The Lost Boy
Author's interview with Robin Williams, February 1996; US junket for *Jack* 1996
Playboy January 1992; *USA Weekend* 3 March 1996; *TV Guide* 16 December 1996

Free at Last
US junket for *Father's Day* May 1997; US junket for *Flubber* November 1997; Siobhan Synnot interview with Robin Williams, February 1998
TV Guide 16 December 1996; *Forbes* 22 September 1997; *Los Angeles Times* 21 November 1993; AP news wire, 3 December 1997

Let's See Some I.D.
Author's interview with Robin Williams, February 1996 and May 1997; Siobhan Synnot interview with Robin Williams, February 1998; Alison Maloney interview with Gus Van Sant, March 1998
Matt Damon & Ben Affleck: *Good Will Hunting* Miramax Books 1997

And the Winner Is...
Siobhan Synnot interview with Robin Williams, February 1998
AP news wire, 9 March 1998; AP, Reuters news wires, 24 March 1998
Oscar telecast, 24 March 1998

INDEX